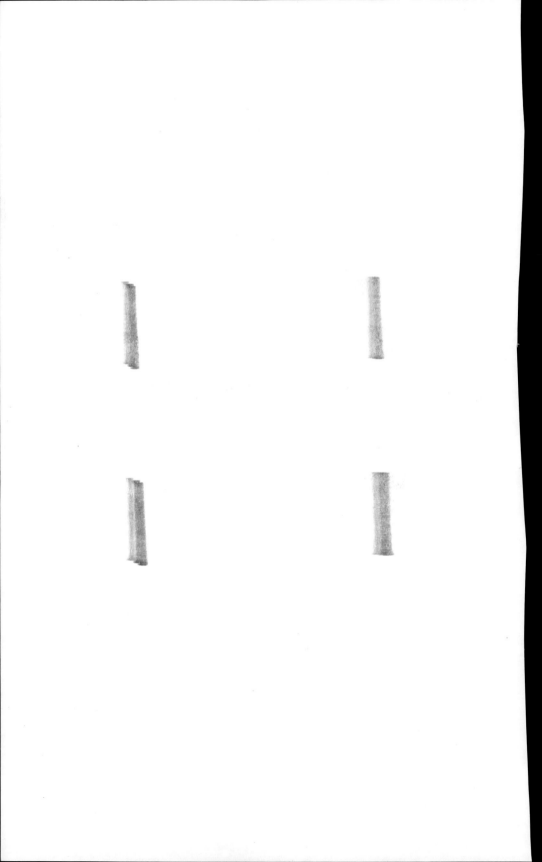

Pragmatism and Reference

Pragmatism and Reference

David Boersema

The MIT Press
Cambridge, Massachusetts
London, England

MIT Press books may be purchased at special quantity discounts for business or sales promotional use. For information, please email special_sales@mitpress.mit.edu or write to Special Sales Department, The MIT Press, 55 Hayward Street, Cambridge, MA 02142.

This book was set in Stone Sans and Stone Serif by the MIT Press, and was printed and bound in the United States of America.

Library of Congress Cataloging-in-Publication Data

Boersema, David.
Pragmatism and reference / David Boersema.
   p.   cm.
Includes bibliographical references and index.
ISBN 978-0-262-02660-4 (hardcover : alk. paper)
1. Reference (Philosophy).   2. Pragmatism.   3. Wittgenstein, Ludwig, 1889–1951.   I. Title.
B105.R25B64   2008
121'.68—dc22   2008017104

10 9 8 7 6 5 4 3 2 1

Contents

Preface

Chapter 1 was originally published as "Is the Descriptivist/Cluster Theory of Reference 'Wrong From the Fundamentals'?," *Philosophy Research Archives* 14 (1988–89): 517–538. Chapter 3, on Wittgenstein, was originally published as "Wittgenstein on Names" in *Essays in Philosophy* 3, no. 2 (June 2002), www.humboldt.edu/~essays. The section on Geach in chapter 3 was originally published in *The Proceedings of the Twenty-First World Congress of Philosophy, Volume 6: Epistemology*, edited by Dermot Moran and Stephen Voss (Ankara: Philosophical Society of Turkey, 2007), pages 37–42. The section on Peirce in chapter 4 was originally published as "Peirce on Names and Reference" in *Transactions of the Charles S. Peirce Society* 37 (2002): 351–362. The section on Eco was originally published as "Eco on Names and Reference" in *Contemporary Pragmatism* 2 (2005): 167–184. The section on James in chapter 4 was originally presented as "James on Names and Reference" at the 2002 meeting of the Society for the Advancement of American Philosophy, held in Portland, Maine, in March 2002. Portions of the section on Dewey in chapter 4 were presented in "Pragmatism, Individuation, and Reference," at the Pacific division meeting of the American Philosophical Association, held in San Francisco, March 2003.

Introduction

I am sitting with a philosopher in the garden; he says again and again "I know that that's a tree," pointing to a tree that is near us. Someone else arrives and hears this, and I tell him: "This fellow isn't insane. We are only doing philosophy."
—Ludwig Wittgenstein, *On Certainty*

I have several goals in writing this book. First, I hope to make a fruitful statement about reference and names, to offer some actual contribution to the philosophy of language. That is, I hope I have something of value to say about these topics. Second, and perhaps more realistic as a goal, I hope to demonstrate the fecundity of pragmatism with respect to its utility in addressing, clarifying, and resolving philosophical concerns about reference and names. That is, I hope I have something to say about demonstrating the philosophical value of pragmatism. Third, and probably even more realistic, I hope to explicate and elucidate the thinking of a number of important pragmatist thinkers to those who have not read or satisfactorily understood them. That is, I hope I have something to say along the lines of clarifying what these important philosophers had to say, especially about reference and names.

Although it is now changing, much of the history of philosophy in America and of philosophical education and training have, if not ignored both pragmatist philosophy and European continental philosophy, relegated them to "also-ran" status. Many prestigious philosophy programs today still do not train their students in the history of pragmatism or in contemporary pragmatist thought. Students—and faculty—who can profess in great detail the nuances of differences between a "causal" account of reference and a "historical" account and a "direct" reference account have no idea what Peirce or James or Dewey had to say about reference, or even that they had anything at all to say about it.[1] I hope that this book is one small corrective to that inattention.

The structure of this book is as follows: In the first two chapters I present what I take to be the descriptivist account of reference and names (at least, what has been called Searle's cluster view) and the causal account (primarily Kripke, but including others). I present what I see as their critiques of one another. I then suggest that they are not as far apart as they take themselves to be. In the third chapter, I outline what I see as a third account of reference and names, namely, Wittgenstein's view. Here I include a section on his student, Peter Geach, as his thoughts on reference have recently been resurrected in the squabbles between descriptivism and the causal view. Though I do not assume that Wittgenstein (or Geach) is pragmatist, or would be comfortable being labeled as "pragmatist," I do see a strong family resemblance between this view and pragmatism. In any case, a Wittgensteinian alternative to the two received accounts is one that many philosophers of language are familiar with. Looking at this alternative is, I believe, a nice acclimation to a straightforward pragmatist view.

This pragmatist view is presented in the middle section of the book, chapters 4 through 6, each covering three pragmatist thinkers. Chapter 4 summarizes the thought on reference and names of the "Big Three" classical American pragmatists: Charles Peirce, William James, and John Dewey. As those philosophers who have read and studied them know, these three thinkers are truly a goldmine of philosophical insight. The breadth and depth of their works are profound. They set out the themes, assumptions, commitments, and details of a pragmatist understanding of reference and names. In chapter 5, I present a survey of three contemporary American philosophers who have written quite extensively on reference and names, and certainly on language in general, and who reflect a pragmatist approach to these issues. These philosophers are Hilary Putnam, Catherine Elgin, and Richard Rorty. Although they vary in their willingness to accept the label of "pragmatist," they all, I believe, exhibit a pragmatist position on these issues. Chapter 6 presents the work of three contemporary continental pragmatist philosophers (again, pragmatist by my accounts, whether or not they would embrace the appellation): Umberto Eco, Karl-Otto Apel, and Jürgen Habermas. In what might come as a surprise to analytically trained philosophers, these three thinkers are not only familiar with contemporary debates about reference and names, they also have had much to say about them. I take these nine philosophers all to be not only representative of pragmatist commitments and views, but to be significantly prolific and influential in their own right. Of course, other philosophers could also have been included here, as they, too, have had important positions on these topics: George Herbert Mead (among the classical American pragmatists), Michael Dummett (among contemporary analytic thinkers), and Paul Ricoeur (among contemporary continental philosophers), for example. Their absence here is simply a matter of editorial choice on my part.

In the final three chapters, I present my own critique of the received accounts of reference and names. I focus on what I see as underlying commitments by both to certain conceptions of individuation, similarity, essences (in the form of haecceities) and sociality of language. Years ago (more than I care to mention!), when writing my doctoral dissertation, one of my faculty advisors remarked that what I had to say was clear, but wrong, from which it could be concluded that I was clearly wrong. I was not prepared to doubt him, but I asked if what I had written was at least interestingly wrong. Apparently it was. I hope this book minimally will meet that standard.

1 The Descriptivist/Cluster Account

"When *I* use a word," Humpty Dumpty said in a rather scornful tone, "it means just what I choose it to mean—neither more nor less." "The question is," said Alice, "whether you *can* make words mean so many different things."
—Lewis Carroll, *Through the Looking Glass*

Bertrand Russell's view of proper names is taken by many philosophers to be a paradigm case of the descriptivist theory of names. For Russell, ordinary proper names are disguised definite descriptions. Ordinary proper names can be replaced by descriptions (which the speaker associates with the name). Common words, even proper names, Russell claimed, are usually really descriptions. That is to say, the thought in the mind of a person using a proper name correctly can generally only be expressed explicitly if we replace the proper name by a description. Russell's view is generally taken to be such that for reference to occur when using a proper name, the description that actually underlies the name must be true of the object to which reference is made. This results in the problems noted below by both John Searle and Saul Kripke. (An important feature of Russell's view of proper names is that he presents it within the context of discussing different kinds of knowledge, knowledge by acquaintance [e.g., immediate sensual knowledge] and knowledge by description [e.g., propositional knowledge]. For Russell, the latter is reducible to the former.)

In *Naming and Necessity* Kripke rejects the Russellian view of proper names as being neither an adequate nor a correct treatment of ordinary (proper) names. Kripke argues (along with many others) that the Russellian view fails to account for the significance of the fact that different descriptions may be (and are) used in place of a name to designate an object. So one person might think of Aristotle as "the teacher of Alexander," another as "the most famous student of Plato," yet another as "the author of the

Metaphysics," and so on. (Even a single speaker might use these various descriptions at different times when referring to Aristotle.) No one of these descriptions could be the meaning of the name "Aristotle" or else the meaning of the name would be in constant flux. Additionally, the notion of proper names as disguised or shorthand definite descriptions is faulty, for if "Aristotle" means "the teacher of Alexander," then the statement "Aristotle was the teacher of Alexander" would be a tautology—something it is not. Indeed, not only is this statement not a tautology, but we could very well discover that it is false. So, says Kripke, being the teacher of Alexander cannot be part of (the sense of) the name "Aristotle."

Kripke then goes on to say that the most common way out of this difficulty with such a view of names is to say that no *particular* description may be substituted for a name; rather, what is needed is a *family*, or *cluster*, of descriptions. A good example of this, says Kripke, is found in Wittgenstein's (1953) *Philosophical Investigations*. (I believe Kripke is mistaken in ascribing the cluster theory to Wittgenstein. This point will be taken up later.) Kripke quotes the following part of paragraph 79 as introducing the idea of family resemblances:

Consider this example. If one says "Moses did not exist," this may mean various things. It may mean: the Israelites did not have a single leader when they withdrew from Egypt—or: their leader was not called Moses—or: there cannot have been anyone who accomplished all that the Bible relates of Moses—. . . But when I make a statement about Moses,—am I always ready to substitute some *one* of these descriptions for "Moses"? I shall perhaps say: by "Moses" I understand the man who did what the Bible relates of Moses, or at any rate, a good deal of it. But how much? Have I decided how much must be proved false for me to give up my proposition as false? Has the name "Moses" got a fixed and unequivocal use for me in all possible cases?

Kripke then states:

According to this view, and a *locus classicus* of it is Searle's article on proper names [Searle 1958, 166–173], the referent of a name is determined not by a single description, but by some cluster or family. Whatever in some sense satisfies enough or most of the family is the referent of the name. (1980, 31)

The Cluster Account

Searle recognized the difficulties facing the Russellian view of names as shorthand definite descriptions, and amended it by claiming that a name refers to an object in virtue of not a *single* description but rather a *cluster*, or disjunctive set, of descriptions. (In this book I will use "disjunctive set of descriptions" to indicate the logical sum, or disjunction, of those descriptions associated with a name.) Says Searle:

Suppose we ask the users of the name "Aristotle" to state what they regard as certain essential and established facts about him. Their answers would constitute a set of identifying descriptions, and I wish to argue that though no single one of them is analytically true of Aristotle, their disjunction is. Put it this way: suppose we have independent means of identifying an object, what then are the conditions under which I could say of the object, "This is Aristotle"? I wish to claim that the conditions, the descriptive power of the statement, is that a sufficient but so far unspecified number of these statements (or descriptions) are true of the object. In short, if none of the identifying descriptions believed to be true of some object by the users of the name of that object proved to be true of some independently located object, then the object could not be identical with the bearer of the name. It is a necessary condition for an object to be Aristotle that it satisfy at least some of these descriptions. (1969, 169)

So, associated with a name "N" is a disjunctive set of descriptions (or descriptive predicates), the satisfaction by an object of some of which is necessary for the object to be the referent of "N." Clearly, the disjunctive set of descriptions that is associated with a name can vary from speaker to speaker and from occasion to occasion; as new beliefs are accepted about an object, new elements may be added to the set of descriptions, and as old beliefs are rejected, some elements may be deleted from the set of descriptions. It is not clear how many of these descriptions must be true of an object for a name to refer to that object, and it is no oversight on Searle's part in failing to specify such a sufficient number. Nevertheless, as Searle says, at least one of the descriptions must be true of an object in order for the name to refer to the object. That is, it couldn't be possible that all of the elements in the set of descriptions associated with a name turn out false and yet reference successfully occur.

The context within which Searle makes the above claims is that of reference as a speech act (i.e., an action performed by a speaker by the use of rule-governed language). The reason he concentrates his remarks on reference, and philosophy of language in general, within this context is that "all linguistic communication involves linguistic acts. The unit of linguistic communication is . . . the production or issuance of the symbol or word or sentence in the performance of the speech act" (1969, 16).[1] In later works Searle places his views of speech acts, and philosophy of language in general, within the context of intentionality and philosophy of mind. Philosophy of language, he says, is a branch of philosophy of mind: "The capacity of speech acts to represent objects and states of affairs in the world is an extension of the more biologically fundamental capacities of the mind (or brain) to relate the organism to the world by way of such mental states as belief and desire, and especially through action and perception" (1983, vii).

Restricting his analysis to singular definite referring expressions (i.e., proper names, definite descriptions, and pronouns), Searle claims that these referring expressions pick out or identify one object (or "particular") apart from other objects (or particulars) and then go on to say something about that object. In discussing the success of a referring expression, he makes the distinction between a *fully consummated reference* and a *successful reference*. A fully consummated reference is one in which an object is identified unambiguously for the hearer; a successful reference (in the sense that we could not accuse the speaker of having failed to refer) is one in which an object could be, on demand, identified unambiguously for the hearer. A question the theory of reference must then answer is: What conditions are necessary for the utterance of an expression to be sufficient to identify for the hearer an object intended by the speaker?

The account of reference that Searle proposes in order to answer this question is capsulized in seven "rules of reference" (listed below). These rules presuppose two "axioms of reference" and a "principle of identification." The axioms are:

A1. The axiom of existence: There must exist one and only one object to which the speaker's utterance of the expression applies.

A2. The axiom of identification: The hearer must be given sufficient means to identify the object from the speaker's utterance of the expression.

The principle of identification is:

P1. A necessary condition for the successful performance of a definite reference in the utterance of an expression is that either the expression must be an identifying description or the speaker must be able to produce an identifying description on demand. (Searle 1969, 88)

Given these three conditions, we can now state Searle's seven rules of reference and consider an example to illustrate his account. Searle (1969, 94–95) states:

Given that S utters an expression R in the presence of H in a context C then in the literal utterance of R, S successfully and non-defectively performs the speech act of singular identifying reference if and only if the following conditions 1–7 obtain:

1. Normal input and output conditions obtain.[2]

2. The utterance of R occurs as part of the utterance of some sentence (or similar stretch of discourse) T.

3. The utterance of T is the (purported) performance of an illocutionary act.[3]

4. There exists some object X such that either R contains an identifying description of X or S is able to supplement R with an identifying description of X.[4]

5. S intends that the utterance of R will pick out or identify X to H.

6. S intends that the utterance of R will identify X to H by means of H's recognition of S's intention to identify X and he intends this recognition to be achieved by means of H's knowledge of the rules governing R and his awareness of C.[5]

7. The semantical rules governing R are such that it is correctly uttered in T in C if and only if conditions 1–6 obtain.

These rules can be exemplified with the following sentence:

(T) Venus is hidden from view by thick cloud cover.

Taking "Venus" as R, it is evident that the rules are satisfied. "Venus" occurs as part of the utterance of T, where the utterance of T is the performance of an illocutionary act (say, that of informing H). Venus exists and an identifying description (e.g., the planet at such-and-such a place in the sky at such-and-such a time) could be offered if needed. Additionally, it is intended that "Venus" pick out Venus (and H knows this).

On the other hand, if not all of the rules are satisfied, then reference has not occurred. For example, if S uttered "Venus" simply as part of a rhyming game (e.g., sounds that rhyme with "wean us"), then rule 5, and perhaps rule 2, would not be fulfilled, and reference would not have taken place.

Having laid out these rules of reference as a proposed theory of reference, Searle turns directly to the problem of definite descriptions and proper names. As noted above, Searle amends Russell's view by claiming that a singular referring expression refers to an object in virtue of not a single description, but rather a cluster of descriptions associated with a name. Again, Searle claims: It is a necessary condition for an object to be Aristotle that it satisfy at least some of these descriptions.[6]

However, Searle's view is more complex than that. There are problems, he says, with the view that names have no senses. If names have no senses, then, as Frege pointed out, there would be no cognitive difference between "a=a" and "a=b." In addition, negative existential statements (e.g., "Cerberus does not exist") are meaningful, but they couldn't be if names have no senses. On the other hand, says Searle, strong arguments militate against the view that names do have senses. If names have senses, at least in the form of being shorthand descriptions, then "descriptions should be available as definitional equivalents for proper names" (1969, 166), but they are not. In addition, if names have senses, then if we substitute descriptions for names, then the following (nonintuitive) result would ensue: some nonanalytically true statements about an object using the name as subject (e.g., "Aristotle was the teacher of Alexander") would turn out to be analytic. Also, the meaning of the name, and perhaps the identity of the object, would change every time there was any change at all in the object, and the name would have different meanings for different speakers. Surely this is not the case.

With strong arguments available both for and against the hypothesis that names have senses, Searle reinterprets the question "Do proper names have senses?" as having two forms, which he labels "weaker" and "stronger." The weaker form is: Are any statements where the subject is a proper name and the predicate a descriptive expression analytic? The stronger form is: Are any statements where the subject is a proper name and the predicate an identifying description analytic? In answering these questions, Searle states:

My answer, then, to the question, "Do proper names have senses?"—if this asks whether or not proper names are used to describe or specify characteristics of objects—is "No." But if it asks whether or not proper names are logically connected with characteristics of the object to which they refer, the answer is "Yes, in a loose sort of way." (1969, 170)

This "loose sort of way" is the necessity that for an object to be X (e.g., Aristotle), it must satisfy the logical sum of the properties attributed to X (i.e., at least one description of the cluster must be true). Searle summarizes his position:

What I have said is a sort of compromise between Mill and Frege. Mill was right in thinking that proper names do not entail any description, that they do not have definitions, but Frege was correct in assuming that any singular term must have a mode of presentation and hence, in a way, a sense. His mistake was in taking the identifying description which we can substitute for the name as a definition. (1969, 170)

Criticisms of the Cluster Theory

Kripke suggests that the cluster theory contains the following six theses:[7]

(1) To every name or designating expression "X," there corresponds a cluster of properties, namely the family of those properties ϕ such that A [the speaker (or hearer?)] believes "ϕX."

(2) One of the properties, or some conjointly, are believed by A to pick out some individual uniquely.

(3) If most, or a weighted most, of the ϕs are satisfied by one unique object Y, then Y is the referent of "X."

(4) If the vote yields no unique object, "X" does not refer.

(5) The statement "If X exists, then X has most of the ϕs" is known a priori by the speaker.

(6) The statement "If X exists, then X has most of the ϕs" expresses a necessary truth (in the idiolect of the speaker). (1980, 71)

Kripke then presents a detailed critical analysis of these theses.

Thesis (1): This, Kripke tells us, is a definition. The import and legitimacy of this definition is to be borne out by theses (2) through (6), and so he does not offer a critical analysis of this particular thesis. Rather, an analysis of the subsequent theses will, if they are shown to be incorrect, yield the incorrectness (or irrelevance) of thesis (1) as well.

Thesis (2): Kripke offers two counterexamples to demonstrate that thesis (2) is incorrect. First, he gives a case to show that the thesis fails to be satisfied. If we consider the name "Feynman," we note that many people who know very little about Feynman are nonetheless able to refer to Feynman when using the name "Feynman." When asked about Feynman, a person might say: "well, he's a physicist or something." The person may not think that this picks out anyone uniquely (and in this case probably wouldn't think that it does). Yet, says Kripke, it seems that such a person is still using the name "Feynman" as a name for Feynman. Second, to show that the thesis is simply false, Kripke offers the following case. We can uniquely pick out Einstein as "the man who discovered the theory of relativity." However, many people can only say of the theory of relativity that it is "Einstein's theory." We are led, then, "into the most straightforward sort of vicious circle" (1980, 82). The problem here is that one property is believed to pick out Einstein uniquely, but only at the cost of circularity, for in this case the property that picks out Einstein contains reference to Einstein within it.

Thesis (3): Kripke asks, "Suppose that most of the φ's are in fact satisfied by a unique object. Is that object necessarily the referent of 'X' for A?" (1980, 83). His answer is: no. To support this, he presents the following example. Suppose someone says that Gödel is the man who proved the incompleteness of arithmetic. Suppose further that Gödel was not in fact the author of this theorem, but rather a man named "Schmidt" was. On the cluster view, says Kripke, when the "ordinary" speaker uses the name "Gödel," "he really means to refer to Schmidt, because Schmidt is the unique person satisfying the description 'the man who discovered the incompleteness of arithmetic'" (1980, 84). So when the speaker talks of Gödel, he is in fact referring to Schmidt.[8] Thesis (3) "seems simply to be false" (1980, 85).

Thesis (4): Concerning this thesis, Kripke states that his previous examples show it to be incorrect. Suppose, he says, that nothing satisfies most, or even any substantial number, of the φs. Does that mean that the name doesn't refer? Kripke says: no, it does not mean that, for just as one may have false beliefs about X that are in fact true of Y, so one may have false beliefs about X that are in fact true of no one—and these false beliefs might constitute the totality of one's beliefs about X. For example, Einstein might be referred to as "the inventor of the atomic bomb." However, possibly no one really deserves to be called the inventor of the device (or, at least, no single person was the inventor). Yet, even if "the inventor of the atomic bomb" were our only belief about Einstein, we would still be referring to Einstein by "Einstein." So this thesis, too, is incorrect.

Thesis (5): About this, Kripke says that it is simply false. Even if theses (3) and (4) happen to be true, this hardly constitutes a priori knowledge that they are true. We certainly believe that Einstein was the man who discovered the theory of relativity, but this belief is hardly true a priori.[9]

Thesis (6): This thesis, according to Kripke, "need not be a thesis of the theory if someone doesn't think that the cluster is part of the meaning of the name" (1980, 65).[10] This thesis, along with thesis (5), seems primarily to say that a sufficiently reflective speaker grasps this theory of proper names. Kripke's attitude toward this *necessity* thesis is the same as toward the a prioricity thesis, namely, it is obviously false. He states: "It would seem that it is a contingent fact that Aristotle ever did *any* of the things commonly attributed to him today, *any* of the great achievements that we so much admire" (1980, 75).

Having investigated each of the theses (1) through (6) above, Kripke concludes:

What I think the examples I've given show is not simply that there's some technical error here or some mistake there, but that the whole picture given by this theory of how reference is determined seems to be wrong from the fundamentals. It seems to be wrong to think that we give ourselves some properties which somehow qualitatively uniquely pick out an object and determine our reference in that manner. (1980, 93–94)

At this point we need to ask whether Kripke's criticisms are legitimate (i.e., are they fair criticisms of what Searle's view is committed to) and, if so, are they debilitating (i.e., can Searle's view be defended or must it be abandoned). In answering these questions each of the theses that Kripke attributes to the cluster account will be investigated in turn.[11]

Thesis (1): "To every name or designating expression 'X,' there corresponds a cluster of properties, namely the family of those properties ϕ such that A believes 'ϕX.'" Kripke regards this, as noted earlier, as a definition, the legitimacy of which hinges on (the fate of) the other theses. Granting this assumption, we will turn to the remaining theses.

Thesis (2): "One of the properties, or some conjointly, are believed by X to pick out some individual uniquely." The motivation for asserting this as a thesis of the cluster account is found in statements such as the following: "In short, if none of the identifying descriptions believed to be true of some object by the users of the name of that object proved to be true of some independently located object, then the object could not be identical with the bearer of the name" (Searle 1969, 169).

As we saw, Kripke offers his Feynman example to show that one can refer even though one does not believe that an object has been uniquely picked out. Such a counterexample does indeed seem to violate the thesis (which does seem to be implied by the Searle quote above). However, in other places, Searle allows for such cases. Before considering these cases, though, a preliminary distinction that Searle makes between the *primary aspects* and *secondary aspects* of reference must be explicated, and this explication requires a detour into the writings of Keith Donnellan (1966).

Donnellan distinguishes between the referential and the attributive uses of definite descriptions. A speaker who uses a definite description referentially uses the description to enable a hearer to pick out whom or what the speaker is talking about and states something about that person or thing.

A speaker who uses a definite description attributively uses the description to state something about whomever or whatever is so-and-so. For example, if a speaker says, "Smith's murderer is insane," meaning that particular person over there, Jones, the speaker would be using the term "Smith's murderer" referentially. On the other hand, if the speaker says, "Smith's murderer is insane," meaning not any particular person, but whoever it was who murdered Smith, the speaker would be using the term "Smith's murderer" attributively.

Back to Searle. In arguing that the referential–attributive distinction is bogus, Searle distinguishes between what he calls the primary and secondary aspects of reference (or, aspects under which reference is made).[12] Searle says:

> Sometimes when one refers to an object one is in possession of a whole lot of aspects under which or in virtue of which one could have referred to that object, but one picks out one aspect under which one refers to the object. Usually the aspect one picks out will be one that the speaker supposes will enable the hearer to pick out the same object. In such cases . . . one means what one says but one means something more as well. In these cases any aspect will do, provided it enables the hearer to pick out the object. (It may even be something which both the hearer and the speaker believe to be false of the object. . . .) (1979, 144)

> provided that the speaker's intentions are clear enough so that we can say that he really knew what he meant, then even though the aspect expressed by the expression he utters may not be satisfied by the object he "has in mind" or may not be satisfied by anything, still there must be some aspect (or collection of aspects) such that if nothing satisfies it (or them) the statement cannot be true and if some one thing satisfies it the statement will be true or false depending on whether or not the thing that satisfies it has the property ascribed to it. (1979, 145)

The primary aspect under which reference is made is that aspect which, if not satisfied, would yield a statement that cannot be true. The secondary aspect is any aspect that the speaker expresses such that the speaker utters it in an attempt to secure reference to the object that satisfies the primary aspect, but which is not intended as part of the truth conditions of the statement the speaker is intending to make. For example, the speaker, looking at someone in the room, says, "Smith's murdered is insane." The speaker and the hearer might agree that the speaker has referred to, and made a true statement about, that particular person being looked at even though that person (and perhaps everyone) fails to satisfy the expression "Smith's murderer." The speaker could, on demand, fall back on another aspect, say, one expressed by "the person I am looking at." If it turns out that there is no person being looked at, only a hologram perhaps, then the speaker could fall back on another aspect, say, one expressed by "the person arrested by the police and accused by the District Attorney as Smith's murderer." If it turns out that there is no such person, then the speaker could fall back on another aspect. Eventually, however, an aspect must be reached such that if no one satisfied it, then the statement could not be true. (And though Searle does not say so explicitly, we must assume that in such a case no one has been referred to.) The primary aspect of reference is this last aspect, the aspect that either works or results in a statement that is false. The other aspects are secondary.

As mentioned earlier, Searle believes that the referential–attributive distinction is bogus. Having introduced his primary–secondary aspect distinction, he explains why. According to Searle, all of Donnellan's cases are cases where the definite description is used to refer. The difference in the cases is that in the so-called referential cases the reference is made under a secondary aspect, and in the so-called attributive cases it is made under a primary aspect. Furthermore, since every statement containing a reference must have a primary aspect, then in the so-called referential use the speaker may still have referred to something that satisfies the primary aspect even though the expression uttered, which expresses a secondary aspect, is not true of that object and may not be true of anything.

Having Searle's primary–secondary aspect distinction in hand, we are now ready to return to Kripke's criticism of thesis (2). It seems that with respect to secondary aspects under which reference is made, Kripke's thesis (2) is not a thesis of the cluster account; however, with respect to primary aspects under which reference is made, Kripke's thesis (2)—and his criticisms of it—are on target, at least for the cluster theory as Searle has posited it.

One might be able to amend Searle's theory, though, and handle the counterexamples Kripke proposed. Both the Feynman and the Einstein-as-discoverer-of-relativity cases work because the speaker has (apparently) no primary aspect under which to refer to Feynman and Einstein respectively. However, if we allow that a speaker in such a situation could appropriately appeal to another speaker or source to supply other aspects by which to refer, then the counterexamples would fail. For example, I may only know Feynman as "a physicist or something" and fully acknowledge that I have not uniquely picked out Feynman, but believe that reference has occurred successfully because I can add something like, "I don't know anything more about Feynman, but Keith does. He can tell you all about Feynman." I can recognize that the set of properties that I associate with Feynman do not uniquely pick out Feynman, but also recognize that someone else could amend the set such that Feynman would be uniquely picked out. (It would not be necessary that Keith be the person from whom I heard about Feynman. I might simply rely on the fact that Keith is a physicist friend on mine whom I know, or have good reason to believe, is familiar with other physicists.) As noted before, though, even if such an amendment to Searle's theory is legitimate, the theory is still committed to the primary aspect under which reference is made as having to be satisfied in order for reference to occur. This would entail that thesis (2) is indeed a thesis of the cluster theory, but Kripke's particular counterexamples would no longer be lethal to that thesis. (Whether or not other counterexamples to the cluster theory—in which this move of appealing to other speakers to secure reference is blocked—are possible or can work will be considered later.)

Thesis (3): "If most, or a weighted most, of the ϕs are satisfied by one unique object Y, then Y is the referent of 'X.'" This thesis, Kripke tells us, says that the speaker's belief noted in thesis (2)—that "ϕX"—is correct. That is, thesis (2) is purely doxastic—it states only that some property (or enough of them) is believed by the speaker to uniquely pick out some object—whereas thesis (3) states that some property (or enough) of them in fact does uniquely pick out some object.[13] The motivation for making this a thesis of the cluster account is statements such as those noted above for thesis (2): if none of the identifying descriptions believed to be true of some object by the users of the name of that object proved to be true of some independently located object, then the object could not be identical with the bearer of the name. This statement clearly implies that if an object is identical with the bearer of a given name (i.e., if Y is [identical with] the referent of "X"), then at least one of the identifying descriptions believed to be true of the object by the users of the name of that object must be true of that (independently located) object (i.e., some of the ϕs are satisfied by Y). As Searle says, "Since the speaker is identifying an object to the hearer, there must, in order for this to be successful, exist an object which the speaker is attempting to identify, and the utterance of the expression by the speaker must be sufficient to identify it" (1969, 82).

Kripke's counterexample to this thesis is Gödel being identified as the man who proved the incompleteness of arithmetic, though, unbeknownst to the speaker, Schmidt was actually the author of the proof. Since the (only) descriptions associated with "Gödel" are in fact satisfied by Schmidt, under the cluster theory, the speaker must be referring to Schmidt by "Gödel."

Searle's (explicit) response to this proposed counterexample is that depending on our intention in a particular context of using the name "Gödel," the referent of "Gödel" could "go in either direction" (1983, 251). Suppose, he says, that Jones proclaims, "On line 17 of his proof, Gödel makes what seems to be a fallacious inference." If we query Jones as to who is meant by (his use of) "Gödel," Jones might respond, "I mean the author of the famous incompleteness theorem." If then informed that Schmidt was the author, what would Jones say? Says Searle:

It seems to me that he might very well say that by "Gödel" he just means the author of the incompleteness proof regardless of who he is, in fact, called. Kripke concedes that there could be such uses. They involve what I have called secondary aspect uses of proper names. (1983, 251)

On the other hand, if Jones says, "Kurt Gödel lived in Princeton" and we query Jones as to whom is meant by "Gödel," Jones will likely be referring to Gödel and not to Schmidt, and will associate a different set of secondary aspect uses than in the first case (and as well, perhaps, a different primary aspect use). In any case, for Searle, it is not a singular, given use, but rather the underlying intentional content that is attached to the name. With the name "Gödel," different intentional contents and primary (and secondary) aspects might be attached to the name for any given use of the name. It seems to me that Searle would say that the reasons Kripke's intuitions are so strong that when we use the name "Gödel" we mean Gödel and not Schmidt is because in most cases the intentional content attached to our use of a name in fact allows us to pick out the "correct" (i.e., intended) object. The fact is that we usually pick out the right object when we use a name; the primary aspect under which reference is made (and usually the secondary aspects) does the job. This should work for "Gödel," too. If it doesn't (i.e., if the intentional content is "incorrect," if the ϕs associated with "Gödel" or at least the primary aspect associated with "Gödel" turns out to identify Schmidt), then, for Searle, we have referred to Schmidt.

It seems to me that the motivation underlying Searle's position here is clear and very intuitive. It is clear why Searle would say that in the cases above where all of the φs (or: the primary φ, or the intentional content) associated with "Gödel" turn out to identify Schmidt, then we obviously have referred to Schmidt. On the other hand, Kripke's insistence that we refer to Gödel by our (every?) use of "Gödel" seems to be based on our belief that we pick out the "correct" object when we use a name.

Once again: if "the author of the incompleteness theorem" is the primary aspect under which reference is made to Gödel, then, for Searle, we have not referred to Gödel in this case, but to Schmidt. But why think that in such a case as this we have referred to Gödel? What is underlying Kripke's claim that even in this situation we are in fact referring to Gödel? It is not clear to me, unless it is the belief that usually when we use "X" we mean, and correct pick out, X rather than Y. However, this hardly runs counter to Searle's view; indeed, he agrees completely.

It is noteworthy that in a footnote Kripke makes some remarks that sound rather conciliatory with regard to his Gödel–Schmidt case and with regard to the cluster theory in general. The note reads:

The cluster-of-descriptions theory of naming would make "Peano discovered the axioms for number theory" express a trivial truth, not a misconception, and similarly for other misconceptions about the history of science. Some who have conceded such cases to me argued that there are *other* uses of the same proper names satisfying the cluster theory. For example, it is argued, if we say, "Gödel proved the incompleteness of arithmetic," we are, of course, referring to Gödel and not to Schmidt. But, if we say, "Gödel relied on a diagonal argument in this step of the proof," don't we here, perhaps, refer to *whoever proved the theorem*? Similarly, if someone asks, "What did Aristotle (or Shakespeare) have in mind here?," isn't he talking about the author of the passage in question, whoever he is? By analogy to Donnellan's usage for descriptions, this might be called an "attributive" use of proper names. If this is so, then assuming the Gödel–Schmidt story, the sentence "Gödel proved the incompleteness theorem" is false, but "Gödel used a diagonal argument in the proof" is (at least in some contexts) true, and the reference of the name "Gödel" is ambiguous. Since some counterexamples remain, the cluster-of-descriptions theory would still, in general, be false, which was my main point in the text; but it would be applicable in a wider class of cases than I thought. I think, however, that no such ambiguity need be postulated. It is, perhaps, true that sometimes when someone uses the name "Gödel," his main interest is in whoever proved the theorem, and, *perhaps*, in some sense, he "refers" to him. I do not think that this case is different from the case of Smith and Jones. . . . If I mistake Jones for Smith, I may *refer* (in an appropriate sense) to Jones when I say that Smith is raking the leaves; nevertheless

I do not use "Smith" ambiguously, as a name sometimes of Smith and sometimes of Jones, but univocally as a name of Smith. Similarly, if I erroneously think that Aristotle wrote such-and-such passage, I may perhaps use "Aristotle" to *refer* to the actual author of the passage, even though there is no ambiguity in my use of the name. In both cases, I will withdraw my original statement and my original use of the name, if appraised of the facts. Recall that, in these lectures, "referent" is used in the technical sense of the thing named by a name (or uniquely satisfying a description), and there should be no confusion. (1980, 85–86n36)

Several points need to be made here. First, although Kripke is obviously going to great lengths to put qualifiers on his remarks (e.g., "perhaps," "in some sense," "*refers*" as opposed to "refers"), he clearly concedes that not every use of the name "X" picks out X, and, in fact, a speaker might pick out Schmidt even when saying "Gödel." While Kripke admits that the cluster theory might be applicable in a wider class of cases than he originally thought, he states that other counterexamples remain to prove the theory false in general. Part of the purpose of this chapter is to suggest that none of the counterexamples that Kripke has given us do the job, and I still see Kripke as bearing the onus to show that they do.

Second, Kripke tries to overcome his concessions to the cluster account by implying that the cluster theory works (or might work) in these Gödel–Schmidt cases because they imply that the names are ambiguous. However, Searle never makes any claim to that effect, nor is it necessary that he do so. Searle claims that we have different primary and secondary uses under which reference is made that result in the variation in reference. For Searle, a name "X" has no meaning at all, so it certainly doesn't have an ambiguous meaning. Rather, we intend to refer to a given object by using a given name and we associate different descriptions with the name. Because a given description might express a given primary or secondary aspect under which reference is made, the same name "X" might be used now to refer to X and later to refer to Y. Kripke's charge of ambiguity here is spurious.

Third, in dismissing even his own concessions to the cluster theory, Kripke emphasizes that we might *refer* to Y with "X," but, of course, there's no confusion of reference here, since "referent" is used in the "technical sense" of the thing named by a name, and happily we still refer to X with "X." It is hard to believe that Kripke thinks that he has explained anything by saying: Well, "X" *refers* to Y, but "X" refers to X. The point is that sometimes Y is picked out when the speaker uses "X." Kripke's *refer*–refer distinction is unhelpful at best, and certainly appears to be question-begging.

Perhaps a better candidate as a counterexample (because it is a more "natural" example than the Gödel case) is one constructed by Donnellan (1972). Consider a case, he says, in which a young child is awakened during a party given by his parents. At this time the child encounters and speaks with one of the party guests and learns the name of the guest to be "Tom." Later, reflecting on the event, the child remarks, "Tom is a nice man." This is the child's only description associated with "Tom," but it does not identify for the parents who Tom is, as they know many Toms. It might even be that Tom is not a nice man, but the child believes him to be so. Now suppose that another man was at the party and this man, whose name is also "Tom," *is* nice. However, the child did not meet this Tom. It seems that if thesis (3) is true, then the child referred to the Tom he did not meet, as this man was the unique object that satisfied (a weighted) most—in this case all—of the ϕs. But this is surely incorrect. Surely the child was referring to the Tom he did meet, even though that Tom did not satisfy the ϕs and another man did.

Again, it seems that Searle's response would be that as discussed above: the aspect expressed by "is a nice man" is a secondary one in this case and could be replaced by the aspect "is the man I met." Probably this aspect would serve as the primary aspect under which reference is made, but if not, then eventually one could be found that would, or else reference would not have occurred. And, again, appeal could (theoretically) be made to other speakers to provide the requisite expression of the primary aspect.

Thesis (4): "If the vote yields no unique object, 'X' does not refer." The motivation for asserting this as a thesis of the cluster account is statements such as the following: "There must exist not more than one object to which the speaker's utterance of the expression applies" (Searle 1969, 83). As noted above, Kripke believes his previous counterexamples show this thesis to be incorrect; just as one can have false beliefs about X that are in fact true of Y, so one can have false beliefs about X that are in fact true of no one or of more than one object. So even if "the inventor of the atomic bomb" is the only description a speaker associates with "Einstein," the speaker nonetheless refers to Einstein by "Einstein."

As seen above, Searle explicitly admits that we sometimes use a description to identify an object even though no unique object is picked out by that description. The reason, for Searle, that a description can work in making reference to an object even though the description may be true of no one or of more than one object is that the description might express a secondary aspect under which reference is made. The particular description may work in identifying to the hearer the object to which the speaker is referring even though the description does not uniquely pick out the intended object. With respect to secondary aspects under which reference is made, then, it seems that thesis (4) is not a thesis of the cluster account.

With respect to the primary aspect under which reference is made, it seems that if no object is uniquely picked out, then "X" indeed does not refer, and thesis (4) is a thesis of the cluster account. But in such a case, why think that reference has been made? If "the inventor of the atomic bomb" is in fact the primary aspect under which a speaker (supposedly) refers to Einstein, then it is not clear why one should insist, with Kripke, that the speaker nonetheless refers to Einstein. As with the Gödel example, it seems that the motivation for claiming that the speaker has still referred to Einstein is that usually we successfully refer to the object to which we intend to refer; again, this is hardly contrary to Searle's position.[14] So, as with theses (2) and (3), thesis (4) seems to be a thesis of Searle's view only if it is restricted to the primary aspects under which reference is made (in which case it is not at all obvious that it is false), and even then only if it is restricted such that reference can be made only through the descriptions that the given speaker associates with a name. These restrictions are certainly subject to challenge.

Thesis (5): "The statement, 'If X exists, then X has most of the ϕs' is known a priori by the speaker." Kripke says only that this is wrong; even if the above theses happen to be true, a typical speaker hardly knows a priori that they are.

Searle says nothing explicitly to the effect that the statement "If X exists, then X has most of the ϕs" is known a priori by the speaker. An initial (minor) amendment to this supposed thesis is in order. The statement needs to be changed to "If X exists, then X has some of (or the primary) ϕs" to be a thesis of Searle's view. It remains to be seen if Searle's view is committed to this amended thesis. In investigating this, several points need to be made. First, Kripke's claim makes sense only if Searle is proposing his view as giving the meaning of a name. That is, only if "Aristotle" means "the most famous student of Plato" or "the teacher of Alexander" or . . . , can this proposed thesis be a thesis of the account. However, Searle sees the disjunctive set of descriptions not as giving the meaning of a name, but rather as being an identifying mode of presentation of the referent of a name. The disjunctive set of descriptions associated with a name is the means of identifying an intended object, not the means of defining a name. (With respect to thesis (6), Kripke notes that if one doesn't think that the descriptions are part of the meaning of a name, but only that they fix the reference, then the thesis need not be a thesis of the cluster account. The same point would hold for thesis (5), and it seems that this could well be the case for Searle, i.e., the descriptions only fix the reference.)

What if Searle's view were committed to the position that the disjunctive set of descriptions associated with a name did give (in some sense) the meaning of a name? Would this thesis then be a thesis of his view, and, if so, would this show a serious weakness in the account? In answering these questions, we need to get clearer on exactly what Kripke is claiming. It is clearly not a thesis of Searle's view if the statement means that a speaker knows a priori that some particular ϕ is true of X. Searle definitely denies that this must be the case. He does, however, say that although no single description is analytically true of a given name, the disjunctive set of descriptions associated with a name is analytically true. The doxastic corollary of this would be that the speaker knows this analytic truth a priori. This reading of Kripke's claim, then, seems not unlikely to be a thesis of Searle's view, for it is not unreasonable to suggest, as Kripke does, that a sufficiently reflective speaker knows (or could come to know) this aspect of names and their uses. However, even if this is a thesis of Searle's view, it is not obvious that this fact carries the unwelcome stigma that Kripke attaches to it. The reason is that this reading of Kripke's claim seems to say nothing more controversial than that the speaker knows ahead of time (a priori, as it were) that some description, though no particular one, is true of X. This is to say very little. In addition, it seems to be a statement not of our knowledge about the object or name in question, but rather our knowledge of the language and how names are used. That is, this reading seems to say nothing more than what Searle readily asserts: if I am to refer by using the name "Aristotle," then I must believe that some of the descriptions I associate with the name are true of the intended object (and I know this fact about names even before I use "Aristotle"). Under this reading of thesis (5), Searle is clearly committed to it; but the apparent ruinous significance of this commitment is lost.

There is another reason to suggest that although thesis (5) may indeed be a thesis of Searle's view, he would be glad to accept it as such (and in fact this could be seen by Kripke as not a point against Searle's view). It is this: if one believes that names have essences (or, rather, that objects named have essences), and if one believes that at least one of the descriptions in the disjunctive set of descriptions associated with a name "picks out" this essence, then one might be more inclined to accept the claim that the disjunctive set is analytically true of the object, and, as a corollary, that the sufficiently reflective speaker knows this analytic truth a priori.

Thesis (6): "The statement, 'If X exists, then X has most of the ϕs' expresses a necessary truth (in the idiolect of the speaker)." As noted earlier, Kripke holds that this *necessity* thesis, like the *a prioricity* thesis (5), is false. Again, if we make the amendment from "most of the ϕs" to "some of the ϕs," such a statement is true of Searle's view, but it is not obvious that this is so objectionable or unintuitive. If Kripke is saying that for the cluster account it must be the case that if X exists, then some description must be believed to be true of X (and is true of X), then indeed Searle is committed to this thesis (assuming Searle is committed to names having meanings). But, again, as with thesis (5), this seems to be a commitment to a fact about language and the use of names, not a commitment to facts about any objects. Furthermore, if one believes that names have essences (or that objects named have essences) and if one believes that at least one description of the disjunctive set of descriptions associated with a name picks out this essence, then this thesis may be not only acceptable, but desirable.

Conclusion

What can be culled from this presentation and analysis of Searle's cluster account of reference? It seems that his cluster account is more sophisticated than it has been given credit for being. Searle's primary–secondary aspect distinction staves off (or at least offers promise of staving off) many of Kripke's objections. In addition, this distinction does not seem an ad hoc device; it has definite intuitive appeal. However, the distinction does not immunize the account from the criticisms that Kripke has raised. Searle's notion of secondary aspects under which reference is made does disarm much of Kripke's attack, but the necessity of bringing in a primary aspect rearms Kripke's objections, for it still seems that much of the basic account that Kripke claims as the cluster account is indeed the view that is held by Searle. Of course, as I have tried to show, even to the extent that Searle holds a version of the account that Kripke attributes to him, it is not obvious that such an account is "wrong from the fundamentals." To those theses to which Searle is committed, it is not obvious that they are false or implausible or even unintuitive. Minimally, something other than Kripke's proposed counterexamples is needed to show that Searle's view should be rejected.

The most evident response to these claims is that even if Searle could successfully defend his view from these particular counterexamples, others could be offered that can do the job. All that is needed is one example where no descriptions (or at least no true descriptions) are associated by the speaker with a given name being used. For instance, the speaker might really know nothing at all about Gödel. So, my attentive apartment neighbor might remark to her friend, "My weird neighbor kept me up last night yelling something about 'that damn turtle' or 'girdle' or 'Gödel' or something like that. I had to pound on the wall to get him to quiet down."

Has my neighbor referred to Gödel? Kripke's causal account of reference, we will see later, completely devoid of descriptivist assumptions, must say: yes. Searle, it seems, would say: no. Why think that reference has *not* occurred? For Searle, the reason is that rule 5 of his view (and perhaps rule 6) has been violated. (Rule 5, remember, is: S intends that the utterance of R will pick out or identify X to H. Rule 6 is: S intends that the utterance of R will identify X to H by means of H's recognition of S's intention to identify X and he intends this recognition to be achieved by means of H's knowledge of the rules governing R and his awareness of C.) Why think that reference *has* occurred? For Kripke's causal account, as will be seen later, the reason is that there is a causal chain linking "Gödel" to Gödel. Apart from or prior to these theories, however, why think that reference has or hasn't occurred? It is clear why one would claim that reference hasn't taken place: the speaker didn't intend to refer to Gödel; she didn't even know that "Gödel" is a name. On the other hand, it is not clear why one would say that reference has occurred.

Perhaps another example would be fairer to the causal account: suppose my obsession with Gödel has gotten to the point that I often blurt out my innermost thoughts concerning him. On one such occasion, while standing at a bus stop, I mutter, "Ha! Gödel couldn't hold a candle to Cantor. Now, there was a mind!" Upon hearing this, a bemused and intrigued stranger next to me asks, "Who is Gödel?" Has the stranger referred to Gödel? Kripke's causal account, it would seem, would say: yes, because there is a causal link from the stranger's utterance of "Gödel" to Gödel. Searle would most likely say: no, because it does not seem that the stranger intended that the utterance of "Gödel" would pick out or identify Gödel. (Searle's rule 5 is violated.)[15] The accounts, then, differ in the answer to whether or not the stranger has referred to Gödel. Which account best matches our pretheoretic intuitions here? It may not be clear, but I must admit that Searle's view comes closer to my intuitions. The very question, "Who is Gödel?" shows that the speaker has no clear referent associated with the name, and in fact the question could be paraphrased with no loss of meaning with a different question: "Whom are you referring to when you say 'Gödel'?" For the immediate purposes, I think the following (minimally) could be said: there is no clear counterexample to Searle's view in which reference occurs and for which the speaker has no descriptions at all associated with a name.

These examples illustrate a general point to which Searle responds (properly, I think) in connection with the variety of proposed counterexamples to his view. The point is this: the cases generally offered as inconsistent with Searle's view are singular, private instances of supposed reference. That is, these cases where references supposedly take place are cases of singular occurrences of a name or singular, isolated statements in which the name occurs. All of the examples in which the speaker has at best (apparently) one description associated with a name are of this sort (e.g., "Feynman is a physicist or something," "Einstein is the inventor of the atomic bomb"). But it seems that such cases (if possible) are far from paradigmatic for reference. We usually have an assortment of descriptions associated with a given name, even if some of them are not illuminating in terms of identifying the object being referred to. In those cases (if any) where we have one or no descriptions associated with a name, it seems more plausible to either appeal to other speakers as a source of reference or simply admit that reference has not occurred. It is in connection with the former alternative that I say that the usual counterexamples to Searle's view are cases of private instances of supposed reference. By that I mean the following: generally, the proposed counterexamples to Searle's view are ones in which reference borrowing is not considered or allowed. Yet, as noted above in response to Kripke's examples, reference borrowing is a natural and common move. To forbid such a move would be to make reference a private matter. This issue will become significant in later discussion, so I only mention it here with the caveat that I see such a condition as untenable.

Although Kripke and others have said little or nothing with respect to the private–public underpinnings of reference, they have dealt explicitly with the issue of reference borrowing. Kripke, for instance, briefly discusses Strawson's (1959) comments on reference borrowing (Kripke 1980, 90–92, 160–161) in connection with his remarks on his noncircularity condition (C). The notion of reference borrowing that Strawson and Kripke discuss is that of appealing to another speaker as the historical source for the present speaker's ability to refer by using a name (e.g., "By 'Gödel' I mean the man who Joe told me about"). This is not the sense of reference borrowing that I am mentioning here and which I will take up in more detail in chapter 9. Although Kripke's condition (C) may well forbid cases of reference borrowing in the Strawsonian sense, it is irrelevant to the sense I am using. That sense of reference borrowing is this: we can appeal to other speakers to provide requisite information or descriptions in order to secure reference, not because they stand in the position of being the historical source of my acquisition or acquaintance of a name, but because they can stand in the position of providing the needed identifying descriptions (which I lack) in order to pick out the intended object. I don't necessarily get my acquaintance with a name from these other speakers, but I get identifying descriptions from them to help pick out the intended object. The other speakers who provide me with these identifying descriptions could very well be different speakers from those from whom I first gained acquaintance with the name. So, I could have first heard of Gödel from Alice, but I now appeal to Betty to provide me with an identifying description so that I (and, perhaps, Carol) can pick out Gödel. Such appeal to other speakers is clearly not in violation of Kripke's condition (C) (or Searle's own noncircularity constraints). Objections to this sense of reference borrowing, it seems to me, make sense only if one presupposes a view of reference as a private matter.[16]

2 The Causal Account

"A man was murdered in the Rockies who called himself Hardross Courage, and who was traveling with my traps. Only you see it wasn't I" [said Hardross Courage].
—E. Phillips Oppenheim, *The Great Secret*

Having analyzed the cluster account of reference and having found it "wrong from the fundamentals," Kripke proposes to present a "better picture" of how reference takes place. "In general," he says, "our reference depends not just on what we think ourselves, but on other people in the community, the history of how the name reached one, and things like that. It is by following such a history that one gets to the reference" (1980, 95). This better picture, which Kripke says is "not a theory" (1980, 96), has nonetheless served as the nascence and kernel of what has come to be called the casual theory of reference. Kripke gives a "rough statement" of such an account:

A rough statement of a theory might be the following: An initial baptism takes place. Here the object may be named by ostension, or the reference of the name may be fixed by a description. When the name is "passed from link to link," the receiver of the name must, I think, intend when he learns it to use it with the same reference as the man from whom he heard it. (1980, 96)[1]

The sense in which this is a *causal* account of reference is that the passage of a name from link to link is said to secure a causal connection between the name of an object and the object. The initial baptismal act of naming the object (by ostension, perhaps) establishes the causal connection in the first place. Later uses of the name must be connected to the object in some sort of causal chain stretching back to the original naming act. As noted above, Kripke does not explicitly propose a *theory* of reference. However, others (e.g., Devitt 1981, 1984, 1987) have attempted to forge a causal theory of reference based on Kripke's picture. According to Devitt:

The central idea of a causal theory of names is that our present uses of a name, say "Aristotle," designate the famous Greek philosopher Aristotle, *not* in virtue of the various things we (rightly) believe true of him, but in virtue of a causal network stretching back from our uses to the first uses of the name to designate Aristotle. It is in this way that our present uses of the name "borrow their reference" from earlier uses. It is this social mechanism that enables us all to designate the same thing by a name. (1981, 25)

This simple statement of a causal account indicates what Devitt takes to be the basic elements of the account. Reference, or designation, is explained in terms of *d-chains* (short for "designating chains"). There are three types of links in a d-chain: (1) groundings, which link the chain to an object; (2) abilities to designate; and (3) communication situations in which abilities are passed on or reinforced (i.e., reference borrowing).

In a grounding, Devitt tells us, a person perceives an object (preferably face to face), correctly believing it to be an object of a certain very general category. The grounding consists in the person coming to have "grounding thoughts" about that object as a result of the act of perceiving the object. A grounding thought about an object, according to Devitt, "includes a mental representation" of that object brought about by an act of perception. The thought is one that a speaker would express using a demonstrative from that language. To use one of Devitt's examples: "Consider the case of our late cat. We acquired her as a kitten. My wife said, 'Let's call her "Nana" after Zola's courtesan.' I agreed. Thus Nana was named" (1981, 26). In this instance, Devitt perceived that cat and correctly believed it to be a cat. Furthermore, it was paramount that Devitt saw it as a member of the very general category that contains cats.[2] Having perceived it, Devitt was causally affected by it. As a result of seeing the object and hence being causally affected by it, Devitt came to have "grounding thoughts" about it (i.e., he came to have a mental representation of the object). The name, having been grounded, can now be used by speakers to refer to the object because a causal link has been established between the initial use of the name and the object, and a causal link can be established between later uses of the name and the initial use. For instance, having named the cat "Nana," Devitt could then exercise his new ability to refer to Nana by saying, "Nana is hungry." He could speak to his friends about Nana, thus enabling them, in turn, to refer to Nana. These friends (and their uses of "Nana") are causally linked to Nana by perceiving (hearing) Devitt's utterances in which reference to Nana is made. Since to perceive is to be causally affected, they are now causally linked in a sense to Nana. These friends now have the ability to refer to Nana *because* of this causal linkage.

The nature of this causal hookup in this chain seems to be based on identity beliefs, says Devitt (i.e., beliefs we would express using identity statements). According to Devitt, noninitial uses of a name become grounded in objects by the user's taking advantage of grounding thoughts. This process of taking advantage can be either direct or indirect, but in both cases advantage is taken by coming to hold identity beliefs. Direct advantage of grounding thoughts is taken by holding an identity belief containing a demonstrative representation like those in the grounding thoughts (e.g., "*that* cat is Nana" or by definite descriptions). Indirect advantage of grounding thoughts is taken when a speaker has nondemonstrative representations of an object, i.e., by holding an identity belief that includes an already grounded nondemonstrative representation (e.g., "the F," knowing that Nana is the F). In both cases of advantage being taken, it is the identity beliefs that lead to the representational thoughts, and these identity beliefs link the thoughts associated with "Nana" to the grounding thoughts and thus to Nana.

Closely connected with the notion of grounding and the uses of a designating term is the ability to designate. Devitt claims that "we should see a person's ability to designate with a term as, basically, his having thoughts that include mental representations which are both of the object and associated with the term" (1981, 130). The ability to designate can be divided into the ability to designate *in thought* and the ability to designate *in speech* (or writing and so forth), with the former being basic. Says Devitt:

For a person to have an ability in thought to designate an object, an ability associated with a physical type, is for him to have a set of thoughts, including tokens which are grounded in the object and which dispose him to use the type. (1981, 132)

for a person to have an ability to designate an object with a sound type is for him to have (a) the power of speaking that type, and (b) a set of thoughts including tokens which are grounded in the object and which dispose him to speak the type. (1981, 131)

So, Devitt's ability to designate his cat—if it is a speech ability—is the ability to utter certain sound tokens. The set of thoughts associated with that type (namely, sound) dispose him to speak it. Likewise, mutatis mutandis, for the ability to designate if it is a thought ability.

We have, then, the first two types of links in a designating chain. The third type of link is that of communication situations in which abilities to designate are passed on or reinforced, that is, reference borrowing. In reference borrowing, says Devitt, the act of perceiving a designation of the object by the term plays the role for the borrower that the earlier act of perceiving the object played for a person present at a grounding; it grounds the term in the object. So when Devitt comments to his friends that Nana is hungry, "Nana" is a designational term, since it has underlying it a representation grounded in the object. On the strength of this utterance, the friends come to have certain thoughts and gain the benefit of that grounding. The friends have mental representations that are of the object in virtue of being causally linked to the object via the act of borrowing. Underlying these representations are designating chains grounded in the object in virtue of appropriate grounding thoughts and identity beliefs.

Criticisms of the Causal Account

In response to the causal account of reference, Searle has said little with respect to Kripke and almost nothing at all with respect to Devitt. He has, however, directed criticisms against aspects of the causal account (e.g., proper names do not have senses) as far back as his 1958 essay. In later works (Searle 1979, 1983) he has leveled specific criticisms against the causal accounts. Among his criticisms are:

(1) The view that proper names have no senses is, minimally, counterintuitive.

(2) Kripke's distinction between speaker reference and semantic reference is bogus (as is Donnellan's distinction between referential uses and attributive uses of definite descriptions).

(3) There are intuitive counterexamples showing that the causal theory of reference fails to give either necessary or sufficient conditions for successful reference.

(4) Kripke's (and Donnellan's) position is really a descriptivist one.

These criticisms need to be looked at in detail.

Criticism (1): The view that proper names have no senses is, minimally, counterintuitive. In the context of existential statements such as "Princeton exists" or "Cerberus does not exist" proper names cannot be said to refer. If they did, the precondition of such statements having a truth-value would guarantee their truth (in the case of affirmative existential statements) or their falsity (in the case of negative existential statements). This, says Searle, is because every existential statement states that a certain predicate is instantiated. An existential statement does not refer to an object and state that it exists; rather it expresses a concept and states that the concept is instantiated. If Cerberus does not exist and if "Cerberus" has no sense, then how can we make sense of "Cerberus does not exist"? Surely—at least, intuitively—the statement "Cerberus does not exist" is true. But this can't be if "Cerberus" has no sense.

Another problem with the view that proper names have no senses is that such a view cannot explain the cognitive difference between identity statements of the form "a=a" and "a=b." That is, if proper names have no senses, but at best only referents, then the assertion "Everest is Chomolumga" could convey no more information than the assertion "Everest is Everest." However, this seems wrong.

Criticism (2): Kripke's distinction between speaker reference and semantic reference is bogus (as is Donnellan's distinction between referential and attributive uses of definite descriptions). According to Searle, Kripke (1977) rejects—or reinterprets—Donnellan's referential–attributive distinction as rather a distinction between speaker reference and semantic reference. For Kripke, if a speaker has a designator in his idiolect, then certain conventions of his idiolect determine the referent in his idiolect. This is the semantic referent of the designator. On the other hand, the object that the speaker wishes to talk about on a given occasion, and which the speaker believes fulfills the conditions for being the semantic referent of the designator, is the speaker's referent of the designator. In Donnellan's attributive cases, speaker reference and semantic reference coincide because the speaker's intention is just to refer to the semantic reference. In the referential cases, however, the speaker's reference and the semantic reference would be different if the speaker is mistaken in believing that they both determine the same object. For example, two speakers see Smith in the distance and mistake him for Jones. One speaker asks, "What is Jones doing?" The other speaker answers, "Raking the leaves." Now, "Jones" is the name of Jones, not of Smith. The semantic referent of "Jones" is Jones, but the speaker referent of "Jones" in this case is Smith.

Kripke's account, says Searle, couldn't be quite right as it stands because in the "referential" use the speaker need not even believe that the object referred to satisfies the expression he uses. For example, to avoid political persecution one might refer to the usurper of a throne as "the King" even though one does not believe the usurper to be the king. Where Kripke goes wrong, says Searle, is in his attempt to analyze both speaker's reference and semantic reference in terms of different kinds of intentions. Kripke states that in a particular idiolect, "the semantic reference of a designator (without indexicals) is given by a *general* intention of the speaker to refer to a certain object whenever the designator is used. The speaker's referent is given by a *specific* intention, on a given occasion, to refer to a certain object" (1977, 264). Searle responds to this attempt:

This is where the account bogs down. In the sense in which I really do have both general and specific intentions (e.g., I have a specific intention to drive to Berkeley tomorrow, and a general intention to drive on the right hand side of the road, ceteris paribus, whenever I drive in the United States) I have no such general intentions about definite descriptions. If my use of definite descriptions required such general intentions I would have to form an infinite number of them since there are an infinite number of definite descriptions I am able to use and understand in my language. (1979, 156)

Rather than speaking of speaker's reference and semantic reference, Searle suggests that the real distinction to be noted with respect to reference is that between primary and secondary aspects under which reference is made (discussed in chapter 1 above).

Criticism (3): There are intuitive counterexamples showing that the causal account of reference fails to give either necessary or sufficient conditions for successful reference.[3] Searle presents several counterexamples. "Madagascar" was originally the name of part of mainland Africa. Mistakenly, Marco Polo used the name to refer to an island off the coast. So, says Searle, the present uses of the name "Madagascar" (by which we now mean to refer to the island, not part of the mainland) satisfy a causal connection that connects it with part of the mainland, but that is not sufficient to enable the name to refer to that part of the mainland. The use of names of abstract entities (e.g., "two") or of "future" entities (e.g., "the K car," while it's still in the planning stages) are examples of reference in which no causal connection is necessary between an object and (the use of) a name.[4]

Criticism (4): Kripke's (and Donnellan's) position is really a descriptivist one. Searle says:

From the point of view of the descriptivist theory, what the causal analysis amounts to is the following: *the causal chain of communication is simply a characterization of the parasitic cases seen from an external point of view*. Let me try to make this clear. Kripke says that at each link in the chain of communication the speaker must have the intention, "when I utter 'N' I mean to refer to the same object as the person from whom I got the name 'N.'" The descriptivist says that one sort of identifying description that one can attach to a name "N" is "the person referred to by others in my linguistic community as 'N.'" Both sides agree that this is not enough by itself: Kripke insists that the chain must terminate in an initial baptism; the descriptivist allows for a variety of ways in which it can terminate, of which an initial baptism is one. Where is the difference? As far as the issue between the descriptivist and the causal theory is concerned there is no difference: Kripke's theory is just a variant form of descriptivism. (1983, 244)

As with the earlier criticisms of Searle's cluster account, at this point we need to ask: are these criticisms of the causal account legitimate, and, if so, are they debilitating?[5]

Criticism (1): "The view that proper names have no senses is, minimally, counterintuitive." As stated, the first counterintuitive result of denying senses to proper names is to make (certain) existential statements non-sensical or paradoxically true. The second counterintuitive result is that the apparent cognitive difference between "a=a" and "a=b" cannot be explained.

Both Donnellan (1974) and Devitt (1981) have responded to the first counterintuitive result. Donnellan makes use of an "admittedly not well-defined" notion of a "block" to sketch a means of dealing with the problem of negative existentials. For Donnellan, there is a "block" in the history of the use of a name when events preclude any reference being identified. An example of a block would be the following: a child who once believed in Santa Claus comes to abandon this belief. What has the child learned? Says Donnellan:

Our account is that he has learned that when in the past he believed something, for example, "Santa Claus comes tonight," and would have thought himself when saying this to be referring to someone, the historical explanation of this belief does not involve any individual who could count as the referent of "Santa Claus"; rather it ends in a story given him by his parents, a story told to him as factual. (1974, 23)

The block, then, is the introduction of the name into the child's speech via a fiction told to him by his parents. Another example is the following: the Homeric poems, suppose, were written not by a single author, but by many people. Perhaps the poems were combined from a patchwork of many writings over time. Suppose further that someone later attributed these poems to a single author, Homer. If this were the historical explanation of our saying, for example, "Homer wrote the *Iliad*," then the block occurs at the point at which the person attributed the poems to Homer.

Armed with the notion of a block, Donnellan proposes the following rule for giving truth conditions of existential statements containing a name:

(R) If *N* is a proper name that has been used in predicative statements with the intention to refer to some individual, then "*N* does not exist" is true if and only if the history of those uses ends in a block.[6]

So we can assign truth-values to negative existentials such as "Cerberus does not exist" even though we deny that "Cerberus" has a sense.

Devitt's responds to the Searlean objection of negative existentials by proposing the following rule:

If e_1 is a singular term, then $\ulcorner e_1$ exists$\urcorner$ is *m*-true$_s$ if and only if there is an object *a* to which e_1 *m*-refers$_s$ (where "true$_s$" means "true relative to the assignment of sequent *s*," "refers" means "refers relative to the assignment of sequent *s*," "*m*-true$_s$" means "trues relative to a structure *m* which maps terms onto the world," and "*m*-refers$_s$" means "refers relative to a structure *m* which maps terms onto the world"). (1981, 186)[7]

Negative existentials are handled by the addition of a negation rule:

If e_1 is a formula and e_2 is a negative symbol, then $e_2(e_1)$ is *m*-true$_s$ if and only if e_1 is not *m*-true$_s$. (1981, 164)

As with Donnellan's rule (R), these rules do not analyze negative existentials in the sense of giving a synonym or translation of them, but they do offer a method of determining the truth conditions of such statements.

Kripke more directly addresses the second counterintuitive result of names having no senses (namely, "a=a" and "a=b" would then have no cognitive difference, but they do). In laying out his argument for why he thinks that names do not have senses, he first attempts to clarify several notions and distinctions that he sees as important: Kripke argues that, contrary to popular usage, a prioricity is not interchangeable with necessity. Both a prioricity and a posterioricity are epistemological concepts, whereas both necessity and possibility are metaphysical concepts. To see that a prioricity is not interchangeable with necessity, consider the following example: Goldbach's conjecture that every even number greater than two is the sum of two prime numbers is either true or false. Furthermore, if it is true (false), then it is presumably necessarily true (false). However, none of us can be said to have any a priori knowledge about the answer to this conjecture. As Kripke puts it, we don't know whether the conjecture is true or false, so we certainly don't know a priori whether it is true or false.

Having given some intuitive appeal for distinguishing a prioricity and necessity, Kripke goes on to suggest that some statements (such as Goldbach's conjecture) are necessary and a posteriori, while others (such as the horsepower example below [which is not Kripke's example]) are contingent and a priori. In giving examples, he brings up discussion of possible worlds and transworld identity. Possible worlds are stipulated by descriptive conditions we associate with them (and are, in a sense, says Kripke, no more than counterfactual situations). Transworld identity is the identity of an object across possible worlds. So, if we say that Nixon might have lost the 1968 Presidential election, we will be asserting a necessary or contingent statement depending on what singular term is used and what is meant to be referred to. That is, some referring terms (for Kripke, all names but not all definite descriptions) are what he calls *rigid designators*, that is, terms that designate the same object in every possible world in which that object exists. "Nixon" is a rigid designator because it refers to the same object in all worlds in which that object exists, but "the winner of the 1968 Presidential elections" is not a rigid designator, because, though Nixon could not be anyone other than Nixon, the winner of the 1968 Presidential elections could have been (and in some possible world, is) someone other than Nixon.

This notion of rigid designation and the earlier distinction between a prioricity and necessity come together in the following way. Some statements, such as identity statements involving names, are necessary and a posteriori, whereas other statements, such as ones involving (some) definite descriptions, are (or could be) contingent and a priori. For example, to say "Siddhartha is Gautama Buddha" is to make a statement that is known a posteriori. That is, we come to discover that "Siddhartha" refers to the same object as "Gautama Buddha." Or, "Hesperus" and "Phosphorus," we find out, refer to the same object, even though we might believe them to refer to different objects. However, if names are rigid designators, then the same object is picked out in all possible worlds in which that object exists. So "Siddhartha" picks out the same object in all possible worlds and "Gautama Buddha" picks out the same object in all possible worlds. Consequently, if the identity is true, then, since the same object is picked out in all possible worlds for each name, the identity is true in all possible worlds, that is, the identity is necessarily true. The truth of the statement "Siddhartha is Gautama Buddha" is (epistemologically) a posteriori and (metaphysically) necessary.

On the other hand, the statement "One horsepower equals the power required by one horse to displace 150 pounds by 220 feet in one minute" is contingent and a priori. For Kripke, such a statement is contingent because it simply fixes the referent of "horsepower" (and given a different horse in different possible worlds, the value might have been different from the value—550 foot-pounds/second—in this world). The value in the actual world was picked out by a particular accidental property (the distance a certain mass could be displaced in a certain amount of time by a certain horse), and so the statement is (metaphysically) contingent. Nonetheless, the statement is—now—known a priori. This is so because once the reference has been fixed, the definition holds; we do not (need to) appeal to any evidence to know the truth of the statement.

Returning, then, to Searle's criticism that the cognitive difference between "a=a" and "a=b" cannot be accounted for unless names have senses, we see that Kripke disagrees. Both identities, if true, are necessarily true (assuming we are dealing with names, i.e., rigid designators). On the other hand, whereas "a=a" is known a priori, "a=b" is known a posteriori, accounting for the apparent cognitive difference. However, Kripke has not introduced senses in accounting for this cognitive difference; hence Searle's criticism fails.

Criticism (2): "Kripke's distinction between speaker reference and semantic reference is bogus." Again, the reason Searle makes this claim is that he sees it as assuming that in referring we have both a general intention to refer to a certain object (whenever the designator is used) and a specific intention to refer to a certain object (on a given occasion). Searle finds this assumption questionable because, he says, we have no such intentions for definite descriptions.

Kripke anticipates this objection and responds (to some extent, anyway) in a footnote (1977, 273n22). What he is trying to show there is that reference is not subjective. That is, it is true that we as speakers mean to refer to a certain object when we use a referring term, but obviously we cannot refer to whatever we want when we use a referring term. A referring term has a history and is objective is the sense that within a language a given speaker's use of the term must conform to the other speakers' uses of that term. For Kripke, the notion of what words can mean and refer to is given by the conventions of our language, and what words mean and refer to on a given occasion is determined by these conventions together with the intentions of the speaker and various contextual features. (This issue of objectivity versus subjectivity of reference will be dealt with in some detail later, so I will only say at this point that I think Kripke is right. It is not clear to me, however, that Searle is lobbying for, or is committed to, subjectivity of reference. His objection seems to be more that on a given occasion we do not have any general intentions to refer in Kripke's sense.)

Kripke continues explicating his distinction by considering just the sort of cases that Searle mentions, for example, the "the King" case. Fearing the secret police, people may well use "the King" to refer to a usurper, or, humoring a lunatic, they may call Smith "Napoleon." Further, such cases shade into ironic or "inverted commas" cases, such as "He's a fine friend" (spoken ironically) or "Napoleon has gone to bed" (spoken of Smith). The point of all these cases is that the more contextual phenomena one includes in the notion of speaker's reference (such as irony, linguistic errors, deliberate misuses of language), the further one gets from any connection with semantic matters. Kripke does not deny, then, that many of these Searlean features are present and important in ordinary discourse, but he does deny that they play the role in semantic analysis that Searle seems to think they do.

Additionally, it seems to me, we could construct intuitive counterexamples to Searle's objections. It seems we often mistakenly refer to someone (e.g., call someone the wrong name, or believe someone's name is "Smith" when in fact it is "Jones"). In such cases we are often corrected (and even correct ourselves): for example, "You mean Jones, don't you? Smith was in Cleveland on that day." Our response often exhibits our acceptance of a speaker reference–semantic reference distinction (e.g., "I'm sorry; I meant to say 'Jones' rather than 'Smith.'" or "I didn't know her name was

'Smith,' I thought it was 'Jones'"). Such examples seem to me to indicate that whom I believe I am referring to and whom the name refers to are not always identical.[8]

Criticism (3): "There are intuitive counterexamples showing that the causal theory of reference fails to give either necessary or sufficient conditions for successful reference." The case of reference to abstract or to "future" objects is said to demonstrate the failure to give necessary conditions for reference, and the case of Madagascar is said to demonstrate the failure to give sufficient conditions for reference.

As noted before, Kripke (at least) does not see himself as offering a theory wherein necessary and sufficient conditions are stipulated. To criticize him for not having done what he didn't attempt to do seems puzzling. Of course, a Searlean reply could be that not only has Kripke not given necessary and sufficient conditions for reference, but, as the above counterexamples illustrate, he couldn't, and that this is clearly a sign that the causal account is weak.

In the addenda to *Naming and Necessity* Kripke explicitly responds to the Madagascar case. He says:

a present intention to refer to a given entity (or to refer fictionally) overrides the original intention to preserve reference in the historical chain of transmission. The matter deserves extended discussion. But the phenomenon is perhaps explicable in terms of the predominantly social character of the use of proper names emphasized in the text: we use names to communicate with other speakers in a common language. This character dictates ordinarily that a speaker intend to use a name the same way as it was transmitted to him; but in the "Madagascar" case this social character dictates that the present intention to refer to an island overrides the distant link to native usage. (1980, 163)

Making this all clear, says Kripke, is a problem for further work, but minimally we must distinguish a present intention to use a name for an object from a present belief that the object is the only one having a certain property. Certainly, however, to say that the problem has not been thoroughly worked out does not entail, contra Searle, that it cannot be.

With respect to the objection that reference to abstract entities illustrates the failure of the causal theory to provide necessary conditions for reference, Kripke (and others) have said practically nothing. Nevertheless, there are a variety of responses that could be made. One could deny that the supposed names of abstract entities are really names. For example, one could deny that "two" is a name. Such a denial might take the form of claiming that all such "names" are really disguised descriptions. So, one might insist that "two" can be translated into set-theoretic notation and defined in such a way as to eliminate the "name." Even if this were to work for number (and it is not at all obvious that it would), it seems much less intuitive that this move could succeed for reference to "future" entities. For example, a recent groom might exclaim, "The curtains in little Saul's room have got to go!" where Saul is, as yet, an unborn (unconceived?) son. There is, at the time of the utterance, no Saul in which "Saul" is grounded. Or, in the initial planning stages of the marketing and manufacturing of the K car, someone might say, "Great idea, Saul! The K car could save this company!" The K car might be, at the time of the utterance, no more than an idea in Saul's mind or only in the initial blueprint stage. In any case, it is not at all clear that "Saul" or "the K car" (where I take "the K car" to function as a name, not as a definite description) can be dismissed as disguised descriptions. A causal account advocate might respond to such cases of supposed reference by taking a nominalistic stance with respect to the entity in question. That is, one could deny that such entities are real and so treat reference to them in the same manner as to other fictional entities, say, by appealing to Donnellan's notion of a block. So, just as supposed reference to Santa Claus resulted in a block, supposed reference to the number two or to the K car might result in a block. In each case, statements containing the "names" can still be assigned truth values even if there are not really objects being referred to. (This tack could apply not only to "future" entities, but to numbers as well, if we insist that what we refer to are not numbers, but numerals or specific tokens.) The cost of taking such a nominalistic position, however, might be too high (because of other difficulties) so that this sort of move would be unsatisfactory.

Another response to Searle's objection might be found in the work of Salmon (1981), though his comments were not directed to this issue. In looking at the notion of rigid designation, Salmon despairs that there are several distinct notions of rigid designation to be found in the literature. The most familiar notion is that a designator is rigid if it designates the same thing with respect to every possible world in which that thing exists. One interpretation of a rigid designator Salmon dubs a *persistently rigid designator*. A designator is persistently rigid if it designates the same thing with respect to every possible world in which that thing exists and it designates nothing with respect to possible worlds in which that thing does not exist. Another interpretation of a rigid designator Salmon dubs as *obstinately rigid designator.* A designator is obstinately rigid if it designates the same thing with respect to every possible world, period. Obstinate designators, Salmon tells us, "may be insensitive to the question of whether their designata exist in a given possible world; they designate the same thing with respect to every possible world, whether that thing exists or not" (1981, 34). Further, Salmon contends that Kripke may very well intend his notion of rigid designation to be that of obstinate rigid designation, and points to the following note in *Naming and Necessity* as evidence:

Concerning rigidity: In many places, both in this preface and in the text of this monograph, I deliberately ignore delicate questions arising from the possible nonexistence of an object. . . . I say that a proper name rigidly designates the referent even when we speak of counterfactual situations where the referent would not have existed. Thus the issues about nonexistence are affected. (1980, 21n21)

The present point of this, with respect to the Searlean objection of reference to abstract or "future" entities, is that if we take names (of numbers, say) as obstinate designators, then there is no problem for the causal account. Reference can be made whether or not the name refers to anything that exists in the world, if the name designates obstinately. Since the actual world is obviously a possible world, and if obstinate designators designate their objects in all possible worlds whether or not the object exists in those worlds, then, if names of numbers are obstinate designators, they designate their objects even if those objects don't exist. For Salmon, names of numbers do designate obstinately (at least for the causal account). He claims:

As is most obvious in the clearest case of a nondescriptional singular term—the free variable whose denotation is fully and directly determined by an assignment of values to variables—there is no reason to suppose that the denotation of a nondescriptional term should change with respect to different possible worlds. . . . Proper names do not denote by, so to speak, rummaging through the individuals in a possible world seeking anyone or anything uniquely meeting certain conditions. Hence, there remains no reason to expect denotation to vary from one world to the next. Instead, one may think of the denotation as being fixed for all time and for all possibilities by an initial dubbing ceremony, or an assignment of values to variables, etc. (1981, 33n35)

Since the actual world is a possible world, there is also no reason to think that proper names denote in it by "rummaging through individuals . . .

seeking anyone or anything uniquely meeting certain conditions." If this is so, then reference to abstract or "future" entities should be no problem for the causal account of reference.

Another response to Searle's objection—and this seems to be Kripke's response—might be that the initial grounding of the causal chain may well be achieved by means of a description that fixes the reference of a name. Once the reference of a name has been fixed by the use of a description, then future uses of the name will link up to that baptismal event. I say that this seems to be Kripke's response because of his comments like the following:

Neptune was hypothesized as the planet which caused such and such discrepancies in the orbits of certain other planets. If Leverrier indeed gave the name "Neptune" to the planet before it was ever seen, then he fixed the reference of Neptune by means of the description just mentioned. At that time he was unable to see the planet even through a telescope. (1980, 79n33)

A page later Kripke notes that the reference could be fixed even if the description used turned out to be false, as when "Phosphorus" had its reference fixed by the description "the morning star" (which is false because Phosphorus [i.e., Venus] is not a star at all). By allowing that the reference of a name can be fixed by a description, then, there is no problem for the causal account to refer to abstract or "future" objects. Since these were the sorts of cases that Searle proposed as counterexamples to the causal account as being incapable of providing necessary conditions for successful reference, it seems that the criticism fails.[9]

Criticism (4): "Kripke's (and Donnellan's) position is really a descriptivist one." Searle claims that the "causal chain of communication" is simply a characterization of parasitic cases of reference seen from an external point of view. That is, for Searle, the causal (or historical) chain plays no explanatory role in an account of reference (or, in Kripke's account of reference). What does matter in an explanatory role is the transfer of intentional content from one speaker or speech act to another. Reference is secured, says Searle, under Kripke's account in virtue of the intentional content in the mind of the speaker who uses a particular designating expression. After an initial baptism, subsequent "intentional contents" are parasitic on the prior ones for achieving reference. Of course, an omniscient observer could give a historical (causal) account of the chain of reference, and hence describe historically (causally) how a later use of the expression refers, but what secures reference is the descriptive, intentional content.

Even if Searle is correct that this is really what is going on with Kripke's account, it is a strange sort of criticism. That is, he seems to be saying that Kripke's account is fine as it stands, but that Kripke is mistaken in thinking that he has offered anything new, anything contrary to a descriptivist theory. Rather he has wrongly identified or overemphasized one aspect of his theory as unique and essential.[10] However, it does not seem that Kripke would agree with Searle's assessment of Kripke's view. While admitting that intentionality plays a role in reference and even that the descriptivist view might suffice for explaining reference in limited contexts (such as an initial baptism), Kripke clearly denies that the descriptivist account is adequate. His view is not descriptivist because he insists that in general "our reference depends not just on what we think ourselves, but on other people in the community" (1980, 95). It is simply false that for Kripke reference is secured in virtue of some intentional content in the mind of the speaker who uses a particular designating expression. Indeed, one of the points of making the speaker reference–semantic reference distinction is to show that reference is not dependent upon the intentional content in the mind of the speaker who uses a particular designating expression.[11]

Conclusion

Just as in chapter 1 above, I was not trying to claim that Searle is right and Kripke wrong when it comes to explicating reference, so now I am not trying to claim that Kripke is right and Searle is wrong. What I have tried to do is to fairly present both the cluster account and the causal account, criticize each from the other's perspective, and respond to those criticisms from within the two theories. That is, I have tried to capture (in an admittedly glossing manner) the debate between the received accounts of reference as I see it, and I have tried to let the authors of those theories speak for themselves as fully as possible (given what they have said in print).

Coda

In the final three chapters of this book, I will emphasize and analyze underlying commitments of the received accounts of reference. In particular I want to argue that both the Searlean cluster view and the Kripkean causal view are committed to, or at least presuppose, certain views with respect to the similarity relation, a principle of individuation, and essentialism, particularly in the form of haecceities. However, before turning to the task of laying out what I take these various notions to be and showing how the received theories are committed to them, I want to look more at the received accounts as they have been presented in these first two chapters. I will argue that even prior to considering any underlying commitments, there is reason to believe that the two views are not nearly so far apart as the debate in the literature would seem to indicate. I also want to make some initial observations and criticisms about the received views before going into the more basic observations and criticisms that I believe are lethal to those theories.

First a review. Minimally, much of the focus and force of the criticisms by the causalists of the cluster account of reference (and of the descriptivist account in general) is that it seems to allow a speaker's intentions to play too key a role in the business of reference. As Kripke says, "It seems to be wrong to think that we give ourselves some properties which somehow qualitatively uniquely pick out an object and determine our reference in that manner" (1980, 93–94). Kripke's speaker reference–semantic reference distinction and his proposed counterexamples to Searle's theory are designed to address this very point. Reference is not the sort of thing, say the causalists, that a speaker secures simply by uttering an expression and intending to pick out some unique object. Rather, reference is a public, historical phenomenon. Merely intending to pick out X while saying "Y" is not enough to refer to X, especially if other speakers have used "Y" to pick out Y and "X" to pick out X. Whether we like it or not, "Gödel" has a history which is intimately tied up with Gödel and not with Schmidt.

On the other hand, Searle has claimed that the causal account is nothing more than a descriptivist account in disguise. The key feature of the account—that which secures reference for the causal theory—is the intention to refer to the same object as that from whom the speaker learned or acquired the name. Granted, one could describe a historical chain of the uses of a name, and so this is a public phenomenon; nonetheless, a speaker's ability to refer to an object by (the use of) a name depends on the speaker's intention to in fact designate the same object by that name as did the person from whom the speaker learned or acquired the name (otherwise the speaker's present use of the name would not become part of the historical chain, but would be part of some other historical chain stretching back to a different object or to nothing at all). Or, in the case of baptism, a speaker's ability to refer to an object by a name depends on the speaker's intention to designate that object by (the use of) a name (e.g., for Devitt, by having the mental representation of the object).

On the surface, then, the two accounts seem clearly at odds. The Kripkean counterexamples show (or are intended to show) that the descriptions that a speaker associates with a name may be totally inadequate or even irrelevant to picking out the actual referent of the name. Indeed, it is held that a speaker could legitimately use a name to refer to an object and yet have no (true) descriptions associated with that name that would uniquely pick out that object. The Searlean counterexamples show (or are intended to show) that a historical chain linking a speaker's use of a name to an object is inadequate as an explanation or account of successful reference. It is held that there are legitimate cases of successful reference (such as to abstract entities) for which historical chains are irrelevant and even nonsensical. For Searle, it is the case that at least one member of the disjunctive set of descriptions associated with the use of a name to an object must be true of the object for reference to successfully occur; for Kripke this is not the case.

Despite the apparent fundamental differences between these two accounts, I want to claim that they are much closer in agreement that they at first appear. Much of the dispute seems to be centered, at least implicitly, on the issue of public versus private reference. That is, as noted earlier, Kripke has accused Searle of, in effect, seeing reference as a private affair for any given speaker. I think, given much of what Searle has said, that Kripke is right, but I want also to accuse Kripke of the same thing. In spite of his insistence that reference depends on "other people in the community, the history of how the name reached one, and things like that" (1980, 95), the causal account is just as compatible with, and in the manner in which it has been presented by its adherents, just as committed to private reference as is the cluster account. Before directly supporting this claim, however, I will present some initial observations and criticisms of the received accounts, which I hope will give a better background for a discussion of public and private reference.

Convergence of the Received Accounts

Are the cluster and causal accounts as divergent as they are usually portrayed as being? I think not. As I will argue later, they share fundamental underlying commitments, but even on a more superficial level, the accounts do not seem to me so far apart. What has been said to be unique to the cluster account is that speakers must have a set of identifying descriptions associated with a name, the disjunction of those descriptions being analytically true of the object referred to by the name. However, in several places Searle remarks that, as far as he is concerned, "the issue is not really about analyzing proper names in *words* at all" (1983, 233). Some cases, for example, reference for children (who often learn names before other expressions), are such that the only "identifying description" a speaker might have that he associates with a name is simply the ability to recognize the object. A young child saying "Mama" might well have no (verbal) descriptions at all associated with the name, and indeed "Mama" might have no significance to the child except when Mama is in sight and can be pointed to. For Searle, "pointing is precisely an example that fits [the descriptivist's] thesis, since pointing succeeds only in virtue of the intentions of the pointer" (1983, 233). That is, for Searle, what is fundamental for reference is that the speaker intends to pick out an object uniquely by the use of a name, and, apparently, as long as the intention is there, the "description" used to pick out an object may not have to be verbal. For Searle, then, ostension seems to count as a means of picking out an object. This sounds very much like Kripke's view that descriptions can be used to fix the reference of a name and that, *pace* Devitt, in the presence of an object we can name an object by having the appropriate "mental representations" while uttering the name. In fact, ostension has seemed in some ways as much a paradigmatic example of the strength of the causal account as of the weakness of the cluster account. Naming by ostension has been seen as a clear case in which a name is used but no description (or disjunction of descriptions) associated with the name is either necessary or sufficient for reference to occur. Now we see Searle arguing that naming by ostension is paradigmatic of the cluster account! This issue of ostension points to a focus of commonality for the cluster and the causal accounts: intentionality.

Two of Searle's seven rules of reference employ intention in successful reference: rule 5 (*S* intends that the utterance of *R* will pick out or identify *X* to *H*) and rule 6 (*S* intends that the utterance of *R* will identify *X* to *H* by means of *H*'s recognition of *S*'s intention to identify *X*, and he intends this recognition to be achieved by means of *H*'s knowledge of the rules governing *R* and his awareness of C). A key element of Searle's view is that a speaker intends to pick out an object by (the use of) a name. (Kripke's objection, remember, is that this is not sufficient to guarantee successful reference, because the speaker might intend to pick out one object by a name but in fact might actually pick out a different object by that name.) As just noted, we see that for Searle this intention to refer to an object by (the use of) a name does not entail that any verbal descriptions must be employed by the speaker; pointing might be fine. So, cases where the speaker supposedly associates no descriptions with the name (as in, for example, some of the cases discussed in chapter 1) are no trouble for Searle because in those cases rules 5 and 6 of his theory are violated (i.e., the intentional element of the speech act of referring is missing). My neighbor, then, does not refer to Gödel simply because she uttered the name "Gödel." The fact that the name "Gödel" has a historical chain stretching back to an initial use of the name (to refer to Gödel) is irrelevant. Furthermore, just as for Kripke, for Searle, intending to refer to an object by (the use of) a name is not sufficient to actually refer to that object. If none of the descriptions in the disjunctive set of descriptions that a speaker associates with a name uniquely picks out an (otherwise independently located) object, then merely intending to pick out that object by (the use of) a name does not secure reference. For Searle, I do not and cannot refer to Aristotle by uttering "Aristotle" simply because I intend to refer to him. I must have at least one description (albeit not necessarily a verbal one) that is true of Aristotle in order to pick him out.

In chapter 1 I presented two cases for which I said that the cluster account denies (but the causal account asserts) that reference takes place. The first case was my neighbor complaining to her friend, "My weird neighbor kept me up last night yelling something about 'that damn turtle' or 'girdle' or 'Gödel' or something like that. I had to pound on the wall to get him to quiet down." The second case was a stranger asking me, "Who is Gödel?" after hearing me mention Gödel's name. For both cases, I claimed that for Searle's cluster account reference does not occur (and the reason is that in both cases the speaker did not intend to refer). I also claimed that under the causal account "devoid of descriptivist assumptions" reference does occur. I now want to clarify those claims.

First, under what I will call a "pure" cluster account of reference, that is, an account in which a speaker's intention to uniquely pick out an object by a name is a necessary and sufficient condition for reference to that object to occur, both my neighbor (in the first case) and the stranger (in the second case) would not have referred (for the reasons I stated in chapter 1). However, Searle is not a "pure" cluster theorist in that sense. I do think that he would claim that in the first case, my neighbor did not refer to Gödel, but I think in the second case, he would allow (insist?) that the stranger did refer to Gödel. This is borne out by his claim that "there are uses of names where one is almost totally dependent on other people's prior usage to secure reference" (1983, 261). In such a case, the stranger could secure reference through my use of the name "Gödel" to refer to Gödel. (This move brings up two important points. First, it makes Searle's position certainly sound more and more like the causalist account. Second, it points to the issue of publicity of reference borrowing and reference in general, an issue that will be addressed explicitly in chapter 9.)

Besides clarifying my initial strong claim about the cluster account on the two cases, I want to clarify my claims about the causal account with regard to these cases. Under what I will call a "pure" causal account of reference, that is, an account in which a causal connection between an object and (the utterance of) a name is both necessary and sufficient for successful reference, both my neighbor (in the first case) and the stranger (in the second case) would have referred (because the historical, causal chain linking their uses of the name "Gödel" to Gödel would have been established). However, neither Kripke nor Devitt are "pure" causalists in this sense. Both, it seems, would deny (at least in the first case) that reference has occurred.[12] Kripke explicitly states (in his rough statement of a better picture of reference): "When the name is 'passed from link to link,' the receiver of the name must, I think, intend when he learns it to use it with the same reference as the man from whom he heard it" (1980, 96).

Devitt (1981) is not nearly so straightforward as Kripke about admitting intention into the causal account. In fact he seems to go to great lengths to avoid committing the causal account to intentions. He states:

It is tempting, and I think correct, to say that when a person uses a name he (mostly) intends to designate whatever was designated by the person from whom he borrows his reference. . . . Such intentions seem as much in need of explanation as designation itself. I do not talk of these intentions but capture the intuitions in another way: the tokens of the name a person produces are tied to the token from which he borrowed his reference by causal links (of the sort discussed) between his mental representations of the object. (1981, 138)

So, even though not actually using intentionalistic language, Devitt nonetheless wants and needs to capture the intuitions of such language in order to guarantee that different speakers are in fact referring to the same object when using a given name.[13] My point here is not to debate whether talk of intentions is necessary in dealing with reference, but to indicate that advocates of both the cluster account and the causal account invoke it (or, at least, invoke the same intuitions that names are not used helter skelter in referring).

Not only does Kripke seem to indicate that a necessary condition for successful reference is the employment of the "proper" intention, he also seems to see the cluster account as appropriate in certain contexts, such as in the fixing of reference (say, during a baptismal event). In Kripke's own example of the naming of Neptune he acknowledges that there may be cases where the cluster-of-descriptions view seems to make sense.

Both of these considerations (the requirement for Kripke of the "proper" intention to refer and the admission of the possibility of using a name to fix the reference *pace* Searle) indicate that the causal account and the cluster account might be closer in agreement than initially thought. But there is more. As noted in chapter 1, Kripke concedes that there may be cases in which "*X*" is used to refer to *Y*. (For example, if someone asks, "What did Aristotle have in mind here?," the speaker is referring—or, for Kripke, *referring*—to whoever wrote the passage even if it turns out not to have been Aristotle.) With that concession, Kripke remarks that the cluster account would be "applicable in a wider class of cases" than he originally thought, even though he still believes it to be ultimately false. Whether or not the cluster account is false, the point here is that again Kripke seems to be softening his blanket opposition to the cluster account.

Another sign of the convergence of the cluster and causal accounts is Kripke's response to the Searlean counterexamples to the causal account involving reference to abstract and "future" objects. Recall that Kripke's apparent way out of the difficulty of referring to such objects for the causal account is to allow that descriptions can fix the reference of a name even if there is no causal hookup to an object. Reference is secured, then, but not in a "purely" causal way, and indeed Kripke's response seems to fit in quite easily with Searle's view.

Devitt, too, in a brief discussion of reference to "future" objects sounds like Kripke (and like Searle). Says Devitt:

> Consider, for example, the situation where there exists a plan or blueprint for a ship or building. We could introduce a name for that future object and it would seem to function like an ordinary designational name. This requires a small modification in our theory: the network for a name may be grounded initially not in the object itself but in some plan to produce the object according to certain specifications. Later, of course, the network becomes grounded in the object so produced.
>
> Those who make these claims about naming future objects [i.e., that the causal theory can't account for reference to them] are struck by the oddity of now naming, say, the first child born in the twenty-first century. The oddity arises, I suggest, because we could not have any particular object in mind using the names so introduced. This is striking because we mostly do have an object in mind in using a name. However, sometimes we don't. . . . (1981, 59–60)

This "small modification" to the account sounds to me at least more like a major concession to the cluster account than a minor adjustment in the causal account.

What is the point of all this? The point is that even at the level of what the cluster and causal advocates present explicitly as their positions, they are not so far apart. Both Searle and Kripke assert that intending to refer to a given object by the use of a name (and indeed intending to refer to the same object as the person from whom one acquires the name) is a necessary condition for successful reference. Both deny that such intention is a sufficient condition for successful reference. Both see ostension as paradigmatic of a correct theory of reference. Both see the use of reference-fixing descriptions as a legitimate mode of reference. Kripke's insistence that we "use names to communicate with other speakers in a common language" (1980, 163) sounds like Searle's claim that we "need to make repeated reference to the same object, even when the object is not present, so we give the object a name" (1983, 231). Both deny (as in the "Madagascar" case) that a historical link between an object and a name is sufficient to secure reference. Both deny (as in the case of abstract objects) that a causal link between an object and a name is necessary to secure reference.

With all of these similarities between the two accounts, we end up getting comments like the following:

Since the point of having proper names is just to refer to objects, not to describe them, it often doesn't really matter to us much what descriptive content is used to identify the object as long as it identifies the right object, where the "right object" is just the one that other people use the name to refer to.

There may be cases . . . where some man really gives a name by going into the privacy of his room and saying that the referent is to be the unique thing with certain identifying properties.

The first, "antidescriptivist" quote is, of course, Searle's (Searle 1983, 250) and the second "prodescriptivist" quote is, of course, Kripke's (Kripke 1980, 94)! But if these two theories actually share many common features, what, then, is the important difference between them? In the way it has been presented in the literature (and primarily from the causalist perspective) the difference is that the cluster account is supposedly committed to private reference and fails to account for the historical, public nature of reference. I want to turn to this issue later, and I will claim that even here the two accounts agree; they both at bottom allow private reference. To the extent that they do, the distinction between the accounts is blurred even more, and the received accounts of reference look more and more like a single received account of reference.

3 A Wittgensteinian Account

Language is a kind of code dependent upon the life rhythms of the species which originated the language. Unless you learn those rhythms, the code remains mostly unintelligible.

—Frank Herbert, *Whipping Star*

Wittgenstein versus Searle

In *Naming and Necessity* Kripke (1980) rejected the Russellian theory of proper names as neither an adequate nor a correct treatment of proper names. Kripke argued (along with many others) that the Russellian view fails to account for the significance of the fact that different descriptions may be (and are) used in place of a name to designate an object. So one person might designate Aristotle as "the teacher of Alexander the Great," another as "the most famous student of Plato," another as "the author of the *Metaphysics*," and so on. (Even a single speaker might use various descriptions at different times to designate Aristotle.) Clearly, the notion of proper names as disguised or shorthand definite descriptions is faulty, for if the name "Aristotle" means "the teacher of Alexander the Great" then the statement "Aristotle was the teacher of Alexander the Great" would be a tautology—something it surely is not. So, said Kripke, being the teacher of Alexander the Great cannot be part of (the sense of) the name "Aristotle."

Kripke then went on to say that the most common way out of this difficulty with names is to say that no *particular* description may be substituted for a name; rather what is needed is a family, or cluster, of descriptions. A good example of this, said Kripke, is found in Wittgenstein's (1953) *Philosophical Investigations*. Kripke quoted the following part of paragraph 79 as introducing the idea of family resemblances:

Consider this example. If one says "Moses did not exist," this may mean various things. It may mean: the Israelites did not have a *single* leader when they withdrew from—or: their leader was not called Moses—or: there cannot have been anyone who accomplished all that the Bible relates of Moses—. . . But when I make a statement about Moses,—am I always ready to substitute some *one* of those descriptions for "Moses"? I shall perhaps say: by "Moses" I understand the man who did what the Bible relates of Moses, or at any rate, a good deal of it. But how much? Have I decided how much must be proved false for me to give up my proposition as false? Has the name "Moses" got a fixed and unequivocal use for me in all possible cases?

Kripke (1980, 31) then stated:

According to this view, and a *locus classicus* of it is Searle's article on proper names [Searle 1958, 166–173], the referent of a name is determined not by a single description but by some cluster or family. Whatever in some sense satisfies enough or most of the family is the referent of the name.

I want to argue here that Wittgenstein did not hold the cluster view of Searle and that Kripke misread the very passage of Wittgenstein's that he quoted, first by wrongly attending to certain notions in paragraph 79, and second by bypassing the more significant claims (which he does not quote) of paragraph 79 and the surrounding paragraphs of the *Investigations*. First, I will reiterate Searle's view and then show that it is not the same view as is found in paragraph 79.

As noted in chapter 1, Searle recognized the difficulties facing the Russellian view of names as shorthand definite descriptions and amended it by claiming that a name refers to an object in virtue not of a single description, but rather in virtue of a cluster or disjunctive set of descriptions:

Suppose we ask the users of the name "Aristotle" to state what they regard as certain essential and established facts about him. Their answers would constitute a set of identifying descriptions, and I wish to argue that though no single one of them is analytically true of Aristotle, their disjunction is. Put it this way: suppose we have independent means of identifying an object, what then are the conditions under which I could say of the object, "This is Aristotle"? I wish to claim that the conditions, the descriptive power of the statement, is that a sufficient but so far unspecified number of these statements (or descriptions) are true of the object. In short, if none of the identifying descriptions believed to be true of some object by the users of the name proved to be true of some independently located object, then that object could not be identical with the bearer of the name. It is a necessary condition for an object to be Aristotle that it satisfy at least some of these descriptions. (1969, 169)

So, associated with a name "*N*" is a disjunctive set of descriptions, the satisfaction by an object of some of which is necessary for the object to be the referent of "*N*." Clearly, the disjunctive set of descriptions that are associated with a name can vary from speaker to speaker and from occasion to occasion; as new beliefs are accepted about an object, new elements might be added to the set of descriptions, and as old beliefs are rejected, some elements might be dropped from the set of descriptions.

As noted in chapter 1, it is not clear how many of these descriptions must be true for a name to refer, but it is no oversight on Searle's part in failing to specify such a sufficient number, for it will depend upon too many specific and contextual factors. However, critics of Searle's view are right in interpreting the view as requiring that at least one of the descriptions be true of an object in order for the name to successfully refer to the object. That is, it couldn't be possible that all of the elements in the set of descriptions associated with a name turn out false and yet reference successfully take place.

Consider again Donnellan's (1972) case, in which a young child is awakened during a party given by the child's parents. During the brief interruption of the child's sleep, the child speaks with one of the party guests, and learns the name of the guest to be Tom. Later, reflecting on the occurrence, the child remarks to his parents, "Tom is a nice man." This is the child's only description associated with Tom, but it does not identify for the parents who Tom is, as they know many Toms. It might even be that Tom is not a nice man, but the child believes him to be so. In such a case, all of the descriptions that the speaker associates with an object are false, yet it seems that reference successfully occurs. If Searle's view forbids the possibility of the entire disjunctive set of descriptions being false, then such a counterexample would seem to refute Searle.

Why would Searle want to forbid such a possibility? Because he wants to retain the position that words (names) have senses, or meanings. If the disjunctive set of descriptions associated with a name is to give the meaning of a name, the possibility of every description in the set being false would entail the possibility of the name losing its meaning, or having no meaning, supposedly something Searle wants to forbid. The purpose of this chapter is not to debate whether or not Donnellan's counterexample works, but to put forth Wittgenstein's view (and contrast it with Searle's).

Turning to Wittgenstein, I want now to argue that Kripke mistakenly identified Wittgenstein's view with Searle's. This is not to say that Wittgenstein's view is not similar to Searle's in many respects; it is. However, the differences are substantial enough that a clear distinction can be made between them, and arguments offered by Kripke and Donnellan against Searle's view do not apply to Wittgenstein's view.

We saw above that Kripke took paragraph 79 of the *Investigations* to be a forceful statement of the view that "the referent of a name is determined not by a single description but by some cluster or family." This paragraph, he said, is where the idea of family resemblances is introduced (though Wittgenstein actually does so in paragraph 67) and is a good example of the view that "what we really associate" with a name is a family of descriptions. There is an important jump made here that involves a clear misunderstanding of Wittgenstein's view. Kripke didn't say much more directly related to this misunderstanding, but I think it is fair to believe that he was guilty on this point. Schwartz (1977), however, explicitly committed the error, namely, taking Wittgenstein to be saying that we only associate names with a family of descriptions and that words have meaning only in virtue of family resemblances. According to Schwartz:

According to one contemporary version [of a descriptionist theory of reference] there is *not a conjunction* of properties associated with each term, but there *is* a *cluster* of properties associated with it. For example, it is held that we cannot define "game" by a conjunction of properties such as having a winner and a loser, being entertaining, involving the gaining and losing of points, because some perfectly acceptable games lack some of these features. According to the cluster theory, something is a game because it has enough features from a cluster of properties like these. A cluster theorist would claim that there need not be any property in the cluster that is sufficient for the application of the term, but he nevertheless holds that the cluster taken as a whole determines the extension of the term. Wittgenstein's position that there are only family resemblances among the individuals in the extension of many ordinary terms can be construed as a version of the cluster theory. (1977, 15)

True, Wittgenstein's view could be construed as a version of the cluster account, but only on a misunderstanding and false representation of Wittgenstein's position. Wittgenstein's point in introducing the notion of family resemblances was to show that it is a mistake to insist that because we use the same word to refer to different objects that there must be some essential property of those objects in virtue of which we use the same word for them all. (Indeed, his immediate concern was to show that it is mistaken to suppose that there is a general form of propositions, something common to all that we call language. As well, it is mistaken to object to the notion of language games since no essence of a language game can be given.) This is not to say that some words have only family resemblances; some words might well have a single (conjunction of) description(s) giving the meaning of a word, for example, "bachelor" ("adult human male who has never been married") or "mule" ("offspring of a female horse and male donkey"). It *is* to say that many words do not have a single (conjunction of) description(s) giving the meaning of a word.

Furthermore, if the cluster account "holds that the cluster taken as a whole determines the extension" of a term, it is obvious that this is not Wittgenstein's view. The major reason for this is that Wittgenstein denies that it makes any sense to even speak of "the cluster taken as a whole." This is because words (at least some words) are not "closed by a frontier" (1953, para. 68); they have, in Waismann's (1965) terminology, an open texture. Open-texturedness leads into the heart of Wittgenstein's view, and this will be dealt with in the next section of this chapter. About this point, I want to say here that this is precisely the issue of greatest divergence between Wittgenstein's view and Searle's view. Where Searle admitted the sense and usefulness of speaking of the logical sum or inclusive disjunctive set of descriptions associated with a name, Wittgenstein did not; rather Wittgenstein spoke of the lack of any fixed meaning of a name.[1]

Wittgenstein's View

We have seen what Wittgenstein's view is not—it is not a version of the cluster account of names—but the question remains of what it is. In this section I will explicate his view, but first I want to stress that Wittgenstein presented (as Kripke said of his own view) a "better picture" than those given by other views, as opposed to an alternative theory.

Above, Wittgenstein's view on names was hinted at when the differences between his view and Searle's were indicated. The hint was the notion of open texture when dealing with (some) words, and it is best to flesh out this notion now. In paragraph 68 of the *Investigations*, Wittgenstein (1953) says:

"All right: the concept of number is defined for you as the logical sum of these individual interrelated concepts: cardinal numbers, rational numbers, real numbers, etc.; and in the same way the concept of a game as the logical sum of a corresponding set of sub-concepts."—It need not be so. For I *can* give the concept "number" rigid limits in this way, that is, use the word "number" for a rigidly limited concept, but I can also use it so that the extension of the concept is *not* closed by a frontier.

What Wittgenstein was getting at is, on the one hand, the projectibility of words—that is, the propriety and legitimacy of using a word or phrase in a novel manner or context (e.g., "feed" as in "feed the parking meter")—and, on the other hand, the lack of distinct boundaries or a clear extension of a word or phrase (e.g., "game").

Waismann, who coined the term "open texture'" (1965, 125), stated that open texture might mean that we could get acquainted with some totally new experience or that some new discovery could be made that would affect our interpretation of certain facts. He offered the following example:

The notion of gold seems to be defined with absolute precision, say by the spectrum of gold with its characteristic lines. Now what would you say if a substance was discovered that looked like gold, satisfied all the chemical tests for gold, whilst it emitted a new sort of radiation? "But such things do not happen." Quite so; but they *might* happen, and that is enough to show that we can never exclude altogether the possibility of some unforeseen situation arising in which we shall have to modify our definition. Try as we may, no concept is limited in such a way that there is no reason for any doubt. We introduce a concept and limit it in *some* directions; for instance, we define gold in contrast to some other metals such as alloys. This suffices for our present needs, and we do not probe any farther. We tend to *overlook* the fact that there are always other directions in which the concept has not been defined. And if we did, we could easily imagine conditions which would necessitate new limitations. In short, it is not possible to define a concept like gold with absolute precision, i.e. in such a way that every nook and cranny is blocked against entry of doubt. That is what is meant by the open texture of a concept. (1965, 126)

The point is this: when it comes to giving an account of (most) words—including names—we are not able to state a set of necessary and sufficient conditions for the applicability of those words. Specifically, for names, we are not able—contrary to both the descriptionists and causalists—to establish these conditions prior to and independently of the use of the names in discourse. So we cannot say ahead of time, as it were, (1) what conditions must be met for a name to refer to an object, nor (2) what, in general, naming is. A mistake of the descriptionists is the attempt to establish those conditions through the notion of a disjunctive set of descriptions associated with a name; a mistake of the causalists is the attempt to establish these conditions through the notion of a causal chain connecting an utterance of a name and an original baptismal act in which an object is referred to by the name. This aspect of open texture is, for both Wittgenstein and

Waismann, an empirical fact about our use of names; we do in fact often use names without any fixed meaning.[2]

This leads to a question that was touched on earlier in laying out Searle's view. The question was: does at least one member of the disjunctive set of descriptions associated with a name need to be true for reference to be successful? Wittgenstein's answer to this was that the question is a faulty one; it displays a misunderstanding of the relationship between names and descriptions. For Wittgenstein, names can be used as abbreviations for descriptions, although in such cases the name would function not as a name, but as a description. For Wittgenstein, names can be explained by descriptions, but are in no way synonymous with them (see Wittgenstein 1953, paras. 43–45). For example, suppose Jones says something about N and Smith wants to know who N is, to whom reference is being made. Jones remarks that N is the man at the bus stop over there. Now, this description does not define "N" in any sense—the description is not a synonym, and no necessary and sufficient conditions of reference are laid down—rather it helps to identify N for Smith, providing instructions for finding out who N is. If the identification fails—if Smith cannot pick out N—another description might be given (perhaps "N has on a gray hat"). These are the sorts of considerations Wittgenstein had in mind when he spoke of various descriptions that we could use to give the meaning of "Moses" and that we use a name without any fixed meaning. Although descriptions explain (identify)—and, in many cases, make possible—the use of names, the meanings, or uses, of the descriptions are not identical with the meaning, or uses, of the name.[3]

The above remarks sound quite similar to what Kripke had to say about descriptions as reference fixers, and indeed they are similar. However, Kripke's view of descriptions as reference fixers seems to miss Wittgenstein's main point, namely, the open texture of names. Kripke claimed:

Now another view might be that even though the description in some sense doesn't give the *meaning* of the name, it is what *determines its reference* and although the phrase "Walter Scott" isn't synonymous with "the man such that such and such and such and such," or even maybe with the family (if something can be synonymous with a family), the family or the single description is what is used to determine to whom some-one is referring when he says "Walter Scott." . . . some of the attractiveness of the [descriptionist] theory is lost if it isn't supposed to give the meaning of the name; for some of the solutions of problems that I've just mentioned will not be right, or at least won't clearly be right, if the description doesn't give the meaning of the name. . . . If, on the other hand, "Moses" is not synonymous with any description, then even if its reference is in some sense determined by a description, statements containing the name cannot in general be *analyzed* by replacing the name by a description, though they may be materially equivalent to statements containing a description. (1980, 31–32)

Attractiveness notwithstanding, one of Wittgenstein's concerns in talking about open texture was precisely that it is mistaken to think that a name can in general be analyzed by replacing it with a description (see Wittgenstein 1953, para. 63). An identifying description helps to pick out the referent of a name for a given speaker or listener in a given context; in a different situation with a different speaker or listener the identifying description might not succeed in picking out the referent, whereas another description might. Nor was it Wittgenstein's view that offering descriptions as identifying descriptions rather than as synonyms of names is intended to replace talk of meaning of names. That is, to replace talk of descriptions as synonyms with talk of descriptions as reference fixers is not to abandon talk of meanings, for Wittgenstein. Again, Kripke seemed to be assuming that for names to have meanings, they must have fixed meanings, which, as noted above, Wittgenstein denied.

Besides this error of supposing that names are synonymous with their identifying descriptions, philosophers have committed the error of supposing that they are able to uniquely pick out objects prior to or separate from the use of identifying descriptions. This, for Wittgenstein, is a mistaken picture of how reference (and language) works. One possible candidate offered against Wittgenstein's claim is that of ostension. Ostension, it is claimed, is a clear example of picking out referents without appeal to any descriptions. However, Wittgenstein went to some lengths (1953, paras. 27–38) to show the misleading nature of such a claim. The gist of his arguments is that ostension can occur only within a given language game, that is, ostensive definitions only work when it is clear what is being defined, and this cannot happen separate from any descriptions. For example, suppose Jones points to a red pencil and says, "This is tove." Smith might interpret Jones's statement as meaning: a tove thing is a pencil, a tove thing is round, a tove thing is wooden, a tove thing is singular, a tove thing is hard, a tove thing is red, etc. Without some background (or additional) information, Smith is unable to understand and use the word "tove" successfully.[4] Ishiguro (1969) gives a nice summary of Wittgenstein's position on this issue:

The *Tractatus* [and the *Investigations*] view entails that it is the use of the Name which gives you the identity of the object rather than vice versa. . . . If the object can be identified by a description we can learn the reference and use of a name by correlating it to the object picked out by the definite description, as indeed we normally do. . . . The *Tractatus* theory of names is basically correct, however, in so far as it is a refutation of views which assume that a name is like a piece of label which we tag onto an object which we can already identify. A label serves a purpose because we usually write names—which already have a use—on the label. (1969, 34–35)

Criticisms of Wittgenstein

Having shown that Wittgenstein's view on names is not that of Searle's, and having indicated what Wittgenstein's view is, I now want to offer some comments in way of assessment of his view.

It was suggested that a main strength of Wittgenstein's view over Searle's was his recognition of the open texture of words, including names. However, I find the treatment of open texture given by both Wittgenstein and Waismann to be rather unsatisfying in terms of clarifying the role of descriptions in naming and referring. What I find unsatisfying is this: neither Wittgenstein nor Waismann make it clear how open open texture is. Granted, we might not be able to find necessary and sufficient conditions for something being a game or a number or a chair (or even being open textured), but to leave matters at that is not very enlightening. For clearly, the texture of "game" is not so open as to include numbers or chairs in its extension, nor that of "chair" to include numbers or games. What would be helpful, and indeed needed, is an explanation of why open texture is not "wide open texture," that is, how open texture is limited and limiting in the extension of a word (name).

Another fundamental point of Wittgenstein's view is that descriptions associated with a name are not synonyms of the name, but rather are identifying descriptions. However, there are problems here. Consider a case in which Jones says, "I wonder if Aristotle wore socks." Smith, who hears Jones's ponderative utterance, knows only that "Aristotle" is the name Jones uses to refer to some ancient Greek philosopher. Looking in his copy of the definitive work on the history of socks, Smith reads that no ancient Greeks wore socks. Smith relays this information to Jones with syllogistic candor: "No ancient Greeks wore socks; Aristotle was an ancient Greek; so Aristotle did not wear socks." Now, did Smith refer to Aristotle? What would Wittgenstein have said? Smith has been able to use the name "Aristotle" and even to say something true and informative about Aristotle, which would lend credence to saying that Smith has referred to Aristotle. Nevertheless, it seems from what Wittgenstein said about descriptions associated with a name that they are called into play only when reference fails or is unclear from the utterance of a name. So when Jones says something about N ("N has on a gray hat"), Jones might have no descriptions in mind associated with "N." But if Smith is unable to pick out N, Jones can use certain descriptions to help Smith pick out N. If this is so, though, then how could Smith refer to Aristotle in the case of informing Jones that Aristotle did not wear socks? (I must stress here that the problem I see is not so much whether Smith did in fact refer to Aristotle, but where the talk of identifying descriptions fits in. I don't see how Wittgenstein's view makes clear the role of identifying descriptions in the context of referring.)

One objection to my interpretation of Wittgenstein's view might be that I have misrepresented the relationship between naming and descriptions. On this Wittgenstein said:

For naming and describing do not stand on the same level: naming is a preparation for description. Naming is so far not a move in the language-game—any more than putting a piece in its place on the board is a move in chess. We may say: *nothing* has so far been done, when a thing has been named. It has not even *got* a name except in the language-game. (1953, para. 49)

However, it seems to me that the question here isn't over the naming of an object, but whether Smith referred to Aristotle, and, underlying that immediate question, what the role is of identifying descriptions in the context of referring. If descriptions are used even as only identifying descriptions, and not as synonyms of names, they are used to pick out objects. But in this case, it doesn't seem as if Smith can pick out the object, even though Smith was successful in salving Jones's curiosity with a true, informative assertion about Aristotle.

This example points to another issue involved in naming, one that is more of a problem for the causal view of names than for Wittgenstein's view. The issue is the place of evidence in reference. Consider the situation: Jones is an incoming student in the first term of graduate study in philosophy. The faculty members whom Jones has so far encountered at Philosophy University have all been bearded and rather elderly. Jones decides to enroll in a course taught by Professor Schmipke. That is, Jones enrolls in a course, the description of which (in the college catalog) states is taught by Professor Schmipke. At the first class meeting, a clean-shaven, young-looking person enters and begins lecturing. During the course of the lecture, Jones overhears several students remark that they think the lecturer is a graduate assistant (being so young-looking). Later that day, Jones sees the same lecturer sitting in an office which Jones knows is not the office of any other member of the faculty. Later yet, Jones passes the same office and sees the same lecturer still there. As Jones continues down the hallway, Jones meets Smith, who asks, "Have you seen Professor Schmipke?" Jones replies, "Yes, he's in his office now, right down the hall."

In this case, Jones successfully refers, as indeed Schmipke is the clean-shaven, young-looking lecturer. Here is what I find important about the example: the causal theory advocate will claim that Jones referred to Schmipke through a causal chain connecting Schmipke to Jones's contact with the name "Schmipke," which Jones read on the course description in the college catalog, and so forth. But what seems involved in this case is the relevance of evidence Jones had that led Jones to infer that this lecturer was Schmipke. It seems much more likely in this case than in many others the causal advocates cite that evidence plays a genuine role in Jones hooking up a name with an object. On the relation between naming and evidence, Steinman (1982) has shown that the causal chain connecting an object and an utterance of its name is not necessary, and has suggested a spectrum of cases that involve this relationship between naming and evidence. Steinman showed the causal chain to not be a necessary condition for reference to succeed with the following example. Suppose Bob is at a party and sees the wife of his friend Dave. During their conversation, Dave's wife informs Bob that Dave names all of his pets "Sal." She also tells Bob that, Dave being a one-pet-at-a-time man, there is never any confusion as to what he is referring to when he utters the name "Sal." (At any time, Dave has at most one pet and that pet's name is "Sal.") Several days later, Bob comes over to Dave's house and Dave shows Bob his new pet goldfish. Upon seeing the fish for the first time, Bob remarks, "Sal sure is a fine specimen!" In this case, Bob's utterance of the name is not causally connected to the object, even though he successfully referred to the object. The evidence that Bob has about the name of the object (Dave is a one-pet man, Dave names all of his pets "Sal," Dave's wife is known to be a reliable person who always tells the truth, etc.) is what made successful reference possible.

Back to the Schmipke case (in which evidence played a part for reference to have occurred, though not to the extent as in the "Sal" case—hence talk of a spectrum of cases), the point is not at all to deny that a causal chain existed between Schmipke and Jones's utterance of "Schmipke." Indeed, the presence of a causal chain connecting utterances of a name with the referent of a name does not seem to me to be a point of contention between the causalists and Wittgenstein. Both would admit that a causal chain exists between an object and the name-utterances (at least in most cases). Where the conflict of views occurs is in the referring status granted to descriptions. The causalists hold that it is in virtue of the causal chain alone that reference occurs; the descriptionists hold that it is in virtue of descriptions associated with a name alone that reference occurs. Wittgenstein held that in some cases it is in virtue of the causal chain that reference occurs and in some cases in virtue of the descriptions associated with the name. This is to say that Wittgenstein held that there is no unique essence to naming. This denial of an essence to naming is one that Wittgenstein dealt with directly in paragraphs 37 and 38 of the *Investigations*:

What is the relation between a name and the thing named? . . . This relation may . . . consist, among many other things, in the fact that hearing the name calls before our mind the picture of what is named; and it also consists, among other things, in the name's being written on the thing named or being pronounced when the thing is pointed at. . . . we call very different things "names"; the word "name" is used to characterize many different kinds of use of a word, related to one another in many different ways. . . . Naming [under Russell's account] appears as a *queer* connexion of a word with an object.—And you really get such a queer connexion when the philosopher tries to bring out *the* relation between name and thing by staring at an object in front of him and repeating a name or even the word "this" innumerable times. . . . And HERE we may indeed fancy naming to be some remarkable act of mind, as it were a baptism of an object.

Tied in with this belief that there is no essence to naming is the main point of difference between Wittgenstein's view and the causalist view. The difference is made explicit in paragraph 87:

Suppose I give this explanation: "I take 'Moses' to mean the man, if there was such a man, who led the Israelites out of Egypt, whatever he was called then and whatever he may or may not have done besides."—But similar doubt [about meaning and reference] to those about "Moses" are possible about the words of this explanation (what are you calling "Egypt," whom the "Israelites" etc.?). Nor would these questions come to an end when we got down to words like "red," "dark," "sweet."—"But then how does an explanation help me to understand if after all it is not the final one? In that case the explanation is never completed; and I still don't understand what he means, and never shall!"—As though an explanation as it were hung in the air unless supported by another one. Whereas an explanation may indeed rest on another one that has been given, but none stands in need of another—unless WE require it to prevent a misunderstanding. One might say: an explanation serves to remove or avert a misunderstanding—one, that is, that would occur but for the explanation: not every one that I can imagine.

The point of these remarks in relation to the problems of naming and reference is this: in some cases (at least) the presence of a causal chain is unnecessary as an explanation of how reference occurs. (The "Sal" case, as noted above, makes the point that the causal chain isn't even necessary in an explanation of how reference occurs.) Causal chains might well serve as descriptions of how reference occurs, and they might even serve, in some cases, as explanations of how reference occurs, but if what we want is an understanding of how we refer by naming, then causal chains are not needed. Wittgenstein's reasoning is that we require explanations in order to solve problems of failure to understand. Explanations serve to remove or avert misunderstandings, but these explanations are needed only in such a capacity; if there were no misunderstanding that needed removing or averting, the explanation would not be needed. So when it comes to naming, the problems that actually occur, such as knowing the correct name of someone or knowing when to use one name rather than another, are ones such that any misunderstandings that might arise (at least, generally) can be handled without having to bring in talk of underlying causal chains. This is not to deny that causal chains might be invoked in some explanations; it is only to claim that in general such explanations aren't necessary to provide an understanding of how naming and reference successfully occur.

Peter Geach

Recently, several philosophers of language have claimed that, at least in some respects, Peter Geach proposed a view about proper names that anticipated important features of the causal account (or historical chain account) that was later set forth by Kripke, Devitt, and others. Quentin Smith (1999), for example, in his essay, "Direct, Rigid Designation and A Posteriori Necessity: A History and Critique," says explicitly that "Geach (1969) . . . originated the causal or 'historical chain' theory of names." In his entry entitled "Proper Names" for the *Routledge Encyclopedia of Philosophy,* Graeme Forbes speaks of the "Geach-Kripke historical chain account" of proper names. In this section, I suggest that, although there are very clear affinities between Geach's view on proper names and that of Kripke, there are several important differences, differences that are significant enough to claim that Geach and Kripke do not share a single account of proper names.

The Causal (Historical Chain) View

To state again Kripke's "rough statement" and Devitt's fuller remarks:

A rough statement of a theory might be the following: An initial baptism takes place. Here the object may be named by ostension, or the reference of the name may be fixed by a description. When the name is "passed from link to link," the receiver of the name must, I think, intend when he learns it to use it with the same reference as the man from whom he heard it. (Kripke 1980, 96)

The sense in which this is a causal theory of reference is that the passage of a name from link to link is said to secure a causal connection between the name of an object and the object. The initial baptismal act of naming the object (by ostension, perhaps) establishes the causal connection in the first place. Later uses of the name must be connected to the object in some sort of causal chain stretching back to the original naming act. As just noted, Kripke does not explicitly propose a *theory* of reference. However, others (e.g., Devitt) have attempted to forge a fuller causal account of reference based on Kripke's picture. According to Devitt:

The central idea of a causal theory of names is that our present uses of a name, say "Aristotle," designate the famous Greek philosopher Aristotle *not* in virtue of the various things we (rightly) believe true of him, but in virtue of a causal network stretching back from our uses to the first uses of the name to designate Aristotle. It is in this way that our present uses of the name "borrow the reference" from earlier uses. It is this social mechanism that enables us all to designate the same thing by a name. (1981, 25)

There are a number of passages in Geach's works that are strikingly similar to the remarks by Kripke and Devitt just noted above. In his 1969 essay, "The Perils of Pauline" (which both Smith and Forbes cite), Geach says:

I do indeed think that for the use of a word as a proper name there must in the first instance be someone acquainted with the object named. But language is an institution, a tradition; and the use of a given name for a given object, like other features of language, can be handed on from one generation to another; the acquaintance required for the use of a proper name may be mediate, not immediate. Plato knew Socrates, and Aristotle knew Plato, and Theophrastus knew Aristotle, and so on in apostolic succession down to our own times; that is why we can legitimately use "Socrates" as a name the way we do. It is not our knowledge of this chain that validates our use, but the existence of such a chain. (1969, 288–289)

In addition, in his earlier book, *Reference and Generality* (1962), Geach makes it clear that he rejects a descriptivist account of proper names, while at the same time proposing a notion of using identifying descriptions as a means of fixing the reference of a name, just as Kripke does:

A proper name can never be an abbreviation for a definite description; though we may of course introduce a proper name as a name for the object described by such a description. A natural way of effecting such an introduction would be to enunciate a proposition with the proper name as subject and the definite description as predicate: "Neptune is the planet of the Solar System next out from Uranus." If we have no other way of identifying the object named than is supplied by the definite description, it may be natural to think of the proper name as short for the description; but this would be wrong. (1962, 150)

Geach contra Kripke

In spite of the quotations provided above, I want to suggest that Geach's view of proper names has a number of important dissimilarities to Kripke's view. First, Geach rejects the view, one held by Kripke, that names are purely denotative and in no way connotative. As early as 1957, in his book *Mental Acts,* Geach claims that such a view is "entirely false" (66) and "forms part of a highly muddled logical doctrine" (68). Nor is this merely an early view that Geach himself later abandons. In "The Perils of Pauline," noted above, he calls the view that names have no meanings as "worthless" (1969, 297). Second, and more significant, Geach insists that one "cannot learn the use of the proper name without being able to apply some *criterion* of identity" (ibid., 69). It is worth quoting Geach at length here, as it shows a crucial difference between his views and Kripke's:

The theory that proper names have no connotation historically forms part of a highly muddled logical doctrine about "connotation and denotation." A clearer way of stating it is to be found in Locke: that there is nothing essential to an individual. . . . The sense of a proper name certainly does not involve anything about the peculiarities of the individual so named, which distinguish it from other individuals of the kind; a baby, a youth, an adult, and an old man may be unrecognizably different, although the same name is borne throughout life. But it is meaningless to say without qualification that the baby, the youth, the adult, and the old man are "the same," or "the same thing," and that this is what justifies us in calling them by the same name. . . . "The same" is a fragmentary expression, and has no significance unless we say or mean "the same X," where "X" represents a general term. . . . What is implied by our use of the same name throughout a period of years is that the baby, the youth, the adult, and the old man are one and the same *man*. In general, if an individual is presented to me by a proper name, I cannot learn the use of the proper name without being able to apply some *criterion* of identity; and since the identity of a thing always consists in its being the same X, e.g. the same *man,* and there is no such thing as being just "the same," my application of the proper name is justified only if (e.g.) its meaning includes its being applicable to a *man* and I keep on applying it to one and the same *man*. (1957, 68–69)

This passage runs counter to the essentialist underpinnings (i.e., a commitment to haecceities) of Kripke's view that names are rigid designators, as is evidenced by the remarks he makes about an example of "this table." Kripke, in the context of explaining and justifying his conception of transworld identity (i.e., the identity of an object across possible worlds, or across counterfactual conditional statements) claims:

I can refer to the table before me, and ask what might have happened to it under certain circumstances; I can also refer to its molecules. If, on the other hand, it is demanded that I describe each counter-factual situation purely qualitatively, then I can only ask whether *a table*, of such and such color, and so on, would have certain properties; whether the table in question would be *this table*, table T, is indeed moot, since all reference to objects, as opposed to qualities, has disappeared. . . . Don't ask: how can I identify this table in another possible world, except by its properties? I have this table in my hands, I can point to it, and when I ask whether *it* might have been in another room, I am talking, by definition, about *it* . . . We can refer to the object and ask what might have happened to *it* . . . we being with the objects, which we have, and can identity, in the actual world. We can then ask whether certain things might have been true of the objects. (1980, 52–53)

What these two points (viz., names do have meanings and they inherently possess criteria of identity) suggest is that Geach's view of proper names is less like Kripke's and more like Wittgenstein's. Not surprisingly, such a view is not a descriptivist one, as has been shown above. Also, as argued above, Kripke and others (e.g., Schwartz) identify Wittgenstein as having a commitment to a cluster version of a descriptivist view of names. But this is mistaken. As Wittgenstein says later in the section partially quoted by Kripke, "I use the name *X* without *a fixed* meaning." For Wittgenstein, the extension of terms is not "closed by a frontier," including a frontier that is a cluster of descriptions. The point for Wittgenstein—and I am claiming this is true for Geach as well—is this: when it comes to giving an account of names, we are not able to state a set of necessary and sufficient conditions for their applicability. Specifically, for names, we are not able, contrary to both the descriptivists and the causalists, to establish those conditions prior to and independent of the contextualized use of the names. How, then, are we to make sense of Geach's initial remarks that have led Smith and Forbes to see his view as a causal/historical chain view? Like Kripke, and Wittgenstein, Geach emphasizes the sociality of language and of names in particular. Where the use of names can (but needn't) be explained by invoking historical usage chains, what is important for Geach is that these chains explain, or clear up misunderstandings, not by tracing usages back to some initial baptism, but by tracing them back to initial situated uses. Merely having a set of descriptions associated with a name fails to accomplish this, but merely having a chain of linked usages fails as well. As there is not space to flesh this out here, I will end by claiming that, along the lines of Wittgenstein, Geach's view of proper names rejects the notion that the semantics of names can be sufficiently understood apart from the pragmatics of them or apart from their social, communicative roles. These points will be elaborated upon in great length in the upcoming chapters, highlighting how various pragmatist philosophers have accounted for names and reference in general.

4 The Big Three: Peirce, James, Dewey

Naming is, perhaps, the most frequent and an especially important sense of meaning.

—C. I. Lewis, *An Analysis of Knowledge and Valuation*

Charles Peirce

Over the past couple of decades several Peirce scholars have suggested a close connection between Peirce's views on names and reference and the causal account of reference (or direct reference) usually associated with Kripke, Donnellan, Devitt, Putnam, and others. For example, Risto Hilpinen (1994, 290) claims: "Peirce's theory of proper names is a 'direct reference theory,'" and Helmut Pape (1982, 339) remarks that *pace* Peirce, "the naming of an object can occur successfully without a description being used to determine its reference." With respect to proper names, both Hilpinen and Pape, along with others (e.g., Thibaud 1987; Liszka 1996), cite the identical passage from Peirce:[1]

A proper name, when one meets it for the first time, is existentially connected with some percept or other equivalent individual knowledge of the individual it names. It is then, and then only, a genuine Index. The next time one meets with it, one regards it as an Icon of that Index. The habitual acquaintance with it having been acquired, it becomes a Symbol whose Interpretant represents it as an Icon of an Index of the Individual named. (*CP*, 2.329)

In this section I want to suggest that although there are similarities between Peirce's views on names and reference and those of the causal account, there are important and overriding differences that indicate Peirce's views are separable from the causal account.

Criticisms of the Causal Account

Although the causal account by now has become the received account of reference, nonetheless there have been various objections and criticisms leveled against it. The present focus will be on aspects of the causal account that appear to be inconsistent with what I take Peirce's views to be. Three points will be raised:

(1) Names as rigid designators: whereas this is usually taken to be a crowning achievement of the causal account, I will argue that it runs counter to Peirce's view of names.

(2) Semantic reference is separable from speaker reference: for the causal account, what a name refers to and what a person refers to, or intends to refer to, might very well be different (this is the point of several of Kripke's counterexamples to the descriptivist view). I take this intuition to be quite correct, but the underlying view of how language works incorporated here is not, I will argue, consistent with Peirce's views.

(3) There are intuitive counterexamples showing that the causal account of reference fails to give either necessary or sufficient conditions for successful reference. These counterexamples include, but are not restricted to, reference to abstract or future entities, that is, cases in which no causal connection can be established.[2] I will argue that Peirce's view of reference and names are not subject to these counterexamples and that his success in dealing with them helps to delineate his views from the causal account.

Peirce on Names

So, what exactly was Peirce's view on names and reference? It is well known that Peirce's writings can be difficult to grasp and hence summarize. Nevertheless, they can be explicated. As noted earlier, Peirce claimed that a proper name is, at least "when one meets with it for the first time," an index. Again, the passage from 2.329:

A proper name, when one meets it for the first time, is existentially connected with some percept or other equivalent individual knowledge of the individual it names. It is then, and then only, a genuine Index. The next time one meets with it, one regards it as an Icon of that Index. The habitual acquaintance with it having been acquired, it becomes a Symbol whose Interpretant represents it as an Icon of an Index of the Individual named. (CP, 2.329)

Indeed, he repeatedly speaks of the indexical nature of proper names. In his paper, "The Logic of Relatives," he speaks of "An indexical word, such as a proper noun or demonstrative or selective pronoun" (*CP*, 3.460), and in his correspondence with Lady Welby he remarks, "I define an Index as a sign determined by its dynamic object by virtue of being in a real relation to it. Such is a Proper Name (a legisign)" (*CP*, 8.335). Peirce even identifies proper names as "rhematic indexical legisigns" (*CP*, 8.341).[3] As a rhematic indexical legisign, a proper name indicates or points to an object while conveying little or no content about that object (or, in less Peircean language, it indicates a referent but not a sense; or, is purely denotative and not connotative). In Peirce's words, it is "any general type or law, however established, which requires each instance of it to be really affected by its Object in such a manner as merely to draw attention to that Object" (*CP*, 2.259).

So far, so good. And what has been said so far is completely consistent with the causal account of reference (names have no meanings; they are purely denotative; their reference to objects in the world is fixed causally). In spite of these similarities, though, I now want to suggest that there are deeper dissimilarities between Peirce's views and those of the causalists.

Peirce versus Causal Reference

As a sign, a proper name involves a representamen, an object, and an interpretant. Peirce's understanding of both objects and interpretants, I believe, distinguish his view from the causal account. Beginning with the latter, interpretants, I will argue that Peirce's understanding of interpretants precludes Kripke's assertion that names are rigid designators.

In denying that "a particular is nothing but a 'bundle of qualities'" (1980, 52), Kripke claims that names are rigid designators. That is, a name designates the same object in all possible worlds in which it designates any object at all. The object might have essential properties, but these are irrelevant to the individualness of the object. Whatever (if anything) might be essential or defining of Nixon, the name "Nixon" always and only picks out a unique, particular object. That is to say, it picks out a haecceity. This, too, is akin to Peirce's remarks:

Some such sign as the word *this*, or *that*, or *hullo*, or *hi*, which awakens and directs attention must be employed. A sign which denotes a thing by forcing it upon the attention is called an *index*. An index does not describe the qualities of its object. An object, in so far as it is denoted by an index, having *thisness*, and distinguishing itself from other things by its continuous identity and forcefulness, but not any distinguishing characters, may be called a *hecceity*. (*CP*, 3.434)

While this sounds perfectly consistent with Kripke's notion of rigid designation, Peirce says more that does not jibe with Kripke. First, in "The Logic of Relatives," he claims: "An indexical word, such as a proper noun or demonstrative or selective pronoun, has force to draw attention of the listener to some hecceity common to the experience of speaker and listener" (*CP*, 3.460). I take this commonality of experience of speaker and listener to be a necessary, and not merely accidental, feature of the haecceity of the object. By saying this, I am not—nor is Peirce—at all advocating an idealist metaphysics. The object, at least the Dynamical Object, might very well exist completely independently of speaker or listener (though, if it is fictive, it might not). Nevertheless, names as signs cannot be rigid designators, if that involves a representamen and object, but no interpretant. And it is the interpretant that I take here to be reflective of the commonality of the experience of speaker and listener. This, I think, is reinforced by further remarks by Peirce on the nature of haecceities:

Otherness belongs to hecceities. It is the inseparable spouse of identity: wherever there is identity there is necessarily otherness; and in whatever field there is true otherness there is necessarily identity. Since identity belongs exclusively to what is *hic et nunc*, so likewise must otherness. It is, therefore, in a sense a dynamical relation, though only a relation of reason. It exists only so far as the objects concerned are, or are liable to be, forcibly brought together before the attention. Dissimilarity is a relation between characters consisting in otherness of all the subjects of those characters. Consequently, being an otherness, it is a dynamo-logical relation, existing only so far as the characters are, or are liable to be, brought into comparison by something besides those characters in themselves. (*CP*, 1.566)

Of course, Nixon is Nixon and the name "Nixon" refers to a particular object, but as a name, "Nixon" also involves an interpretant. It is this semiotic element that is inconsistent with the concept of rigid designation, since the interpretant is the "effect of the sign," or even, as the Final Interpretant, "that which would finally be decided to be the true interpretation if consideration of the matter were carried so far that an ultimate opinion were reached" (CP, 8.184). We cannot, for Peirce, simply ignore or eliminate this semiotic element of names; yet that is exactly what treating names as rigid designators does. Indeed, when Peirce (1998, 480) claims that a sign's "Interpretant is all that the Sign conveys," he surely rejects names as rigid designators, since names convey more than the mere existence of an object.

This leads to an even deeper difference between Peirce and Kripke, namely, a difference on how reference and language work in general. Where Kripke and others want to separate out the semantic features of reference, Peirce emphasizes the semantic, pragmatic, and semiotic features of reference (and, for that matter, of names). These differences can be enunciated by looking at what he says about signs and representation:

"Representation" and "sign" are synonyms. The whole purpose of a sign is that it shall be interpreted in another sign; and its whole purpose lies in the special character which it imparts to that interpretation. (*CP*, 8.191)

As Christopher Hookway puts it: "A thought , utterance, or other sign denotes an object only because it can be interpreted in subsequent thought as a sign of that thing" (2000, 126). This is not a conflation of semantic reference with speaker reference, which is how Kripke and others try to handle the sociality of language. Rather, the point is that denotation is not "merely" a semantic function. Not simply *our* ability to denote, but a sign's ability to denote, is possible because there are inseparable pragmatic and semiotic elements inherent in semantics. Names don't denote all on their own! (Though, for the purposes of some analysis, we might want to focus on semantic features, by abstracting them away from other features, say, speaker intention.) This, I take it, is much the point that Hilary Putnam (1981) makes in the following example. Suppose, he says, that in crawling across the sand an ant traces a particular pattern of lines which we depict as a recognizable caricature of Winston Churchill (or suppose the ant traces a particular pattern of lines which we depict as a recognizable shape resembling the name "Winston Churchill"). Would we say the ant has referred to Winston Churchill? (I would even add, would we say the line pattern refers to Winston Churchill?) Putnam says: no. What might seem to be missing for reference to have occurred is the element of intention. However, this will not do. As Putnam says:

But to have the intention that *anything* . . . should *represent* Churchill, I must have been able to *think about* Churchill in the first place. If lines in the sand, noises, etc., cannot "in themselves" represent anything, then how is it that thought forms can "in themselves" represent anything? (1981, 2)

Just as physical representations (e.g., lines in the sand) have no necessary connection to objects, so mental representations also have no necessary connections to objects. Words, signs, are included here: a discourse might seem to be, say, a description of a tree, but if it was produced by monkeys randomly hitting keys on a keyboard for millions of years, then the words would not refer. This pragmatic view is echoed by Catherine Elgin:

intending to produce an effect by getting one's audience to recognize one's intention to produce that effect is not, or at least is not always, required for reference. Someone talking in his sleep or under the influence of anesthesia or, for that matter, someone who is unconsciously "thinking out loud" may have no such intention. Whether to say that such a person refers depends on how his words are interpreted. If we can make no sense of his utterances we put them down to inchoate ramblings. If their interpretation is straight-forward, we take his utterances to be sentences, and the terms in them to refer. It is the availability of a reasonable interpretation rather than the intention with which they were produced that is crucial in decided whether his words refer. (1983, 17)

The relevant points, here, with respect to Peirce, I take it, are that Kripke's desire to make reference a purely semantic issue is mistaken. As signs, names refer, even as indices, only because of the sociality of signs—only because they involve interpretants (and interpreters).

These remarks, that Peirce's understanding of interpretants distinguishes his view from the causal account, are further supported, I believe, by Peirce's understanding of objects and the role of information connected to objects. With respect to objects, Peirce says the following:

We must distinguish between the Immediate Object,—i.e. the Object as represented in the sign,—and the Real (no, because perhaps the Object is altogether fictive, I must choose a different term, therefore), say rather the Dynamical Object, which from the nature of things, the Sign *cannot* express, which it can only *indicate* and leave the interpreter to find out by *collateral experience*. For instance, I point my finger to what I mean, but I can't make my companion know what I mean, if he can't see it, or if seeing it, it does not, to his mind, separate itself from the surrounding objects in the field of vision. It is useless to attempt to discuss the genuineness and possession of a personality beneath the histrionic presentation of Theodore Roosevelt with a person who recently has come from Mars and never heard of Theodore before. (*CP*, 8.314)

Signs are not singular, isolated entities; they cannot properly be understood in a purely synchronic way. They are diachronic and communal. The very ability of them to represent and to be informative rests on this diachronic communality. There is an inherent continuity of signs, both in terms of their diachronicity and in terms of their communality. Nor is this the touted sense of names' referring via a community of speakers, associated with Kripke. His communality is after the fact, so to speak. For him, the reason we can now refer to Nixon by the name "Nixon" is the causal network that the community of speakers has built up over time. But this communality, for Kripke, is not inherent in his view of the nature of names.[4]

Earlier in this section I said that there were three points I wanted to make: first, that Kripke's notion of names as rigid designators runs counter to Peirce; second, that Kripke's insistence on understanding names in purely semantic ways runs counter to Peirce; and third, that Peirce's views are immune to several criticisms of the causal account of reference, specifically that the causal view cannot account for reference to abstract and future objects (since how could we be causally affected by them?). (Also, how can we make sense of names of abstract or future objects?) The solution to the question of how reference can be made to objects that do not exist, either in the sense of future objects (the one-hundredth President of the United States) or in the sense of nonphysical objects (the number two) is simply that these can be, for Peirce, Dynamical Objects, as can fictional objects. As such, they can be treated as any other Dynamical Object and be understood in terms of his analysis of signs and semiosis.[5]

William James

A core concern among contemporary analytic philosophers of language is the topic of reference, along with related issues of meaning and truth. Although the ideas of William James on these latter issues, including his disputes with Bertrand Russell, are somewhat legendary, he wrote little directly on the topic of reference. Nevertheless, a conception of reference, including an underlying notion of the semantic and pragmatic features of language, can be extracted from James's works. Robert Burch (1979), in his essay "James and the 'New Theory of Reference,'" has suggested that several important features of the causal account of reference (or direct reference), which is usually associated with Kripke, Donnellan, and others, were anticipated by ideas of William James. I disagree, at least with some important details of his suggestion. In this section, I will outline Burch's account for how James anticipates central features of the causal account. Having done that, I will argue that James's ideas relating to reference are not as closely aligned with the causal account as Burch suggests. I claim that Burch has not fully made his case for these connections, and further that those ideas that can be culled from James on the issue of reference reveal a view that is sufficiently different from and superior to the causal account.

Burch's View

Burch claims that there are three positive features of the Kripke–Donnellan theory that James anticipated. The first feature is that the referential unit is considered to be an act—a speech act, writing act, or (possibly) a mental act. Says Burch: "Language itself is not what refers, as Russell perhaps thought; it is persons who refer with language, in speaking, writing, and (possibly) thinking. Being an event in history, the referential act is in the continuous stream of temporal experience, and it has concrete causal and explanatory relations with the rest of the world" (Burch 1979, 284).

The second feature is that the doctrine of reference goes hand in hand with a doctrine of truth. This is as it should be, says Burch, since the truth of an assertion obviously depends in some strong way on the successful accomplishments of the assertion's referential acts.

The third feature is that reference is established by something like a causal or referential chain, as exemplified in the earlier quotes by Kripke and Devitt, rather than being established by some sort of "inner, mental act of pointing that hits its target automatically" (ibid., 285).

Having identified these features of the causal account of reference as ones anticipated by James—and having noted that there are other features of the account, such as Kripke's thesis that names are rigid designators, that are not anticipated by James—Burch then proceeds to flesh out what James's ideas of reference are and attempts to show that these ideas are similar enough to the modern causal account to warrant holding them as anticipations of it. He makes his case about James by first detailing James's view of truth, particularly James's view of truth as a version of a correspondence account of truth. There are three keys components of James's correspondence account: first, there is the term designating that which is to correspond to reality; second, there is reality itself; and third, there is the correspondence relation.

The first component, the thing that is true, is, for James, often characterized as a belief, thought, or idea. The central point here is that the thing that is true is concrete, historical, and temporally present in the world, as opposed, say, to Russellian "propositions." As Burch puts it: "Truths are possessions of particular human beings at particular times and places" (ibid., 287).

The second component, reality, is the world of pure experience, which for James includes relations as well as properties and objects. The third component, the correspondence relation itself, is, in James's terminology, an *ambulatory* relation, one in which "there is a continuous path or a successive series of steps by which the one *relatum* leads up smoothly or stepwise to the other" (ibid., 289). This ambulation is constitutive of the relation of truth, and, indeed, is the fundamental pragmatic notion of "workings," that is, the understanding that truth happens to an idea. As Burch claims: "To a great extent, James's notion of 'working(s)' simply *is* this notion of ambulation, along continuously connected intermediaries, between the true idea and reality" (ibid., 290). The agreement between truth and reality is constituted by the "workings" of true ideas, and these workings in turn are ambulatory relations connecting true ideas with the realities of which they are true.

Having briefly laid out James's view of truth, Burch uses this to make an explicit account of a Jamesian view of reference. As Burch puts it:

My central claims about James's theory of reference are that for James, the *agreement* of an idea *with* reality and the *reference* of an idea *to* reality are inextricably intertwined, and that both involve the same chain of empirical intermediaries stretching between the idea and the rest of the world. The same notion of "workings" underlies both truth and reference. (Ibid., 291)

And, indeed, James says as much in *The Meaning of Truth*:

Reference, then, to something determinate, and some sort of adaptation to it worthy of the name of agreement, are thus constituent elements in the definition of any statement of mine as "true." You cannot get at either the reference or the adaptation without using the notion of workings. (James 1970, 218)

It is, for Burch, this notion of workings and James's insistence on a chain of empirical intermediaries that especially demonstrates the kinship (and anticipation) of James's ideas with the new causal account. Again, in Burch's words: "the existence of a chain of empirical links running continuously from the referring act to the referent is actually constitutive of the reference. That is to say, the existence of such a chain is a necessary condition of a successful reference. Without it, one has at best only intended reference" (Burch 1979, 293).

Finally, Burch argues that this position of James is held not only for reference in general, but also for proper names. This is exemplified in the discussion, in James's *The Meaning of Truth*, of the case of Julius Caesar. In underscoring his position that a statement's truth invokes the concept of its workings, James asks how it can be that my statements about Caesar can be true and can refer to the original person, Caesar. His answer is there are (or would be) "finite intermediaries between the two original facts. Caesar *had*, and my statement *has*, effects; and if these effects in any way run together, a concrete medium and bottom is provided for the determinate cognitive relation. . . . The real Caesar, for example, wrote a manuscript of which I see a real imprint, and say, 'the Caesar I mean is the author of *that*.'" (James 1970, 222). Burch concludes by asking: "What could make it any clearer that the heart of the 'new' theory of reference was genuinely new only to James?" (1979, 293).

Concerns and Criticisms

I think that Burch is absolutely right that James's ideas about reference resonate with the new causal account. I also agree with much of his characterization of just what James's ideas about reference are. However, in the final analysis, Burch is mistaken on several counts. I will argue that, although he is essentially correct in his portrayal of James's position, James's position is less like the causal account than Burch asserts. First, I suggest that Burch has mischaracterized the causal account in some respects. Second, I will flesh out what I see as James's position on reference and why I see it as distinct from and superior to the causal account.

So why isn't Burch's account of the causal view correct? It is not correct on two of the three features that he discusses: first, that reference is a speech act, and second, that reference is so intimately associated with truth. To the first claim, that reference is a speech act, Kripke, Donnellan, Devitt, and others have all insisted that there is a clear difference between the semantic meaning (or referent) of a term/name and the speaker's meaning (or referent). So: I might mean to refer to James when I utter the name "Peirce," but the name "Peirce" refers to Peirce, not to James. Of course, referring is an act made by a speaker, but for the causalists, the semantic reference of a term/name is not at all the sort of thing that speech-act theorists are talking about. The name, once established (say, in a baptismal act) has a semantic life of its own, independent of how I use it or misuse it. This is important, I believe, in distinguishing James's position from the causal account, and I will return to this below.

The second feature of the causal account that Burch identifies is the intimate connection between reference and truth. He rightly points out that the truth of sentences is dependent upon the terms in the sentence referring. Nevertheless, the nature of the relation between reference and truth is more than this. For one thing, terms/names refer, but they are not true; sentences are true, but they do not refer. Because of this, Kripke simply does not discuss truth, or theories of truth, in fleshing out his picture of reference. For him, it simply is not necessary. In addition, though this point is not crucial for the present concerns, there is the question of whether the truth of a sentence is in fact dependent upon the successful reference of its terms. For example, suppose that after a quarrel, I want to say something disparaging about my friend Richard Robin. So, I sneeringly refer to him as "Peirce," as in: "Well, I see fine Mr. Peirce decided to show up to work today." My utterance is true (he's here!), though, of course, the name unsuccessfully (improperly) refers. (Or, one might say that the utterance, along with the speaker's reference, is true, while the sentence, along with its semantic reference, is false.)

As with Burch, though, my main concern here is with James's ideas of reference. What are they? Burch quite correctly points out that the concept of workings underlies and is central to James for both truth and reference. He is also right to insist that, for James, any account of reference must be intimately connected with an account of truth, precisely because both depend on workings. (And this is exactly one of the differences between James and Kripke.) As noted earlier, James explicitly remarks: "You cannot get at either the reference or the adaptation without using the notion of the workings" (1970, 218). As Burch points out, these workings involve empirical intermediaries between the individual belief and an object referred to or believed to be true.

However, these intermediaries are not the historical causal links going back to some baptismal naming ceremony, as they are for Kripke. Rather, the sociality of the intermediaries is, for James, of a different sort. First, for James the point is that the connections between the name and the object cannot simply be a matter of private mental associations. This sounds very much like the causal account, but not quite. As Burch himself points out, James's notion of workings is future-oriented, not past-oriented. He says that this is still a version of the causal view (in which the intermediaries are obviously past-oriented causal connections) because the past (and future) is the only means of access to the past. I take James's position somewhat differently. Workings are future-oriented; truth happens to sentences and reference happens to terms/names because of how we use them in the future, not simply because of a past causal chain of uses. Of course, there might well be a past chain of uses of a name, but, for James, those cannot be constitutive of the name's ability to refer (much less a speaker's ability to refer by using that name). The sociality of reference, indeed the sociality of language generally, is for James the future-oriented workings. Past referrings, "older truths" as James says, are clearly a significant part of the future orientation, but they do not define or constitute it. The very possibility and fact of reference change speaks on behalf of James's position and against Kripke's. As Gareth Evans (1985) showed, the reference of the name "Madagascar" changed from its original object, namely, a portion of the African mainland, to the island offshore. In addition, reference to abstract objects (such as numbers) or to future objects (such as, say, my first grandchild) is unproblematic under James's notion of workings and his future-oriented view of the sociality of reference. So, although both James and Kripke insist on reference as a social, public function of language, and object to reference as a purely private, mental affair, they conceive of the sociality of language in different ways. James's, I believe, is superior.

This difference can be highlighted by reference to James's "skrkl" example, given in *The Meaning of Truth*. He proposes that we take an example of a term that has no possible workings, an utterance of the (to us, nonsensical) term "skrkl." Perhaps I say, "Peirce was quite a skrkl." Either my claim is true, or false, or "irrelative" (i.e., not relatable to anything). James says:

> For it not to be irrelevant (or not-cognitive in nature), an object of some kind must be provided which it may refer to. Supposing that object provided, whether "skrkl" is true or false [i.e., refers or not] of it, depends, according to Professor Pratt [for our purposes, Professor Kripke], on no intermediating condition whatever. The trueness or the falsity [read: the semantic reference] is even now immediately, absolutely, and positively there. (1970, 171)

I take, then, the sort of causal chains enunciated in the causal account of reference to be something different from the needed intermediaries outlined in James. His sociality has to do with the future uses of a term/name as constitutive of its reference at least as much as its past and present uses.

This is related to another difference between the causal account and James's ideas, namely, the nature of truth. Although I think that Burch is completely correct to insist that James's pragmatic view of truth is properly seen as a correspondence view, I would characterize it a bit differently. Clearly, for a statement to be true, it must connect to reality. In addition, however, James is explicit about truth as a form of expediency. As he says in "Pragmatism's Conception of Truth": "'The true,' to put it very briefly, is only the expedient in the way of our thinking, just as 'the right' is only the expedient in the way of our behaving" (1995, 86). This axiological base for truth points to the coherentist aspects of James's notion of truth. So, he claims: "A new opinion counts as 'true' just in proportion as it gratifies the individual's desire to assimilate the novel in his experience to his beliefs in stock" (1995, 25). I would characterize this position as the view that, for James, truth is not a dyadic relation simply between reality and the statement (or belief) or a dyadic relation simply between a past stock of statements (or beliefs). Rather, it is a triadic relation between reality, a past stock of statements (or beliefs), and the present statement (or belief) at issue. Likewise for reference. It is not simply a matter of being part of a causal nexus and having a semantic correspondence. Nor is it simply a matter of having a set of beliefs or descriptions associated with a term/ name. Reference presupposes an ability by speakers to use language, and this language use is dependent upon purposive, social behavior.

"Vicious Abstractionism"

I have argued in this section that Burch has not made his case that James anticipated much of the causal account of reference. I first suggested that Burch's portrayal of the causal account is not quite accurate, and I second claimed that James's ideas are actually different in important ways from the causal account. I have only hinted at why I take James's ideas to be not just different from, but superior to, the causal account. I will finish this section with one fuller hint in this direction.

One element of Kripke's view is the unimportance of the question of haecceity and individuation of objects, unimportant in the sense that he adopts a view as given. His notion of rigid designation (that a name refers to the same object in all possible worlds in which it refers at all), I believe, rests on a particular conception of individuation and a conceptual comfort with haecceities and bare particulars. For example, he says: "Unless we assume that some particulars are 'ultimate,' 'basic' particulars, no type of

description need be regarded as privileged. . . . Don't ask: how can I identify this table in another possible world, except by its properties? I have the
table in my hands, I can point to it, and when I ask whether *it* might have
been in another room, I am talking, by definition, about *it*" (1980, 51, 53).
I confess that I, at least, have qualms about this, but more importantly for
now, I believe that James does, too. For example, in "Two English Critics"
(in *The Meaning of Truth*), James criticizes what he sees as Russell's "vicious
abstractionism":

> The abstract world of mathematics and pure logic is so native to Mr. Russell that
> he thinks that we describers of the functions of concrete fact must also mean fixed
> mathematical terms and functions. A mathematical term, as a, b, c, x, y, sin., log.,
> is self-sufficient, and terms of this sort, once equated, can be substituted for one
> another in endless series without error. Mr. Russell . . . seem[s] to think that in our
> mouth also such terms as 'meaning,' 'truth,' 'belief,' 'object,' 'definition,' [and I
> would add 'reference'] are self-sufficients with no context of varying relation that
> might be further asked about. . . . But may not real terms, I now ask, have accidents
> not expressed in their definitions? And when a real value is finally substituted for
> the result of an algebraic series of substituted definitions, do not all these accidents
> creep back? (1970, 276–278)

I take James here to be concerned with the sort of formal stipulation of reference or identity independent of the concept of workings, as it applies to
both the object itself and our beliefs about it. This, I take it, holds for James
in the case of Russell and, had he known of him, in the case of Kripke. A
fuller discussion of the issue of haecceities will come in chapter 8.

John Dewey

In his introduction to Dewey's *The Quest for Certainty*, Stephen Toulmin
claims that these lectures "show us just how different John Dewey's philosophical methods and arguments were from those of William James and
Charles Sanders Peirce, and so how misleading it can be to lump them
all together, as the single school of 'pragmatists'" (LW.4.ix).[6] In spite of
Toulmin's warning, and in spite of the differences between Dewey and
(other) pragmatists, he is almost universally grouped with Peirce, James,
and others as being among the classical American pragmatists. I will do so
here for the purposes of outlining an alternative conception of reference
and names to the prevailing received views. While there certainly are differences between Dewey and Peirce and James, there is enough of a family

resemblance among their views on reference and names to warrant grouping them together under a pragmatist rubric. In this section I will argue
that Dewey's views on reference and names, along with his views on the
neighboring issues of haecceities, meaning, and even language in general,
all show him to be closely aligned with those views of Peirce and James
and Wittgenstein. Indeed, Dewey had much more to say explicitly and
directly about these various topics than did either Peirce or James. In addition, it offers a corrective to the current received models of names and
reference, namely, the descriptivist view (associated with Searle) and the
causal view (associated with Kripke).

Dewey on Language

Late in his life, Dewey remarked that "We take names always as namings: as
living behaviors in an evolving world of men and things. Thus taken, the
poorest and feeblest name has its place in living and its work to do, whether
we can today trace backward or forecast ahead its capabilities; and the best
and strongest name gains nowhere over us completed dominance" (LW:
16.7). This quotation points to a number of features not only of Dewey's
view of names, but of his view of language in general, a view that underlies
his understanding of names. First, by claiming that names are namings, it
points to his insistence that "things" be understood as processes, especially
when those "things" (such as language) are human creations and artifacts.
Second, as living behaviors they are organic reactions to the world—they
are part of our engagements as agents in the world. Third, names, language,
behaviors, all have "work to do." They are the result of, and also a means
of, our inquiry (which is never disinterested) and our purposive agency.
Fourth, names have capabilities. They are, as for Dewey all language is,
tools. We use them in the context of our purposive conduct.

These four features highlight Dewey's overall understanding of language, which, in *Knowing and the Known* (1949), he defines as follows:
"Language: To be taken as behavior of men (with extensions such as the
progress of factual inquiry may show to be advisable into the behaviors of
other organisms). Not to be viewed as composed of word-bodies apart from
word-meanings, nor as word-meanings apart from word-embodiment. As
behavior, it is a region of knowings. Its terminological status with respect
to symbolings or other expressive behaviors of men is open for future
determinations" (LW.16.266).

As a number of Dewey scholars (e.g., Sleeper [1986]; Burke [1994]; Tiles [1988]) have noted, Dewey's conception of language is grasped only in the context of his theory of inquiry and the naturalistic, evolutionary stance that he takes as the starting point for all inquiry. Besides being a process, language, for Dewey, is also an organic reaction to the world. It is worth quoting Dewey at length on this point. From *Experience and Nature* he claims:

Language is a natural function of human association; and its consequences react upon other events, physical and human, giving them meaning or significance. Events that are objects or significant exist in a context where they acquire new ways of operation and new properties. Words are spoken of as coins and money. Now gold, silver, and instrumentalities of credit are first of all, prior to being money, physical things with their own immediate and final qualities. But as money, they are substitutes, representations, and surrogates, which embody relationships. . . . Language is similarly not a mere agency for economizing energy in the interaction of human beings. It is a release and amplification of energies that enter into it, conferring upon them the added quality of meaning. . . . Gestures and cries are not primarily expressive and communicative. They are modes of organic behavior as much as are locomotion, seizing and crunching. Language, signs and significance, come into existence not by intent and mind but by over-flow, as by-products, in gestures and sound. The story of language is the story of the *use* made of these occurrences; a use that is eventual as well as eventful. . . . The heart of language is not "expression" of something antecedent, much less the expression of antecedent thought. It is communication; the establishment of cooperation in an activity in which there are partners, and in which the activity of each is modified and regulated by partnership. (LW.1.138–141)

In terms of language having "work to do," Dewey is explicit about this when he speaks of naming: "Naming does things. It states. . . . Naming selects, discriminates, identifies, locates, orders, arranges, systematizes. Such activities as these are attributed to 'thought' by older forms of expression, but they are much more properly attributed to language when language is seen as the living behavior of men" (LW.16.134). This view of naming, and of language generally, is certainly reminiscent of (though it predates) Wittgenstein's notion of language games as well as the speech-act views of Austin and Searle.

The fourth feature of language noted above, that of language as a tool, is ubiquitous throughout Dewey's writings. As early as 1897 (EW.5.73) and as late as 1949 (LW.16.134), he describes language as a tool. As a tool, language is purposeful; it is used to accomplish something. In addition, like tools, language has physical features that are separable from their use in the purposive behavior of the tool-user.

Dewey's emphases, then, when focusing on language, are varied. One emphasis is on the nascence of language. As his remarks about gestures and cries noted above reveal, he takes language to be one of many organic behaviors that emerged out of our interactions with our natural and social environments. In his 1922 *Human Nature and Conduct*, he reiterates this position: "Men did not intend language; they did not have social objects consciously in view when they began to talk, nor did they have grammatical and phonetic principles before them by which to regulate their efforts at communication. These things came after the fact and because of it. Language grew out of unintelligent babblings, instinctive motions called gestures, and the pressure of circumstances. But nevertheless language once called into existence is language and operates as language. It operates not to perpetuate the forces which produced it but to modify and redirect them" (MW.14.56).

Besides pointing to the nascence of language, Dewey, as already noted, emphasizes the sociality of language, both in its genesis and in its functions, especially its communicative function.[7] Both these emphases are captured by his characterization of language as a behavior in "the region of knowings," and this is why commentators have insisted that his understanding of language be placed in the context of his theory of inquiry.

Another emphasis of Dewey is on the publicity of language, indicated in his definition mentioned above as having a terminological status "open for future determination." This points to publicity in two respects. First, "terminological status" refers to its terminal status, that is, what, say, a name will ultimately mean or refer to. Second, "terminological status" refers to a word's status as a linguistic term, say, as a name. In both senses, what Dewey is getting at is that what counts as being a linguistic term and what is its meaning or reference is a matter of future determination, that is, by its public, social functioning in the interactive discourse of language users. It is not a matter of simply what a single person means "in his head" so to speak, nor is it a matter of simply the given semantic content or role it has had in the past. This, I take it, is a crucial distinction between Dewey's view of language and of names and reference, indeed of a pragmatist view in general, and the received views of language, names, and reference.

Dewey on Names

The features and emphases found in Dewey's view of language generally, viz., as arising out of purposeful engagement with the world, as being public and a matter of future determination, as being instrumental, are also seen explicitly in his conception of names. Just as he insisted that language is a form of living behavior, so he insists on viewing names most often in the context of naming:

Naming we take as behavior, where behavior is process of organism-in-environment. . . . Except as behavior—as living behavioral action—we recognize no name or naming whatever. Commonly, however, in current discussions name is treated as a third type of "thing" separate both from organism and from environment, and intermediate between them. In colloquial use this makes little difference. But in the logics and epistemologies, a severed realm of phenomena, whether explicit or implicitly introduced, matters a great deal. Such an intervening status for "name," we, by hypothesis, reject. (LW.16.133)

As with language generally, naming is not simply behavior, but purposeful behavior. Namings, and names, are possible and understandable only as forms of purposive activity. They are interest-laden, which he makes clear in *Knowing and the Known*, where he enunciates three conditions for a good understanding of names and namings: (1) names are to be based on such observations as are accessible to and attainable by everyone; (2) the status of observation and the use of reports upon it are to be tentative, postulational, hypothetical; and (3) the aim of the observation and naming adopted is to promote further observation and naming which in turn will advance and improve (which, as he says, "excludes all namings that are asserted to give, or that claim to be, finished reports on 'reality'" [LW.16.46]).

This focus for Dewey on *namings* is important. This very term is intended to stress the process-nature of what we take as names. Names, as means we use to function in the world, are purposive, behavioral processes. How something can become a name is a crucial feature of what a name is. We can, of course, for various purposes overlook this underlying process-nature of names and simply use them to designate objects or events in the world (or, for that matter, objects and events not "in the world"), but their process-nature is what allows names to function as names nonetheless. For example (again from *Knowing and the Known*): "Name, as a 'thing,' is commonly spoken of as a tool which man or his 'mind' uses for an aid. This split of a 'thing' from its function is rejected" (LW.16.133).

Contra Causal Reference

How, specifically, do Dewey's views on names and reference differ from the received views? Much as Wittgenstein insists on seeing reference (or referring) in the context of explanation and in the context of forms of life, Dewey speaks similarly:

The *word* "reference" ranges, I think, from a loose use, e.g., "alluding to," "mentioning," "speaking of," to an "overt" event of *Application* (as overt as applying a plaster to the back, or mucilage to stick pieces of paper together), i.e., bringing events in direct "connection" that were previously only connected by intermediates. This *bringing* into direct connection is what I take to be *experiment* as *test*. . . . Or a *name* can be firm only when *con*firmed, tested, in this fashion. "Light," a name; "light" as electric-magnetic hypothesis, arrived at by mathematical reasoning, a symbol-term; "light" *is* electric-magnetic; a *name* arrived at by an operational event of direct application of events to one another as directed or dictated by hypothesis, and testing the validity of the latter. (Letter to Arthur F. Bentley [September 13–15, 1943] in Ratner and Altman 1964, 175)

Dewey considers the ordinary language housing of the notions of reference and names, and sees there some value, namely, in understanding "refer" etymologically as carrying or bearing back. But, since symbols are human products, products of purposive inquiry, he goes past the ordinary language housing and insists on the testing and confirmation of uses of names, of referrings. Clearly, then, reference is not a private matter. This is important to remember in light of remarks he makes relating names and descriptions. This is important because, though some of what he says seems to be strictly in line with a descriptivist view of names (and reference), this is only tentatively the case. His allusions to descriptions (much like Wittgenstein's) must be understood in the context of purposeful, public inquiry. So, just what does he say about names and descriptions? Again, it is worth quoting him at length:

Description: Before passing to specification it will be well to attend to the status of names and naming with respect to descriptions. Phrasings develop around namings, and namings arise within phrasings. A name is in effect a truncated description. Somewhat similarly, if we look statically at a stable situation after a name has become well established, a description may be called an expanded naming. The name, in a sense which is useful if one is careful to hold the phrasing under control, may be said to name the description, and this even more properly at times than it is said to name the object. For naming the object does not legitimately, under our approach, name an object unknown to the naming system; what it names is the object-named (with due allowance for the other forms of knowing on the sensorimanipulative-perceptive level of signal); and the object-named is far more fully set forth in description than by the abbreviated single word that stands for the description. . . . Bertrand Russell and several of his contemporaries have had a great deal of trouble with what they call "descriptions" as compared with what Russell, for instance, calls "logical proper names." Fundamentally Russell's "proper names" are analogous of the cue—reminiscent of primeval yelps and of the essences and entities that descend from them, to which it is that Russell wishes to reduce all knowledge. At the far extreme from his form of statement stands specification as developed out of characterization by expanding descriptions which in the end have attained scientific caliber. It is to Specification rather than to survivals of primitive catch-words that our own procedure directs itself in connection with progress of knowledge. Our most advanced contemporary cases of scientific identification should certainly not be compelled to comply with a demand that they handcuff themselves "logically" to a primitive type of observation and naming, now scientifically discarded. (LW.16.146–147)

There is a lot to unpack here, though much of it has been stated already. First, it is patently clear that, for Dewey, to say that a name is "in effect a truncated description" is not at all the sort of view that is associated with Russell or Searle. Dewey's point is that a name functions in a way so as to identify an object. But objects are not simply bare particulars; they are what he has dubbed an "object-named," that is, portions of the world, aspects of our knowings, that we find important enough in the context of our inquiries to label. Names can provide a much more convenient label for us than descriptions, especially as our inquiries firm up our ontology. So, names are not just truncated descriptions (or clusters of descriptions) that a speaker might have associated with an object. They are part of our efforts to specify objects in line with our epistemic and practical concerns. Following the just-quoted passage, Dewey characterizes "specification" as "the type of naming that develops when inquiry gets down to close hard work, concentrates experimentally on its own subject matters, and acquires the combination of firmness and flexibility in naming that consolidates the advances of the past and opens the way to the advances of the future" (LW.16.148).

A second point to be gleaned from Dewey's remarks about names as truncated descriptions is his rejection of the Russellian notion of proper names. This is particularly important because it is not simply a rejection of *Russell's* notion of proper names, but more widely is a rejection of taking logical names (or logical constants) as functioning as names, or namings, in any genuinely fruitful way. This is part of his overall conflict with Russell. For the purposes of looking at Dewey's views on names and reference, the point here is that this is part of a rejection of treating logical name-letters as functioning as names for objects, except in a derivative way. To couch this in the context of the causal view of reference, this is a rejection of names as rigid designators and a rejection of the conception of haecceity that underlies the notion of rigid designators.

Kripke (along with many others) explicitly is committed to treating proper names as names of particulars, and as will be noted below this entails commitments that Dewey rejects. The name "Aristotle" refers to Aristotle, independent of any descriptions that might be associated with Aristotle. We can represent Aristotle in the context of formalized sentences by using a particular name-letter, or logical constant, because that name-letter carries no commitment with it other than to designate a particular object. It is just this sort of haecceity that Dewey questions. For example, in *Logic: The Theory of Inquiry*, he states, "A singular as a mere *this*, always sets a problem. The problem is resolved by ascertaining *what* it is—that is, the kind it is of. This fact alone is enough to show the identity of the two apparently different matters of determining the temporal endurance of an event and determining its kind. 'This' is an intellectual puzzle until it is capable of being described in terms of what, linguistically, is a common noun. The description *is* qualification of the singular as one of a kind" (LW.12.248). Indeed, as early as 1890 in his essay, "Is Logic a Dualistic Science?," he speaks approvingly of Venn's criticisms of this underlying haecceitic notion of objects:

And Mr. Venn shows clearly and decisively, to my mind, that in the most elementary recognition of an object processes of analysis and synthesis of very considerable complexity are involved. . . . In like manner, Mr. Venn attacks what he well calls the "alphabetic" view of nature; the idea that objects come to us, so sharply discriminated and separated that one may be represented by A, another by B, and so on. "Generally speaking what we mark out by the letters A, B, C, are more or less fictitious entities, that is, they are manifold groups, held together in a mental synthesis with the cohesive assistance of name. . . . The mere reference to individuals as the basis or starting point of our instruction presupposes that something has already been done to recognize and constitute these A, B, C as individuals." (EW.3.78)

It is clear that, for Dewey, name-letters (and names) can function to represent objects only against a full background of assumptions about the objects named. It simply is not the case that we can just say that "Aristotle" names Aristotle independent of this background. *That* an object is is not given in isolation of *what* an object is; for Dewey, a named object is always what he calls a named-object. Being a named-object presupposes context, or what he calls "features of a situation":

Let us return then to the hypothesis that in actual use names call attention to features of a situation; that they are tools for directing perception or experimental observations. The first thing to be noted is that the "situation" is referred to only in the (literally) *most general way*, as the limiting including thing within which specific things are pointed out. . . . The *situation* as such in short is taken for granted. *It* is not stated or expressed. It is implicit, not explicit. Yet it supplies meaning to all that is stated, pointed out, named. . . . Recur now to the actual naming or pointing. It discriminates, distinguishes something; makes it explicit, states or expresses it. That which is pointed to gives the meaning of the word or directive gesture. But the *lone* thing pointed at has no meaning. We always distinguish one thing *from* something. All explicit names point out then a comparison-contrast of at least two things. A this by itself . . . has no meaning. It is not an expression or statement, but merely another thing, a noise or figure. (MW.13.414–415)

This difference in view between Dewey and Kripke is highlighted by the remarks the latter makes about an example (already noted here in this and earlier chapters) of "this table." Kripke, in the context of explaining and justifying his conception of transworld identity (i.e., the identity of an object across possible worlds, or across counterfactual conditional statements) claims:

I can refer to the table before me, and ask what might have happened to it under certain circumstances; I can also refer to its molecules. If, on the other hand, it is demanded that I describe each counter-factual situation purely qualitatively, then I can only ask whether *a table*, of such and such color, and so on, would have certain properties; whether the table in question would be *this table*, table T, is indeed moot, since all reference to objects, as opposed to qualities, has disappeared. . . . Don't ask: how can I identify this table in another possible world, except by its properties? I have this table in my hands, I can point to it, and when I ask whether *it* might have been in another room, I am talking, by definition, about *it*. . . . We can refer to the object and ask what might have happened to *it* . . . we being with the objects, which we have, and can identity, in the actual world. We can then ask whether certain things might have been true of the objects. (1980, 52–53)

For Kripke, an object is simply what it is. Its identity is separable from our identification. The point carries over, of course, to transworld identity versus transworld identification. Although we might use or need certain properties or descriptions to enable us to identify some object, its identity, what it is, is independent of those identifications. Dewey's point, however, is not that there is no difference between identity and identification. Rather, it is that the concept of identity of an object cannot function in isolation from our identifications of that object. When Kripke insists that this table is the same one that he spoke of an hour ago, and we ask, "Which table?," he can only repeat, "*This* table!" Likewise, for Kripke, "Aristotle" simply picks out Aristotle. Independent of any and all means we have of identification, Aristotle just is Aristotle; he is given. It is this notion of a simple, given object that Dewey questions, as we saw above.

Connected with this issue of objects being given, Kripke and others seem to take our awareness of this given object as quite straightforward. Or, another way of saying this is that they take not only the object as given but also the process of our awareness of the object as given. It is usually characterized as simply a matter of ostension, of simply seeing or pointing (as in, "*This* table," accompanied by a pointing gesture). Dewey's remarks on ostension and pointing make it clear that he takes this process as not nearly so straightforward. Pointing, Dewey claims (MW.13.389), is ambiguous; it might mean a direct act or the function of evidence, but (LW.12.58) words themselves provide no evidence for existence. As he says in *Democracy and Education*, "We cannot procure understanding of their meaning by pointing to things, but only by pointing to their work when they are employed as part of the technique of knowledge" (MW.9.230). This remark reinforces his insistence that language, and now even pointings, make sense only in the context of purposive inquiry. Pointing presupposes not just purposive inquiry, but, as noted above for named-objects, a situation: "It is impossible merely to point *at* something. For anything or everything in the line of vision or gesture may be equally pointed *at*. The act of pointing is wholly indeterminate as to its object. It is not selective within a situation, because it is not controlled by the problem which the situation sets and the necessity for determining the conditions which then and there point to the way in which it shall be resolved" (LW.12.126). Indeed, the very notion of a given requires the context of situation: "The point just made has its logical meaning in disclosure of the ambiguity of the word *given* as that is currently employed in logical texts. That which is 'given' in the strict sense of the word 'given,' is the total field or situation. The given in the sense of the singular, whether object or quality, is the special aspect, phase or constituent of the existentially present situation that is selected to locate and identify its problematic features with reference to the inquiry then and there to be executed" (LW.12.127).

Of course, we can point out objects successfully in everyday, ordinary contexts. Most of the time we understand the situation well enough to recognize the salient aspects of a situation for pointing to be successful. As Dewey says,

"Pointing" on the basis of previous mutual understanding is one thing, but the kind of understanding (or definition) that might be developed from pointing alone in a communicational vacuum, offers a very different sort of problem. Nevertheless, regardless of all such absurdities the ostensive definition, since Mill's time, has gained very considerable repute, and is, indeed, a sort of benchmark for much modern logic, to which, apparently, the possession of such a name as "ostensive definition" is guarantee enough that somewhere in the cosmos there must exist a good, hard fact to go with the name. The ostensives, and their indefinables and ultimates, seem, indeed, to be a type of outcome that is unavoidable when logic is developed as a manipulation of old terminologies using "definers," "realities," and "names" as separate components, instead of being undertaken as an inquiry into a highly specialized form of the behaviors of men in the world around them. (LW.16.181–182)

The point of this present discussion is that Dewey rejects the Kripkean view that there are objects that are simply givens and that names pick out these given objects in a purely semantic, denotative manner. Not only does Dewey see names as more than mere denotative labels, he also sees the objects of those names as being part of a situation. The identity of haecceities, bare particulars, objects can be seen after the fact of inquiry, as it were, and as separable from our identifications of them, but only in the context of communicative, public, purposive inquiry. As Tom Burke (1994) and others have insisted, Dewey's criticisms of much of contemporary logical theory must be understood in the context of his naturalistic demand that logical theory (including logical characterizations of individuals) be housed within the motivations and constraints of inquiry. To put this another way, although identity and identification are not identical, they are separable only for particular purposes; they are not inherently separate. So, Kripke's insistence that we just have this table, or that Aristotle is just Aristotle, is something that Dewey finds highly context-sensitive. Yet it is just this notion of given individuals that underlies Kripke's notion of names as rigid designators. Names designate rigidly, for Kripke, because they (must) pick out *the same object* across worlds. But, for Dewey, what counts as the same object, indeed, what counts as the object at all, is not simply given, as it is for Kripke. The issue of identity across worlds, then, is of a kind with the issue of identity across time (in this world). Dewey is very clear that this issue of identity across time, or sameness, is part of the larger issue of the nature of inquiry. Once again, it is worth letting Dewey speak at length for himself:

Take the grounded proposition that the evening and the morning star are the same planet. This is not an idea of a fact given in immediate experience. It is not an aboriginal datum within the experience. It is warranted in and by a highly complex set of observations as these are systematized by certain conceptions of the structure of the solar system. The case of the identity of the sun is simpler but it is of the same order. The only conclusion which can be drawn from logical theory from these considerations is that the problem of the sameness of the singular object is of the same logical nature as the problem of kinds. Both are products of the continuity of experiential inquiry. Both involve mediating comparisons yielding exclusions and agreements and neither is a truth or datum given antecedent to inquiry.

They are not only products of the same operations of inquiry but are bound up together. *The determination that a singular is an enduring object is all one with the determination that it is one of a kind.* The identification of a sudden light as a flash of lightning, of a noise as the banging of a door, is not grounded upon existential qualities which immediately present themselves, but upon the qualities with respect to *the evidential function* or use in inquiry they subserve. What is recurrent, uniform, "common," is the power of immediate qualities to be *signs*. Immediate qualities in their immediacy are, as we have seen, unique, non-recurrent. But in spite of their existential uniqueness, they are capable, *in the continuum of inquiry*, of becoming distinguishing characteristics which mark off (circumscribe) and identify a *kind* of objects or events. (LW.12.248–249)

All of this discussion over the past several pages has been to say that Dewey rejects the view of names as rigid designators that is associated with Kripke and the causal view of names. In addition, Dewey questions the strong semantic meaning versus speaker meaning view that Kripke holds, along with the corollary that words (names) can have meaning, or can refer, on their own, separate from their housing in inquiry.

5 Contemporary Americans: Putnam, Elgin, Rorty

A concern with explaining the possibility of *communication* can lead to a concern with *reference* and *representation*.

—Robert Brandom, *Articulating Reasons*

Hilary Putnam

It has been claimed that recently there has been a renaissance of pragmatism in the philosophical community. Not only have a multitude of books and articles on pragmatism been published in the past several decades, but notable thinkers across philosophical traditions have embraced or at least paid homage to it, thinkers ranging from Quine, Putnam, and Rorty to Habermas, Ricoeur, and Apel. Nevertheless, though in one sense this claim of renaissance is true, it is misleading—misleading because pragmatism has been with us continuously since Peirce is said to have coined the term in 1870s. Russell and Dewey engaged in rousing debates on epistemology, logic, and truth throughout the early decades of the 1900s; Quine championed pragmatism via his brand of naturalism over the past fifty years. Habermas and Apel have advocated pragmatism in some form or other since the 1960s. So, although pragmatism as a philosophical tradition, or perhaps school, has been overshadowed throughout much of the twentieth century by other traditions and schools (e.g., logical empiricism, ordinary language analysis, phenomenology, structuralism, critical theory), it has not been absent and has not lacked influence.

One of the most notable neo-pragmatists is Hilary Putnam. As will be seen below, although there has been a waxing and waning at different times in his career of being labeled "neo-pragmatist," he would have welcomed this label during much of his philosophical career.[1] At one time claiming that his basic philosophical position should have been termed "pragmatic realism," he has throughout five decades of writings frequently identified the classical pragmatists as sources of inspiration and insight. Pragmatist themes abound in his works: the rejection of genuinely disinterested inquiry, the rejection of a fact–value dichotomy, the rejection of essentialism. Even today, after abandoning pragmatic realism, he cites William James in particular as an especially important forerunner of his direct, or natural, realism. In addition, Putnam is uniquely positioned in a discussion of pragmatism and reference, as his work on reference has been at the center of the rise of the causal, or direct, reference view, just as his later writings have been at the center of questions and interpretations of this view.

Meanings Ain't in the Head

Though Putnam wrote numerous, often fairly technical, pieces for two decades prior to the 1975 publication of his essay, "The Meaning of 'Meaning,'" it was this latter that made Putnam's writings on reference renowned and resulted in his being acknowledged as one of the founding architects of a new theory of reference.[2] Consistent with, though independent of, Kripke's criticisms of the descriptivist view of reference, Putnam put forth his own critique of descriptivism. Here Putnam lays out his famous Twin Earth thought experiment, which highlights several features of his early views on reference, especially the necessarily social dimension of cognition and reference: the linguistic division of labor, the rigidity of natural kind terms, the cognitive significance of stereotypes, the commitment to realism. Although at this time Putnam did not focus on the pragmatist aspects of these features, as we will see, they are there. Indeed, as Putnam's own views and assessment of his own views changed, he came not so much to abandon these features as to reinterpret them through a pragmatist lens.

Putnam begins "The Meaning of 'Meaning'" claiming: "Language is the first broad area of human cognitive capacity for which we are beginning to obtain a description which is not exaggeratedly oversimplified. . . . The most serious drawback to all of this analysis, as far as a philosopher is concerned, is that it does not concern the meaning of words. . . . The reason that the prescientific concept of meaning is in bad shape is not clarified by some general skeptical or nominalistic argument to the effect that meanings don't exist. Indeed, the upshot of our discussion will be that meanings don't exist in quite the way we tend to think they do" (1975b, 215–216).

He ends the essay by remarking:

If there is a reason for both learned and lay opinion having gone so far astray with respect to a topic which deals, after all, with matters which are in everyone's experience, matters concerning which we all have more data than we know what to do with, matters concerning which we have, if we shed preconceptions, pretty clear intuitions, it must be connected to the fact that the grotesquely mistaken views of language which are and always have been current reflect two specific and very central philosophical tendencies: the tendency to treat cognition as a purely *individual* matter and the tendency to ignore the *world*, insofar as it consists of more than the individual's "observation." Ignoring the division of linguistic labor is ignoring the social dimension of cognition; ignoring what we have called the *indexicality* of most words is ignoring the contributions of the environment. Traditional philosophy of language, like much traditional philosophy, leaves out other people and the world; a better philosophy and a better science of language must encompass both. (Ibid., 271)

What lies between? Twin Earth and all its implications! Twin Earth is like our Earth except that the liquid called "water" there has a chemical composition of XYZ, not H_2O. Though Twin Earthlings might have the same phenomenal properties associated with "water" that Earthlings have (odorless, colorless liquid), the term "water," says Putnam, does not have the same extension across these two worlds. "Water" on Earth refers to H_2O, whereas "water" on Twin Earth refers to XYZ. The extension of the term "water" is not determined by the intension of the term; additionally, the intension of the term is not determined by what individual speakers might have associated with it. Likewise, Putnam says, beech trees and elm trees are different species. A speaker might intend to refer to a beech while using the term "elm," but "elm" refers to elms, not to beeches. Quite simply, individual speakers can be mistaken about the meaning and extension of the terms they use. Calling a beech an elm, and being firmly convinced that I'm right, doesn't make it an elm. Again, the extension of the term "elm" is not determined by the intension, nor is the intension determined by what individual speakers might have in mind. As Putnam majestically and succinctly puts it: "Cut the pie any way you like, 'meanings' just ain't in the *head*!" (ibid., 227).

A larger message to get from this thought experiment is that, along the lines of Kripke's rigid designators, natural kind terms (like "water" or "elm") are rigid in their meaning, in what they refer to (though Kripke avoids talk of meaning[s]). Of course, "elm" doesn't refer to elm trees all on its own; it is a word, a human artifact. How, then, does "elm" have its meaning and extension? It has it by virtue of paradigms, stereotypes, and the linguistic division of labor. A paradigm, for Putnam, is simply an exemplar or sample or token that functions for speakers in a linguistic community to assign a meaning to a term, whereas a stereotype is a set of beliefs associated with them. For "water," that might be a sample of water, for "elm" a specific nearby tree, for "gold" perhaps a particular nugget, for "tachyon," say, a stipulated definition. We, as individuals and as a language community, might use this stereotype to fix the meaning of the term (likely based on phenomenal properties of the stereotype). But the extension of the term then has a life of its own, so to speak, apart from the cognitive associations of specific speakers. As the language community comes to know more and more about those things referred to, the extension of the term might well change; for example, whales are not fish, but mammals. (Of course, a change of the extension of a term is not the same thing as the nascence of ambiguity or vagueness of a term. Some paradigms can be discovered not to be in the extension of a term.) There is a linguistic division of labor, says Putnam, and "experts" determine the meaning and extension of these terms. As Putnam says, "We could hardly use such words as 'elm' and 'aluminum' if no one possessed a way of recognizing elm trees and aluminum metal; but not everyone to whom the distinction is important has to be able to make the distinction. . . . The features that are generally thought to be present in connection with a general name—necessary and sufficient conditions for membership in the extension, ways of recognizing if something is in the extension ('criteria'), etc.—are all present in the linguistic community *considered as a collective body;* but that collective body divides the 'labor' of knowing and employing these various parts of the 'meaning' of 'gold'" (1975b, 227, 228). Words, like Wittgenstein said, are tools, but they should be thought of as less like a screwdriver and more like a steamship; they are tools that we use, certainly, but they are ones that require collective, cooperative use.[3]

With respect to proper names, Putnam remarks that:

it is instructive to observe that nouns like "tiger" or "water" are very different from proper names. One can use the proper name "Sanders" correctly without knowing anything about the referent except that he is called "Sanders"—and even that may not be correct. . . . But one cannot use the word tiger correctly, save *per accidens*, without knowing a good deal about tigers, or at least about a certain conception of tigers. In this sense concepts *do* have a lot to do with meaning. (1975b, 247)

Here Putnam's view of names as being purely denotative, shared by Kripke, is clear (though, contra Kripke, he does not take a purely denotative view of natural kind terms). Nevertheless, in his 1973 "Explanation and Reference," Putnam enunciates some distance between his view of names and Kripke's. After acknowledging a "heavy indebtedness" to Kripke's work on names and identifying the essential aspect of Kripke's view on names as a historical chain connecting the user of a name to the bearer of the name, Putnam then gently demurs:

Now then, I do not feel that one should be quite as liberal as Kripke is with respect to the causal chains one allows. I do not see much point, for example, in saying that someone is referring to Quine when he uses the name "Quine" if he thinks that "Quine" was a Roman emperor, and that is all he "knows" about Quine; unless one has *some* beliefs about the bearer of the name which are true or approximately true, then it is at best idle to consider that the name refers to the bearer in one's idiolect. (1975b, 203)

Even here, with respect to names, Putnam insists on the collective sociality of reference (and the ability to refer): "Indeed, what is important about Kripke's theory is not that the use of proper names is 'causal'—what is not?—but that the use of proper names is *collective*" (ibid.).

Realisms

In his 1985 Paul Carus Lectures, published two years later as *The Many Faces of Realism*, Putnam proclaimed: "The key to working out the program of preserving commonsense realism while avoiding the absurdities and antinomies of metaphysical realism in all its familiar varieties (Brand X: Materialism, Brand Y: Subjective Idealism, Brand Z: Dualism . . . . .) is something I have called *internal realism*. (I should have called it pragmatic realism!) Internal realism is, at bottom, just the insistence that realism is *not* incompatible with conceptual relativity" (1987, 17).

This passage highlights what some have seen as a later, different Putnam from the Putnam of "The Meaning of 'Meaning,'" whereas others have seen it as a maturation of the earlier Putnam. Beginning with his 1976 John Locke Lectures, published in 1978 as the bulk of *Meaning and the Moral Sciences*, and delivered only one year after publication of "The Meaning of

'Meaning,'" Putnam's stance on a number of issues displayed a rethinking, or at least a reevaluation, of his earlier work. As will be seen, his writings throughout the late 1970s and all of the 1980s reveal not a complete break with his earlier work, but certainly a different take on the issue of reference and its attendant metaphysical and epistemological commitments. The openly pragmatist turn that Putnam takes during this time can be seen in how he treats a constellation of topics—truth and assertability, individuation and similarity, explanation and understanding—as well as what he says explicitly about the new (causal) theory of reference and Kripke.

Starting with the passage quoted above, what does Putnam take realism to be and what does he take conceptual relativity to be? He distinguishes metaphysical realism from internal (pragmatic) realism. In "Realism and Reason," his 1976 Presidential Address to the Eastern Division of the American Philosophical Association, he characterizes metaphysical realism as "less an empirical theory than a model"; a model that is, or purports to be, a model of the relation of any correct theory to all or part of the world. Metaphysical realism is the view that there is a single, correct symbolic representation of the world. There is *a* way the world is, and our best science will ultimately (we hope) capture that. This metaphysical realism, which Putnam likes to suggest is realism with a capital "R," is not only opposed to all forms of irrealism, but is also opposed to common sense, or realism with a small "r" (since in our best science, we will represent the world as being constituted by, say, quarks and leptons rather than by tigers and gold). Underlying metaphysical realism is the notion that nature is partitioned in a particular way, that similarities are given, that we will discover (we hope) the individuals and kinds that compose the furniture of the world. Internal realism rejects these features. Just as there can be alternative mappings of a geographer's description of the Earth (e.g., mercator, polar), so there can be alternative yet equivalent descriptions of the way, or ways, the world is. Internal realism is not committed to there being one, and only one, true theory of the world. Our symbolic representations of the world are, in effect, answers we give to questions about the world; they are explanations we give for our passive and active engagements with the world. But explanations are interest-relative.

With the relativity of cognitive goals and interests, there is conceptual relativity, but, as noted above, for Putnam this is not incompatible with (internal) realism. To illustrate this compatibility, Putnam offers the following example. Consider a world with three individuals, x_1, x_2, and x_3. Given these individuals, how many objects are there in this world? There are at least two legitimate answers, he says: three and seven. The explanation that provides the answer of "three" takes the three individuals (i.e., x_1, x_2, x_3) to be the only objects that there can be in the world. The explanation that provides the answer of "seven" allows that objects can include the mereological sums of individuals as well as the individuals (i.e., x_1, x_2, x_3, x_1+x_2, x_1+x_3, x_2+x_3, $x_1+x_2+x_3$). This is not simply a verbal difference of how to define "object," but an ontological and conceptual difference of what counts as being an object. As Putnam puts it: "The logical primitives themselves, and in particular the notions of object and existence, have a multitude of different uses rather than one absolute 'meaning'" (1987, 19). From the insistence on this conceptual relativity, though, it does not follow that anything goes, that all is relative. Three individuals were given, not three hundred or any old number. The larger moral is that

elements of what we call "language" or "mind" *penetrate so deeply into what we call "reality" that the very project of representing ourselves as being "mappers" of something "language-independent" is fatally compromised from the very start.* Like Relativism, but in a different way, [Metaphysical] Realism is an impossible attempt to view the world from Nowhere. In this situation it is a temptation to say, "So we make up the world," or "our language makes up the world," or "our culture makes up the world"; but this is just another form of the same mistake. If we succumb, once again we view the world—the only world we know—as a *product*. One kind of philosopher views it as a product from a raw material: Unconceptualized Reality. The other views it as a creation *ex nihilo. But the world isn't a product. It's just the world.* (Putnam 1990, 28)

Given this brief statement of internal realism, it is apparent what Putnam takes to be realist about his position—we engage in the world that is independent of our representations of it—as well as what is internal about his position—our engagement with the world is always mediated through interest-relative representations. These two aspects of his position become clearer as he elaborates on attendant philosophical concerns of truth and assertability, of our partitionings of the world, and of how these relate to both explanation and understanding.

About truth, Putnam insists that abandoning metaphysical realism does not entail abandoning truth, even a traditional correspondence theory of truth. Rather, he says, it involves a shift to the notion of warranted assertability. By the early 1980s (e.g., with the publication of *Reason, Truth and History*), he characterized truth as "an idealization of rational acceptability" and as "ultimate goodness to fit" as well as (in *Realism and Reason*) "idealized justification." We can still *define* truth as correspondence *pace* Tarski, because his definition is neutral. But our *understanding* of truth is not neutral. To define truth as correspondence to facts is consistent with any ontological view. The schema that '*S*' is true iff *p* (where *p* is a proposition and *S* is the name of the proposition) is acceptable to Tarski ('Grass is green' is true iff grass is green) as well as to Goodman ('Grass is grue' iff grass is grue). Where the work occurs, and how we understand this, is with the notion of satisfaction (for Tarski) or reference (for Putnam). What is it for this schema to be satisfied? Answering that leads us away from a purely formal realm into one of ontological and epistemological commitments. As Putnam puts it, it involves not just formal theory, but total theory, "our total theory of knowledge, where this involves our theory of nature and our interactions with nature" (1978, 37). Our correct mapping(s) of language to the world is not one-to-one, but many-to-one. These mappings are not just given, they are our attempts to represent our environment(s). As such, they are interest-relative, and they function in and as our explanations of nature and our interactions with nature. As Reuben Abel remarked, "explananda are not part of the world; they exist only as a function of human curiosity" (1982, 87). For Putnam, what counts as an explanation (an explanation per se, not merely a good explanation) depends on background knowledge and our reason for asking the question. "So 'why-questions'—and hence explanations—*presuppose ranges of interest*" (Putnam 1978, 43). This issue relates directly to the issue of truth as correspondence, including the two supposed components of correspondence, namely, language and the world. The metaphysical realist conception of truth as correspondence is that a sentence is true when it hooks up to "the way things are (independent of our perspective, interests, goals, etc.)," and Putnam asks, what sort of explanation is this? But, says Putnam, this conception of correspondence simply does no work, and it presupposes, rather than explains, metaphysical realism. Putnam claims this view is unintelligible. It is worth quoting him at length:

First, I contend that there is not *one* notion of an "object" but an open class of possible uses of the word *object*—even of the technical logical notion of an object (value of a variable of quantification). The idea that reality itself fixes the use of the word *object* (or the use of the word *correspondence*) is a hangover from prescientific metaphysics. Second, the idea of the world "singling out" a correspondence between objects and our words is incoherent. As a matter of model-theoretic fact, we know that even if we somehow fix the intended truth-values of our sentences, not just in the actual world but in all possible worlds, this does *not* determine a unique correspondence between words and items in the universe of discourse. Third, even if we require that words not merely "correspond" to items in the universe of discourse but be causally connected to them in some way, the required notion of "causal connection" is deeply *intentional*. When we say that a word and its referent must stand in a "causal connection of the appropriate kind," then, even in cases where this is true, the notion of "causal connection" being appealed to is fundamentally the notion of *explanation*. And explanation is a notion which lies in the same circle as reference and truth. (1990, 173)[4]

Of note in this passage is Putnam's contention that the very notion of "object" is not one that is simply given, which, of course, was one of the points of the above example of three (or seven) objects in a world composed of x_1, x_2, and x_3. What we will take to be objects (including individuals, kinds, events, processes, and so on) is not simply given, and is certainly not explained by appeal to correspondence or metaphysical realism. Additionally, what counts as "the same" object or what counts as similarity between objects (hence making them similar enough to be the same kind of object) is also not simply given or explained nonpragmatically.

On Causal Reference

During the period between Putnam's Locke Lectures (1976) and his Gifford Lectures (1990), he reexamined and critiqued his earlier views on reference, sometimes roundly criticizing aspects of those views and other times insisting on the fundamental soundness of them. One aspect of his view that remained unwavering is his rejection of a descriptivist view of names and of an "internalist" view of reference. So, in the Locke Lectures he remarks, "it seems to me that it is not *wholly* wrong to think of reference as a causal-explanatory notion" (1978, 17). In *Representation and Reality*, he claims "reference is *socially* fixed and not determined by conditions or objects in individual brains/minds. Looking inside the brain for the reference of our words is, at least in cases of the kind we have been discussing, just looking in the wrong place" (1988, 25). In the 1989 "Why Is a Philosopher?" (reprinted in Putnam 1990, 105–119) he says, "Words acquire a kind of 'direct' connection with their referents, not by being attached to them with metaphysical glue but by being used to name them even when we supposed the identifying description may be false, or when we consider hypothetical situations in which it is false" (1990, 109).

Besides consistently denying a descriptivist view, Putnam's pragmatist turn retained, and in fact augmented (though perhaps with different emphases), his insistence on the sociality of reference (i.e., the linguistic division of labor) and the "contribution of the environment":

> As I see it, "meanings ain't in the head"; the actual nature of the paradigms enters into fixing reference, and not just the concepts in our heads. Another important feature of both Kripke's theory and mine is that reference is determined *socially*. To determine whether or not something is really gold a native speaker may have to consult an expert, who knows the nature of gold better than the average person does. The chain of historic transmissions which preserve the reference of a proper name in the Kripke theory is another form of social cooperation in the fixing of reference. The idea that the extensions of our terms are fixed by collective practices and not by concepts in our individual heads is a sharp departure from the way meaning has been viewed since the seventeenth century. (1983, 75)

(Again, as noted in note 3 above, Kripke takes exception with Putnam's claims about the appeal to experts and to the linguistic division of labor.)

While retaining these features of an understanding of reference, Putnam reinterprets them such that he says repeatedly during this time (1976–1990) that he would like to distance himself a bit more from Kripke than he had in the past. Indeed, as will be detailed below, Putnam openly criticizes a number of aspects of Kripke's view. Before getting to those criticisms and his own pragmatist view of reference, it is important to point out that Putnam distinguishes a "causal theory of reference" from the "picture" that he attributes to his earlier views and to Kripke. Where Putnam repeatedly chastises the causal theory of Fodor (1990), Devitt (1981), and others,[5] he insists that these attempts at a causal theory are quite different from his and Kripke's nondescriptivist picture. So, in *Renewing Philosophy*, he states:

> I should note here in passing that Kripke and I have both denied quite consistently that what we are proposing is a theory of reference in Fodor's sense, that is to say, a definition of reference in causal terms. What Kripke and I have defended is the idea that certain sorts of words can refer only if there is a causal connection between them and certain things or certain kinds of things. But we have never tried to *reduce* reference to causation. (1992, 221n4)

This disclaimer notwithstanding, Putnam during this time does distance himself from Kripke on a number of grounds. First, Kripke makes it clear that once "the appropriate historical connections exist" (Kripke 1986, 247), the semantic reference of a term is fixed and nothing within or about the community of speakers is relevant to that reference. The entire community of speakers could turn out to be wrong about what is referred to by a term and nevertheless succeed in referring, again, provided the appropriate historical connections exist. Putnam, though, claims that appropriate historical (causal) connections do not determine reference because what counts as the *appropriate* connections, and especially having the intentions to determine which connections are appropriate, *presuppose* the ability to refer. He says, "if I say 'the word "horse" refers to objects which have a property which is connected with my production of the utterance "There is a horse in front of me" on certain occasions by *a causal chain of the appropriate type,'* then I have the problem that, if I am able to specify what *is* the appropriate type of causal chain, I must *already* be able to refer to the kinds of things and properties that make up that kind of causal chain" (Putnam 1981, 66). Of course, Kripke's position is that whether I can specify appropriate causal chains is irrelevant to whether or not the causal chains exist. And this points to a deeper difference between their views, namely, one of the nature of language generally. That difference is that Kripke takes there to be a distinct difference between the semantics of a term and the pragmatics of a term, indeed between semantics and pragmatics of language generally. For Putnam, that distinction is blurred, to say the least. We can, of course, for particular purposes, focus on the semantics of a term (or the syntax of a sentence) in isolation from the pragmatics, just as, for particular purposes, we can focus on the color of a lamp shade in isolation from its shape. But, from that fact, it doesn't at all follow that the semantics of the term is what determines the reference of it. One of Putnam's larger concerns about reference generally is to account for how we are able to refer, how language connects with the world. Throughout his writings, and especially during this time period, he insists that words by themselves (i.e., semantics alone) cannot do this. This is the point of his claim that a discourse on paper might seem to be a perfect description of trees, "but if it was produced by monkeys randomly hitting keys on a typewriter for millions of years, then the words do not refer to anything" (Putnam 1981, 4). Again, for particular purposes, we might focus on the semantic meaning or reference of a term separate from speaker meaning or reference, but it does not follow from this that reference is captured by semantics, and it also does not follow that simply having appropriate (whatever constitutes that!) connections determines reference.

A further separation of Putnam's views from Kripke's revolves around the notion and presuppositions of rigid designation. Rigid designation takes as a given that an individual can be identified and individuated and that that individual has cross-world identity independent of its accidental features. This, for Putnam, is a commitment to both "objective" individuation and essentialism. He rejects both. This is especially, though not only, apparent in his 1989 essay, "Is Water Necessarily H_2O?" (reprinted in Putnam 1990, 54–79). Here he argues that Kripke takes it that there is a fact of the matter as to what it is to be a particular individual. For Kripke, we can simply, and appropriately, say that Aristotle just *is* Aristotle and that he is the same individual across possible worlds. What makes him the same individual across possible worlds must be that there is some essence to him. If the name "Aristotle" is a rigid designator, it must designate the same individual across possible worlds, some there must be a given haecceity for it to designate. This, Putnam says (1983, 64) is the most controversial part of Kripke's view and one which Putnam claims (1983, 220) presupposes essentialism. For Putnam, we can speak of relative essences, that is, what is essential to something given a description or category. So, relative to "that statue," we can speak of a particular shape as being essential, or relative to color, we can speak of "that hue" as being essential. Perhaps, as Kripke would like, even relative to some purpose, we could identify something's origin as being essential, but, again, that would be against a background of a description or category. (We can't simply say the origin of "that," but of "that X.")

So, although Putnam continues to see the contributions of the language community and of the world as constitutive of reference, and sees these as fundamental components of Kripke's view, he places them in a larger context (i.e., beyond "simply" semantics) than does Kripke. Taking an image from Wittgenstein, he summarizes his views at this time:

Of course, from my point of view the "epistemological" and "ontological" are intimately related. Truth and reference are intimately connected with epistemic notions; the open texture of the notion of an object, the open texture of the notion of reference, the open texture of the notion of meaning, the open texture of reason itself are all interconnected. It is from these interconnections that serious philosophical work on these notions must proceed. (Putnam 1988, 120)

The Latest Putnam

Since the mid-1990s, Putnam's writings have focused on the importance of the philosophical issues relating to perception. In his more recent book,

The Threefold Cord, he remarks that "in the course of the past fifteen years [i.e., approximately 1980–1995]" he has come to appreciate the fundamental importance of the nature of perception, and that when he wrote *Reason, Truth, and History*, he did not fully appreciate the importance of connecting issues of perception with those of reference (since at bottom they are the same issue, that of connecting our thoughts to the world).[6] At the same time, much of his published work since the mid-1990s has been centered on pragmatism, particularly on William James.[7] As with the pragmatist turn he appeared to make in the mid-1970s, which he characterized under the banner of internal (or pragmatic) realism, this perceptual turn in the mid-1990s promotes a new banner, what Putnam calls direct (or natural) realism. Of course, just as his earlier pragmatist turn was not a complete rejection of his previous views, but a reworking and reevaluation of some aspects of them (and, indeed, a retention of some, such as the linguistic division of labor), so, too, this new turn is not a total rejection of earlier views and does not suddenly appear full-blown as a dramatic break from those earlier views. For example, in *Representation and Reality*, published in 1988, he comments that in *Reason, Truth, and History*, he failed to show the interdependence of epistemic notions and truth. However, he does hint that, in some senses, he might still be an internal realist if that means finding unintelligible—which he does still find unintelligible—the claim that there is a fixed totality of all objects, of all properties, or a sharp distinction between what we "discover" and what we "project" about the world, and a fixed relation of "correspondence" (Putnam 1999, 183n41).

The direct (natural) realism that the latest Putnam wants to defend is a commonsense notion of perception, that the objects of normal, veridical perception are "external" things and aspects of an "external" reality. This carries with it a rejection of what he calls an "interface" conception of both perception and conception. That is, Putnam rejects that there is some sort of realm of interface between what's "out there" (e.g., tables and trees) and what's "in here" (e.g., impressions in the mind, mental representations, patterns of neuronal activity). Rather than there being an interface between us and the world, and then having that interface itself being in need of some explanation, Putnam suggests that we understand perception (and conception) in transactional terms, in which we interact with objects, knowable and known via their genuine properties. For Putnam, we are "aware of ourselves as in *interaction* with our perceptual objects. I am aware of a series of visual, tactile, etc., *perspectives* on the chair without ceasing to perceive the chair *as* an object that does not change as those perspectives change" (1999, 159). Speaking approvingly of James, Putnam reiterates: "Reality in itself does not consist of two radically different sorts of thing—subjects and objects—with a problematic relation. Rather it consists of the data—the phenomena—and it is just that these can be thought about in different ways" (1996, 157). Echoing Wittgenstein's project that (all-too-much) philosophy needs to be showing the fly the way out of the fly bottle (showing philosophers how their presuppositions get them into conceptual quagmires), Putnam remarks that direct realism is not so much a theory of perception (or conception or reference) as it is a denial of the necessity for (and explanatory value of) positing "interfaces," internal representations in perception and thought.

Citing James's persistent claim that we are *agents*—situated knowers, goal-directed doers—Putnam uses an example from James to connect the issue of perception (and conception) to truth and reference:

James wrote that he never denied that our thoughts have to fit reality to count as true, as he was over and over again accused of doing. In [a] letter he employs the example of someone choosing how to describe some beans that have been cast on a table. The beans can be described in an almost endless variety of ways depending on the interests of the describer, and each of the right descriptions will *fit* the beans-minus-the-describer and yet also reflect the interests of the describer. And James asks, Why should not any such description be called true? James insists that there is no such thing as a description that reflects no particular interest at all. And he further insists that the descriptions we give when our interests are not theoretical or explanatory can be just as *true* as the ones we give when our interests are "intellectual." "And for this," James wrote, "we are accused of denying the beans, or denying being in any way constrained by them. It's too silly!" (Putnam 1999, 5)

Clearly, the beans-under-(interest-laden)-description issue is reminiscent of objects-under-a-description issue that has agitated so much controversy about reference. For all of his rejection of aspects of his earlier internal realism (rejection because he now sees this earlier internal realism as itself flawed by an "interface" model of perception), Putnam still sees reference as a complex of abilities, taking neither causal connections nor descriptions as *constitutive* of the referential relation or of the elements in that relation. Rather, it is still the case for him that there is no unique true description of the world, that the objects in the referential relation are always instances of kinds of objects (i.e., they are experienced as categorized in some way or other). His resolve is still (see, e.g., 1999, 119) that of semantic externalism (meanings still ain't in the head!). What we speak about, just as what we perceive (and conceive), is not simply a matter of there being a pure, semantic words–world relation. We encounter objects-under-a-perspective, just as we refer to objects-under-a-description. We recognize that they are the same objects under all those perspectives or descriptions. The objects are there; they are real. They are (part of) the situations in which we are agents. But we cannot perceive them or refer to them in a noninterested way or noncategorized way.

As James insisted, seen in the passage above, truth is certainly a matter of capturing reality (though a reality experienced by an active agent). Putnam, too, contends that "in the case of the great majority of our everyday assertions, assertions about the familiar objects and persons and animals with which we interact, truth and idealized rational acceptability do coincide. The reason that they so often coincide is not, however, that truth means idealized rational acceptability, but that, first, it is built into our picture of the world itself that these statements can be verified under good conditions (when they are true); and, second, the existence of statements of this kinds is a conceptual prerequisite of our being able to understand a language at all" (1995, 299).

Catherine Elgin

Because of her close association with Nelson Goodman in terms of intellectual stances and in terms of a working relationship (having coauthored a number of works with him and having written frequently about Goodman), Catherine Elgin has appeared as something of a Thomas Huxley to Goodman's Darwin. Seeing her merely, or even primarily, in such a role does not do justice to her own writings, especially in the area of reference. Like Goodman, she extols a strong nonrealism, a view she often terms "constructionalism" (and occasionally, "constructivism"[8]). Like Goodman, she has persistently argued against a number of entrenched doctrines, particularly various dichotomies (such as realism–relativism, scheme–content, fact–value, sciences–arts). Like Goodman, she has lobbied for ontological pluralism. In addition, however, from her earliest writings on depiction and pictorial representation in Wittgenstein's *Tractatus* to her latest essays on parsimony, she has fleshed out a rigorous and sophisticated view of reference, a view, I will suggest in this section, that resonates well with a pragmatist take on reference and names (though she herself does not label her work or philosophical allegiances as "pragmatist").

The title of a recent essay, "Interpretation and Understanding" (2000a), captures, in a succinct way, the foci of her work. Our epistemic goal, as knowers of the world, is not simply knowledge, but understanding. So, our goal, as epistemologists, should be to provide an account of the cognitive processes and accomplishments of understanding, not simply an account of the necessary and sufficient conditions of knowledge. Likewise, our practical goal, as agents in the world, is not simply to follow rules of behavior, but to construct guides to action. So, too, our goal, as philosophers of action, should be to provide an account of how we engage in and make sense of action in the world. Nor is there a dichotomy here of cognitive versus practical goals. Both are interest-oriented; both involve interpretation of data within contexts; both relate facts and values. In a nutshell, both involve interpretation and understanding. As she states at the beginning of her essay:

According to a familiar and not unattractive theory of language, to understand a word is to interpret it correctly, the correct interpretation being the one that correlates it with the right referent. The correct interpretation of "elephant" maps the word onto members of the class of elephants, not the class of bumble bees; the correct interpretation of the name "Julius Caesar" maps the name onto the emperor, not onto his dog. To understand a denoting symbol is to know what in the world it refers to; and to understand a sentence is to know how things must stand for the sentence to be true. . . . the understanding that the correct interpretation supplies determines precisely what is to be investigated. It specifies exactly what about the world we want to know. . . . The question is whether such knowledge is paradigmatic of linguistic competence in general. I suggest that it is not. I will argue that to understand a word, sentence, or other symbol, it is generally neither necessary nor sufficient to assign a unique, determinate reference. Our semantic competence consists in knowing both more and less than the familiar account suggests. Reference fixing is often partial and is often the outcome of empirical investigation rather than a prerequisite for it. The result is that the process of settling on an interpretation and arriving at an understanding of the fact(s) it concerns is a constructive interplay, fraught with contingencies. (Elgin 2000a, 175–176)

Besides noting interpretation and understanding as focal points, this passage also speaks to a constellation of topics that Elgin assimilates into her overall view: that there is not a single, correct way that language hooks up with the world, that ontological issues are not inherently separable from epistemic concerns (though for particular concerns, the ontological or epistemological issues can wax or wane in their saliency), that a correct (or, better) interpretation and understanding is constructed (though not out of thin air) and is contingent (i.e., it can be reconstructed). In addition, though it is relatively subtle in this particular passage, there is a pronounced criticism of the received views of reference, both the descriptivist view and the causal view. I will explicate her overall views in light of these topics.

Constructionalism

Convinced that the battery of arguments given by Quine, Davidson, Sellars, Goodman, and others has demonstrated the failure of foundationalism, Elgin insists that we are not subsequently committed to a free-floating relativism, in which there are no, or only socially prescribed, standards of belief, value, and action. Between an absolute foundationalism and an arbitrary relativism lies a constructionalist standpoint. What we construct are accounts of the world, or, better, accounts of our experiences. And an experience, indeed the very world, is not a simple given, or collection of givens. Experiences themselves, as we conceive them, are informed by prior meaning, meaning provided by our language, our interests and goals, our classifications and partitionings. Without some sort of organizing principles, we lack the cognitive (including emotional) resources to make any sense of experiences.

Drawing an analogy from John Rawls's remarks on types of procedures, Elgin formulates an epistemic *perfect procedure* as having "an independent criterion for a correct outcome and a method whose results—if any—are guaranteed to satisfy that criterion" (1996, 4). This procedure she likens to foundationalism, a view in which there is one true way the world is and there is a method (or perhaps methods) by which our beliefs, values, and actions hook up with that world. Truth is a matter of such correspondence. Knowledge is having our beliefs tethered to this world in an acceptable way so as to make our beliefs true. Since the world is the way it is, independent of us, our cognitive goal is to establish the appropriate means to ensure that our beliefs correspond to that world.

Again, without here going through the arguments that have been offered against this view, let us note Elgin's identification of one response to this view as an epistemic *pure procedural* view. A pure procedural view "has no independent standard for a correct outcome. The procedure itself, when properly performed, determines what result is correct. And unless the procedure is actually performed, there is no fact of the matter as to which outcome is correct" (1996, 4). She identifies this view with Rorty, Kuhn, Feyerabend, Wittgenstein, and others. While rejecting foundationalism, Elgin also rejects this relativist view. Rather, she adopts a view that she likens to an *imperfect procedure*. An imperfect procedure "recognizes an independent criterion for a correct outcome but has no way to guarantee that the criterion is satisfied" (ibid.). So, although she shares the relativists' negative conclusions that foundationalism is deeply flawed, she does not share their "positive" conclusions that mere coherence and consensus are the standards of evaluation and assessment of beliefs, values, and action. Foundationalism and relativism are the flip sides of the same absolutist coin, with both identifying some form of absolutism as the proper conception of knowledge, ethics, and so on. The difference between them is that foundationalists think such absolutist standards can in fact be met and relativists think they can't be. For example, foundationalists such as Descartes will take certainty as an (or even as the) appropriate standard for knowledge and insist that such a standard can be met (via the cogito). Skeptics, while accepting that certainty is a/the appropriate standard, deny that it can be met. Both, though, share a commitment to such a rigorous (for Elgin, illegitimate) standard. Opposed to such a standard is the constructionalist's fallibilist view. We often have cognitively credible reasons, beyond simply consensus, to act as warrant for our beliefs, values, and actions. Not skepticism, but fallibilism, is the recognition of the variability of credence of our evidence for what we accept. As she states:

Imperfect procedural epistemology construes inquiry as a matter of pulling ourselves up by our bootstraps. The considered judgments that tether today's theory are the fruits of yesterday's theorizing. They are not held true come what may but accorded a degree of initial credibility because previous inquiry sanctioned them. We may subsequently revise or reject them, but they give us a place to start. Such an epistemological stance recognizes neither a beginning nor an end of inquiry. As epistemic agents, we are always in medias res. (Ibid., 15)

Not denying that we take beliefs and sentences to be true or false, Elgin suggests that truth, and philosophers' perennial attempts to define or characterize truth, would be better replaced by the notion of "rightness." Truth, as a goal of inquiry, is only one among a buffet of epistemic desiderata, along with simplicity, predictability, and consistency, among others.

Truths are cheap and easy; we can find them anywhere and everywhere. They are hardly what constitute the acquiring of understanding. Indeed, most truths are irrelevant to any given inquiry and are epistemically inert. Beyond truth doing very little epistemic work, the standard attempts to account for truth have proven to be fatally flawed. Although a coherence view of truth recognizes the important interconnections between truth and justification, it ends up taking the relativists' denial of any standards outside of social consensus. There is no principled way to distinguish truth from consistent fantasy if coherence is taken as necessary and sufficient. On the other hand, a correspondence view of truth either does no work or rests on unwarranted presuppositions. To simply offer a Tarskian disquotational account does not enhance our understanding. After all, "Snow is white" is true iff snow is white, but "Snow is white" is also true iff grass is green. In addition, we could accept the claim that "Grass is grue" iff grass is grue. Such an account of truth presupposes facts of the matter, and it is just which facts that matter, and how they matter, that is of concern to Elgin. Rather than truth lying in wait to be discovered, especially, say, by science, there are truths, and right sorts of truths, that are constructed by our (best) theories and practices.

As mentioned above, not truth, but rightness, is the concept that better yields a standard for understanding. Rightness is a matter of fitting and working, not so much a matter of fitting *onto* an independent reality, but more a matter of fitting *into* a context or set of categories. This is not a mere rephrasing of a coherentist position, as Elgin is firm that there is a clear difference between making something *up* and making it *into* something. As she remarks, we can make rags *into* rugs, meats and vegetables *into* stews, sentences *into* arguments, but that does not mean that we make *up* those rags and foods and sentences (1997, 174). The working of rightness speaks to the overall understanding that is (hoped) to be gained. It is not just practicality or know-how, since this does not necessitate understanding ("running a machine successfully does not amount to understanding it in all ways," Elgin 1983, 159). Understanding is not just having a list of known truths; it is having the information and ability to successfully proceed, based on what is currently adopted and known to have been useful in accomplishing our past and present goals. As Elgin characterizes it, "understanding" is a versatile term "for a skill, a process, an accomplishment" (1983, 161).

Expanded Reference

Elgin has long argued for a conception of reference that encompasses much more than simple denotation. For over two decades she has championed the view that things other than speakers and words refer; samples, pictures, and salt shakers can (and do) also refer. She has claimed that reference is not only, or even primarily, literal; metaphorical reference is ubiquitous. She has maintained that reference never occurs in isolation; it occurs in the context of schemes and systems. In the midst of this effort to show an expanded conception of reference, Elgin explicitly and implicitly rejects the received views of reference, both the descriptivist view and the causal view. Before I lay out her expanded conception, I will here explicate this rejection.

Over the course of her writings, Elgin has said little about descriptivism in general or Searle in particular.[9] She has said more, though still not a great deal, explicitly about Kripke and the causal view. What she does say about Searle focuses on the issue of intentions. In *With Reference to Reference* (1983) she notes Searle's focus on intentions in the context of his speech-act theory. In spelling out what constitutes a speech act, she says, Searle contends that an utterance must be a product of both convention (since language is social) and intention (since speakers attempt to communicate). Reference, under such a view, is not in itself a speech act, but is part of a (larger) speech act, such as asserting, questioning, commanding, and the like. But, says Elgin, neither component of such a speech act (i.e., intention nor convention) is as straightforward as Searle might think. Says Elgin:

First, intending to produce an effect by getting one's audience to recognize one's intention to produce that effect is not, or at least is not always, required for reference. Someone talking in his sleep or under the influence of anesthesia or, for that matter, someone who is unconsciously "thinking out loud" may have no such intention. Whether to say that such a person refers depends on how his words are interpreted. If we can make no sense of his utterances we put them down to inchoate ramblings. If their interpretation is straightforward, we take his utterances to be sentences, and the terms in them refer. It is the availability of a reasonable interpretation rather than the intention with which they were produced that is crucial in deciding whether his words refer. (1983, 17)

As for convention, Elgin counsels against taking it, in the guise of (social) use, as either determinative or basic for reference. We cannot say how speakers refer, she reminds us, without first understanding how their language refers. How the linguistic community uses words is an important element in what they mean and what they refer to, but use does not constitute meaning or reference, and a fortiori, a given speaker's use does not constitute a word's meaning or reference. ("Whatever a semantic system is, it is not just a summary of past uses of terms," ibid., 15.) In her 1990 essay, "Facts That Don't Matter" (reprinted in Elgin 1997), she reiterates her objections to Searle's intentionalist view, claiming that Putnam's Twin Earth case shows that it is mistaken. With respect to an Earthling and a Twin Earthling, each can intend to refer to (or, for a speech-act theorist, each can intend to assert of) a certain liquid by speaking of "water," but we refer to different things, since on Earth water is H_2O and on Twin Earth water is XYZ. Our psychological states might be indistinguishable, but our reference is not. Echoing Putnam, she insists that reference is "not determined by what is in the head" (1997, 87). Her conclusion regarding Searle's view, then, is:

I do not then take intentions, whether individual or social, to be authoritative for a system of reference. Although the intentions of its speakers undeniably influence the course of its development, the resulting language has a character that is independent of the intentions of the agents who produced it. Accordingly, accounts of the referential structure of the language need not be framed in terms of those intentions. As a result, we can distinguish between what a speaker intends to refer to and what he actually refers to. (1983, 18)

This last passage could easily lead a reader to think that Elgin aligns herself with Kripke and the causal view. This, however, is not so. From the opening page of *With Reference to Reference*, she proclaims that her concerns are "rather with geography than with genesis" (1983, 1). Given this focus, most of her work is on explicating her expanded conception of reference rather than critiquing the causal view. Nevertheless, she does offer explicit disapproval of a number of features of the causal view. Two features in particular that she criticizes are (1) reference fixing (i.e., "reliance on a matter of historical fact") and (2) rigid designation (i.e., "intuitions about modal matters"). As will be noted below, both criticisms are part of a larger disagreement.

With respect to reference fixing—which Kripke has allowed to occur even via a descriptivist notion of intending to pick out an already identified object perhaps by descriptions associated with it—especially for natural kind terms (but also for names), Elgin objects that "as soon as we talk about 'things like this' (for any 'this'), we have a problem of projection. Granting that a given individual is to be included in the extension of 'cow,' what else is to be included? How is the term 'cow' to be projected to cover new instances?" (1983, 12). Following Goodman, her position is that projectibility of a term is not something that is given; there isn't a single, correct way to extend a term, and we certainly don't *discover* the (or a) correct way to project. *Pace* Gareth Evans, she holds that the meaning, reference, and extension of a term are dynamic. Reference is understood only in the context of our symbol systems, themselves a function of our interests, goals, values, beliefs, and the like. So, reference fixing, even via some baptismal event, can and does occur only in such contexts. Likewise, the subsequent reference is also a function of such contexts. Historical usage could be, and sometimes is, an important factor in future determination of reference, but it is not determinative or constitutive.

Besides rejecting an underlying metaphysical realism in the causal view, Elgin opposes the underlying essentialism of Kripke's view of names as rigid designators.[10] For Kripke, although it is the case that Aristotle might not have been a philosopher, it is not, indeed cannot be, the case that Aristotle was not who he was. "Aristotle" refers to Aristotle, the same individual, in all possible worlds in which it refers at all. Elgin, though, claims that Kripke's position is based on basic essentialist (and realist) intuitions about haecceities, about how objects are individuated and classified. For Kripke, we simply have *this* man, where the category "man" is not crucial, but the "this" is. For him, there is a given particular there. It might be that in order to identify it for the purposes of talking about it, we need to place it in a category (e.g., *man*), but the individual object is what it is, independent of those categories and independent of how we categorize it. Elgin's differences with this view are twofold. First, she takes intuitions to be on the same footing as other types of beliefs (opinions, convictions, prejudices, etc.). They waver, clash, evolve, and obviously can be epistemically unreliable. Kripke's notion of rigid designators, his modal argument, is not so much an argument as a presupposition. Second, Elgin rejects the notion that we have individuals that are inherently individuated, that we have bare particulars. "Individuation depends on schematization. In structuring a domain, we mark out individuals and kinds. We thereby determine what counts as the same thing, what counts as a different thing of the same kind, what counts as a different kind of thing" (1997, 15). Her position is not that we create individuals in the sense that nothing exists unless and until we develop categories. Rather it is that we experience objects always and only in the context of categories, never as bare particulars.

Elgin also has concerns about the use of causation in the causal view of reference. It is not simply a matter that no satisfactory account has been given for just what such causality is. Instead, it is that causality itself is not realist. Of course, things and events in the world cause other things and events, but just as the objects of experience must be placed in categorical contexts, so, too, must the very notion of causality. As she puts it, "'cause,' like every other word, admits of multiple interpretations. Along with the rest of our claims, causal judgments map onto the world in numerous ways, yielding divergent models that satisfy our operational and theoretical constraints. Causal statements are part of the structure that requires interpretation, not mechanisms that supply interpretation" (1997, 92).

Furthermore, Elgin's remarks here are not just about causal discourse as opposed to causality. Drawing from Quine's "gavagai" example, intended to demonstrate the indeterminacy of reference, Elgin states:

The difficulty is not just epistemic. For the attempt to divorce causality from causal discourse is doomed. Causality is whatever relation the verb "cause" refers to. So long as the reference of "cause" is indeterminate, so is the relation of causality. If the causal theory of reference is true, then under one admissible interpretation, rabbits in the vicinity cause the natives to have a word for rabbit; under another, rabbit stages in the vicinity cause them to have a word for rabbit stages. Under the first, then, "gavagai" refers to rabbits; under the second, it refers to rabbit stages. The reference of "cause," like that of "gavagai" and "refers," is determinate within an interpretation, indeterminate apart from one. Since the causal theory of reference cannot secure an independent, univocal interpretation of "cause," it affords no escape from indeterminacy. The world then does not determine the reference of natural-kind (or any other) terms. (1997, 93)

Clearly, Elgin finds both of the received views of reference to be flawed. She does so not only for the specific problems that have just been illustrated, but also for what she takes as their narrow overall conception of what reference is. With overall understanding as her goal, with its attendant focus on effective fecundity for further understanding, Elgin sees the purpose for wanting an account of reference as going beyond getting a tidy semantic theory. This broadened sense of purpose brings with it an extended conception of reference. Acknowledging reference as "the central metalinguistic concept," she argues that the reference of a term depends not on its use in a single sentence (and, subsequently, not on an analysis that focuses on isolated sentences), but on its role in language as a whole. And language as a whole, as she claims, is interconnected, with the differences between literal and metaphoric uses or descriptive and expressive uses or factual and fictive uses being not different languages, but all part of a single language. What is needed, then, is an analysis and understanding of reference that accounts for, and incorporates, metaphoric reference as well as literal reference, expressive reference as well as descriptive reference, fictive reference as well as factual reference. Indeed, as will be seen below, reference can be nonverbal as well as verbal. It is reference in the context of symbol systems that is important. To offer such an account is her positive project.

To illustrate this expanded sense of reference, Elgin offers the following mundane example. A Monday-morning quarterback, while verbally recounting a particular play that happened the day before, manipulates her breakfast crockery to nonverbally accompany her report. Her coffee mug represents the fullback, while the sugar bowl, cereal dishes, and juice glass stand for the defensive line. Elgin claims that both "the fullback" (or, if named, say, "Schmoe") *and the coffee mug* refer to the fullback. As she says, this is not surprising; we do this sort of thing all the time and listeners comprehend. Surely, it is appropriate to say that the mug refers to the fullback in this case. It does so, again in this case, not because of any causal or necessary connection between the mug and the fullback, but because it functions in the context of a narrative wherein the use of such an object as a mug is understood to play the role of the fullback. The mug's use and referring capacity is transient and ad hoc, but it is not different in kind from the use and role of the term "the fullback," which, also, is transient and ad hoc (though in fact less so for us). This is not simply a return to a use theory of meaning or reference. There is an appropriate sense of use as it applies to meaning and reference, but not one that is captured in the earlier Searlean sense. Rather, for Elgin, "being so used involves intersubjectively accessible factors such as understanding the symbol, learning the symbol, applying the symbol, correcting and being corrected in misuses of the symbol, and so on" (1991a, 94).

Nonverbal objects, then, can refer. Probably the most common example of this is pictures. We all recognize that a particular portrait is of, say, Winston Churchill. As Putnam noted, mere lines (or patches of color) by themselves cannot refer, and Elgin's view is the same. Nevertheless, pictures do refer, not in an uninterpreted way, but in the context of an interpretation, which is also true of any referring expression, including names and definite descriptions. Nor do pictures refer because of some inherent Peircean iconicity or indexicality (i.e., because they bear a one-to-one correspondence or causal connection to a particular object). They refer because of their symbolic nature, and as symbols, they are referential only because they function within a symbolic system and are interpreted within a symbolic system. An important point about this, however, is that any account of reference will then need to provide an account of how pictures refer just as much as how names refer.

Just as common as pictorial reference is reference via exemplification. Samples, exemplars, tokens, and instances refer by exhibiting, or exemplifying, salient features of whatever it is they refer to, where the salience is contextual and interpreted. So, a paint chip on a manufacturer's sample card, while it instantiates many predicates and is a token of many types, exemplifies those aspects of its type that we deem of interest, in this case, most likely color (rather than, say, shape). The sample functions to pick out, or refer to, those features of the world that matter to us such that they are exemplified by this sample.

Another extension beyond standard notions of reference, and one that is closely related to exemplification, is metaphorical reference, an example of what Elgin calls complex reference. A denoting symbol, she notes, can function both literally and metaphorically, even to the same object. A person of great size and achievement, for example, is both literally and metaphorically a person of weight. Metaphor is related to exemplification because metaphors function via likening. In calling Juliet "the sun," Elgin tell us, Romeo highlights features she shares with the (literal) sun, such as being glorious or being the point around which his life circumnavigates, while ignoring other features that she does not share with the (literal) sun, such as being the largest gaseous blob in the solar system. Juliet and Sol are linked by their joint exemplification of salient features.

These various extensions of standard treatments of reference display and follow from an underlying meaning holism. This is evident in several aspects of how Elgin characterizes the cross-referential features of symbols. For instance, in her discussion of Israel Scheffler's criticisms of philosophical absolutes, she describes the notion of "mention-selection":

Mention-selection is a mode of cross-reference whereby a symbol refers, not to its denotation, but to mentions thereof. I pull out a photograph and say, "This is my son, Sam." It's not Sam, of course, but a picture of him. In saying of the picture,

This is Sam,

I use "is" mention-selectively, so that one symbol that denotes him—his name—refers to another that does the same—his picture. (1993, 10)

Mention-selection relates back to the fact of metaphorical reference via likening, as when a piccolo trill can refer to a birdcall. In addition, mention-selection points to a key element of Elgin's (and Goodman's) conception of meaning, namely, the primary extension and the secondary extension of a symbol. The primary extension of a symbol is what is standardly taken as what is denoted by that symbol, for example, the class of all cats for the symbol "cat." The secondary extension of a symbol is the compounds containing what is denoted by that symbol, for example, cat-pictures, cat-stories, cat-descriptions, and the like. Especially important about this, for Elgin, is that "If Goodman is right, the stories we tell, and the pictures we paint, affect the meanings of the words we use. If I'm right, they also affect the choices we make about which extensions to assign to our terms" (2000a, 180). Where Goodman emphasizes the logical independence of primary and secondary extensions, Elgin contends that much of their cognitive significance derives from their interanimation. For her, not only do new factual applications of a symbol provide "fodder for fiction," but also new fictional applications influence further findings of fact (much as the cognitive significance of metaphor). Here Elgin's constructionalism is in full view (not that it is ever hidden!), as she insists that the primary extension of a symbol is not sufficient ("affords no rationale") for drawing categorical boundaries where we do. Such partitionings, and especially our understanding of them, are dependent also on secondary extensions of symbols. Interpretation, then, is not simply a matter of determining a unique, correct referent of a symbol. Rather:

[Interpretation] is holistic—depending on how the symbol functions in context, what is presupposed about its primary and secondary extensions and its linguistic and extra-linguistic milieu. . . . Interpretation and understanding inextricably intertwine. And their deliverances are apt to be open-ended. Previously accepted usage supplies precedents. But available precedents do not always determine how to go on. . . . By the choices we make, then, we construct the categories that fix the fact that Caesar was, or that he was not, a tyrant; the fact that arthritis is, or that it is not, a disease; the fact that a coyote is, or that it is not, a dog. In so doing, we participate in the construction of the world that we and our descendants inhabit. (Ibid., 182–183)

Pragmatism?

So, is Elgin's constructionalist view pragmatist? I believe it is—at least, there is enough about her view that is consistent with pragmatism for me to include her among neo-pragmatist philosophers. She never refers to herself or her views as pragmatist, and, in fact, at times she distances herself from what she takes as pragmatist doctrines. For example, in her discussion of rightness and truth, she (or she and Goodman together) remarks that "while our talk of working may echo pragmatism, we are by no means trying to reduce rightness, as some pragmatists try to reduce truth, to practicality" (Goodman and Elgin 1988, 158–159).

Nor does she draw directly from the classical pragmatists in formulating her own position. James is never mentioned in any of her writings. Dewey is mentioned explicitly only once, when she introduces imperfect procedural epistemology as "prepared to criticize, modify, reinterpret, and—if need be—renounce constituent ends and means" (Elgin 1996, 12), where she footnotes Dewey's *Human Nature and Conduct*. On several, but not more than several, occasions she speaks of Peirce, but even then what she says is not particularly laudatory. For example, she claims that Peirce's account of the type–token distinction carries with it a commitment to Platonism, because it sees types as abstract entities. Also, though it is a more muted criticism of Peirce, Elgin objects to the inference from Peirce's classification of signs as being iconic, indexical, and symbolic that some signs, namely icons and indices, somehow refer directly and immediately to objects. All signs, she says, are symbolic (see especially "Icon and Index Revisited" in Elgin 1997).

In spite of these points, I want to suggest that Elgin's view is very much aligned with pragmatism. Her focused emphasis on understanding as our appropriate cognitive goal, her insistence that this pursuit is interest-laden, and her persistent contention that how we engage in the world is inherently and necessarily via interpretation are all reminiscent of pragmatist stances. Even her and Goodman's condemnation of traditional epistemology as coming from "the quest for certainty" (Goodman and Elgin 1988, 4) and her ubiquitous rejection of dichotomous, either-or approaches are strikingly similar to those of the classical pragmatists, especially, though by no means exclusively, Dewey. Her antiessentialism, her rejection of inquiry as ever being disinterested, her demand that categories of experience, along with the ontological commitments of principles of individuation and construction of similarity relations—all are concerns held in common with the pragmatists. "The evaluation of classificatory schemes and the systems of thought they figure in then contains an ineliminably pragmatic moment" (Elgin 1997, 13). That she holds the projectibility of symbols, their future workings, as open-ended and determinative (to the extent that they are determined) of their meanings and reference are all consistent with pragmatism. Her frequent underscoring of reflective equilibrium, of a balancing of theoretical advances and effective past and present under-standings, is just the sort of philosophical methodology that we find over and over in the writings of each of Peirce, James, and Dewey. This is not at all to say that Elgin's position is merely a rehashing of pragmatist themes and doctrines. Her expansion of the sphere of reference is truly hers (and Goodman's); her detailing of how and why various components of her position—such as exemplification, mention-selection, semantic density, projectibility—are not spelled out by these earlier thinkers, certainly not in her detailed and programmatic way. Nonetheless, in content, tone, and sentiment that are very reminiscent of Dewey, she ends her book, *Considered Judgment,* with these remarks:

We cannot hope to understand the material world without understanding what other people make of it. And our theories of nature, ourselves, and each other inform one another. As we learn more about a domain, we learn more about which methods, values, and categories advance our understanding of it, which intellectual abilities are useful, and about whose judgment deserves to be trusted. As we refine our talents, judgments, and methods, we discover more about the domain. Each tenable theory provides a platform from which to launch new investigations. None affords a permanent resting place. The task is endless. (1996, 220)

Richard Rorty

During the second half of the twentieth century, a handful of books appeared that shook the professional philosophical community, shook it in the sense that practically everyone in that community knew of it, read it, and responded—usually with gusto—to it. Wittgenstein's *Philosophical Investigations* was one such book; Kuhn's *The Structure of Scientific Revolutions* was another, as was John Rawls's *A Theory of Justice.* These works were global in their philosophical impact, garnering widespread attention and generating strong allegiances or impassioned criticism. Their reach extended beyond professional philosophers as well to other areas and disciplines within academia, and, indeed, beyond academia. Another such book was Richard Rorty's *Philosophy and the Mirror of Nature* (1979, hereafter *PMN*). Though Rorty had published actively for two decades before this work appeared and many of his prior essays carried the same content and tone as *PMN*, his impact and fame—or infamy—was secured with its publication. In the two decades since its publication, Rorty has extended the messages and "walked the talk" of *PMN* by focusing more and more on social and political concerns, frequently addressed to nonacademic audiences, rather than on epistemic issues that still agitate many philosophers (for example, even the titles of his two more recent books, *Achieving Our Country* and *Philosophy and Social Hope*, reflect this focus).

Rorty has been condemned as a prophet of the end of philosophy, as a purveyor of irrationalism, as an advocate of relativism. At the same time, he has been put forward, by himself as well as by others, as a new Dewey, a thinker concerned with the problems of people and not merely the problems of professional philosophers. Frequently describing his own philosophical views as being "negative," that is, opposed to other (mistaken) views, Rorty has labeled his stance and his commitments as antirepresentationalist, antiessentialist, antirealist, antifoundationalist, and antirelativist. On the "positive" side, he has embraced pragmatism, irony, contingency, solidarity, nominalism, and edificational thinking. What he means by these and how they relate to reference and names, especially to a pragmatist conception of reference and names, will be the subject of what follows.

Reference versus Talking About

From his earliest publication, a 1959 review of Alan Pasch's *Experience and the Analytic: A Reconsideration of Empiricism*, Rorty has promoted and proffered his sense of a pragmatist take on philosophy. His claim about Pasch's central theme (a "pragmatic reconstruction") anticipates and captures much of his own subsequent position, a position that continues to be fleshed out and evolving today. Pasch's central theme, he says, "is that a question is always a question within a context, that a context is always one among alternative possible contexts, and that one selects one's context to fulfill a purpose" (1959, 77). Already here, at the beginning of

Rorty's professional career, we can see his insistence on the axiological bases for all inquiry, on multiple representations of the world, and on a refusal to accept atomistic accounts of the world. These "negative" commitments are evident in his early (1961a,b) essays that focus on categories and their relation to language ("Pragmatism, Categories, and Language" and "Realism, Categories, and the 'Linguistic Turn'"). And it is here where we first encounter Rorty's take on reference, in the context of a discussion of Peirce and Wittgenstein, at least a Wittgensteinian take via David Pears, on naming. Peirce, says Rorty, thought that most theories about naming were wrong because they block the way of inquiry by appealing to one form or another of "just seeing." Naming, connecting words to objects, is not, for Peirce, a matter of absolute necessity or sheer arbitrariness. We do not have any understanding of naming prior to some explanation or categorization schema (Peirce's language is to speak of naming as being possible because Thirds are real). The present concern is not with unpacking this or evaluating it, but with noting that as early as 1961 Rorty raises awareness of the issue of naming and indicates one form of pragmatist approach to naming. Of course, Rorty soon became disenamored with Peirce (if he wasn't already at this time), and after the initial publication of Kripke's views in 1972, the topic of naming, and reference in general, he was vastly reanimated.

Rorty's most explicit and sustained discussion on these issues came in his 1976 essay, "Realism and Reference." In this essay we find much of the philosophical outlook that becomes more renowned in *PMN*, for example, questions about the purpose(s) of philosophizing, enunciation of the differences between inquiry and truth (with a clear assessment of the diminished value of the latter), criticism of the fact–value and fact–language distinctions, and a condemnation of representationalism. (See chapter 6 of *PMN* for a reiteration of these points.) He even uses the expression "Mirror of Nature" as part of his later-famous renunciation of philosophical projects arising in the seventeenth century concerning the relationship of mind (later, language) and the world.

Citing the works of many prominent philosophers, Rorty contends that these folks are seemingly convinced that there is a live issue to be argued between realism and idealism, or realism and pragmatism, "or at any rate realism and something unwholesomely relativistic" (1976, 323). Says Rorty:

The central notion of this newest realism is "reference," as a notion essential to the understanding of truth, and its paradigm problems are those produced by the interlocking of this notion with those of identity and necessity. Substitutability of identicals in modal and belief contexts, assignment of truth-values to statements using proper names, and related issues have engendered an interlocking set of controversies constituting "philosophy of language." Whereas in an earlier period the puzzles created by the errors of our ancestors were thought of as problems for epistemology, connected to issues about phenomenalism-vs.-direct perception, realism-vs.-instrumentalism, and the like, they are now thought of as problems arising in connection with language. (1976, 323–324)

Rorty then distinguishes three senses of "refer." The first sense ("reference$_1$") is the commonsense notion of reference, the sense of "talking about," in which questions of the existence of the referent are irrelevant. Here we can talk about, refer to, Santa Claus just as appropriately as we can refer to Saul Kripke. A second sense of reference ("reference$_2$") is an intermediate notion in which one can talk about only what exists, but the truth of what one says is not determined by the discovery of what one is talking about. Rather, Rorty says, the subject is changed. Here we might talk about, refer to, water without talking about, referring to, H_2O. (That is, we take ourselves here to be talking about the colorless, odorless, etc. liquid that we drink and swim in; if it turns out that this "really is" H_2O, we don't take ourselves to have been talking about H_2O. Chemical composition might well be an essential property of water, but it is not an essential property of what we are talking about in referring$_2$.) Finally, there is a third sense of reference ("reference$_3$") that is the technical, philosophical sense of reference. Here the semantics of a term are separable from the pragmatics of it and the epistemological connections it might have. He agrees with Kripke that reference, even in the first sense of "talking about," cannot be captured just by a speaker's intentions. As Rorty phrases it, the correct answer to the question, "Whom is he talking about?" cannot simply be, "Whomever he thinks he is." If this is the descriptivist view, including the sophisticated Searlean cluster version, it cannot suffice (though there will be cases in which this is quite fine). However, from this negative conclusion, it does not follow, says Rorty, that the causal picture suggested by Kripke (and Donnellan) supplants it. Indeed, this latter picture attempts to replace reference$_1$ with reference$_3$, and this attempt is simply misconceived. Reference$_3$, for Rorty, like its predecessor "knowledge by acquaintance," is another realist attempt to conjure up a grappling-hook between us and the world; it is a notion, he says, that should be discarded, not taken seriously and made precise. It is here where Rorty makes mention of the "Mirror of Nature":

Reference$_1$ is clear enough for any purpose save the gratification of the needs of a certain research program. Reference$_3$ is a term of art, given sense contextually in the development of this program—a program which, I suspect, can only suffer from being linked to outworn philosophical projects. These projects arose in the context of the seventeenth century image of the mind as a Mirror of Nature, and of skeptical problems about testing the accuracy of representations of this Mirror. (Ibid., 334)

The pragmatist focus, in James's sense, of asking about the "cash value" of a project is evident in this passage. What work does reference$_3$ do? For a philosopher of language with representational worries, perhaps it clarifies and makes more rigorous the notion of "talking about," but, for Rorty, it does little, if anything, for anyone else. And this point—what work does it do?—is fundamental for Rorty.

The same year (1979) in which *PMN* was published, another essay by Rorty appeared, "Is There a Problem about Fictional Discourse?" (reprinted in Rorty 1982, *Consequences of Pragmatism*, hereafter *CP*). In this essay, he once again argues that most philosophers of language are entrapped in the "mind–language represents the world and we need to explain how" picture. Here he terms it the Parmenidean Picture, in which we insist (presume) that if we talk about something, there must be something we are talking about, that language, to be meaningful, must correspond to a nonlinguistic reality. Where in "Realism and Reference" (1976) Rorty focuses on the ontological commitments underlying reference, in this essay, while addressing the "problem" of how talk about fictional entities could possibly correspond to the world (since they are fictional, i.e., non-existent!), he zeroes in on the underlying issue of truth versus warranted assertability, or truth versus justification. Most people (no doubt, everyone other than certain philosophers) would say that the sentence "Sherlock Holmes was born in England" is just as true as "Gladstone was born in England." But if truth is correspondence, and if reference is a grappling-hook, then the Homes sentence seems to be a problem. The problem isn't simply about this sentence or about fictional discourse, but in fact about what to say about truth in general. If truth is correspondence, then the Holmes sentence is problematic; but if truth is simply warranted assert-ability, "we have what may seem a less difficult problem; we need merely distinguish the situation, or conventions, or presuppositions, relevant to asserting" a sentence (*CP*, 110). The various attempts to wrestle with this issue, from Russell's "On Denoting" on through Searle's cluster view to the Kripke–Donnellan causal picture (what Rorty calls a "physicalist semantics") have led to two alternatives: a "pure" language-game approach that dispenses with the notions of correspondence and reference altogether and a rigidly physicalist approach that interprets correspondence and reference in terms of physical causality. The result of the first approach is to "separate semantics from epistemology so drastically that semantics will have no interesting distinctions to make between truth about fact and about fiction," while the result of the second approach is to "bring semantics together with a realistic epistemology of 'picturing' which, in the manner of Donnellan, will disallow truth about fiction altogether" (*CP*, 127). The real problem for both approaches, says Rorty, is that they take reference to involve more than simple commonsense "talking about." Rather than look for a more precise account of reference as correspondence, we should abandon the search because there is no problem to be solved here.

In his 1980 review of Kripke's *Naming and Necessity*, Rorty's criticisms of the physical semantics approach are somewhat muted, in the sense that he claims that neither the causal theorist nor the pragmatist has or can refute the other's position. Instead, the issue of how we will proceed in our understanding of names and reference will depend upon what questions we care to have answered about them. To the extent that the causal picture as provided by Kripke is meant as an empirical claim about how people in fact do refer and use names, Rorty says that it is not at all clear if Kripke's view is accurate. It's just not clear, for Rorty, if the "man in the street" is going to be of much help in determining if Kripke's intuitions about, say, haecceities is correct.[11] Both at the "narrow 'technical' level" of philosophers of language and at the more general level of reflecting on inquiry per se, we have a stand-off. In Wittgensteinian manner, for Rorty it is less a case of having a problem solved, or even needing to be solved; rather it is a case of a pseudo-problem that needs to be dissolved. We must show the fly the way out of the fly-bottle.[12]

What Pragmatism Is and Is Not

Rorty ends *PMN* by urging philosophers to abandon their view of philosophy (or, Philosophy) as the queen of the sciences, and to recognize their appropriate role as joining in the human conversations in which the goal is not acquisition of timeless truth but edification. By the early 1990s he adopted the phrasing of "coping" with the contingencies of the world as the goal of inquiry. The goal is (or should be) "a matter of acquiring habits of action for coping with reality" (1991a, 1). Several important elements are contained in this briefly stated goal. First, inquiry is never disinterested, never done for its own sake. Second, there is an insistence on developing habits, not simply bits of knowledge. Problems, questions, interests, goals do not exist in isolation. Rorty at times speaks of a spectrum from habit to inquiry, not in the sense that they are mutually exclusive, but in the sense that habit allows us to proceed (1) so as to be able to fruitfully ask further questions and (2) so as to not be misled by insincere inquiry (e.g., Cartesian doubt about the existence of commonsense objects or other minds). Third, there is a clear recognition of a reality there with which we must cope. This last point is important because Rorty himself (and, he claims, pragmatism in general) is often labeled as idealism, relativism, or some form of irrationalism. Throughout many of his writings, Rorty has been persistent that these labels are wrong-headed. (Of course, many critics point to claims made by Rorty, saying that these labels follow from the very things he says, such as: "I am inclined to agree with Foucault, against Putnam, that 'What is truth?' and 'What is rationality?' are not eternal questions, but misguided ones" [1984b, 7]; or when he claims, "it is contexts all the way down" [1991a, 100] or that "socialization, and thus historical circumstance, goes all the way down" [1989, xiii].)

So, just what does Rorty take pragmatism to be or espouse? More often than not, Rorty characterizes it by what it is not, by what it opposes. In "Pragmatism, Relativism, and Irrationalism" (in Rorty 1982), he claims it is antiessentialist, it is anti-fact–value dichotomy, it opposes the notion that there is any methodological difference between morality and science, and it is antirealist, at least in the sense that there are no constraints on inquiry save conversational ones. In a positive sense, pragmatism is the enunciation of inquiry as a means to engage in the world so as to flourish. It is worth quoting him at length:

The purpose of inquiry is to achieve agreement among human beings about what to do, to bring consensus on the ends to be achieved and the means to be used to achieve those ends. Inquiry that does not achieve coordination of behaviour is not inquiry but simply wordplay. To argue for a certain theory about the microstructure of material bodies, or about the proper balance of powers between branches of government, is to argue about what we should do: how we should use the tools at our disposal in order to make technological, or political, progress. So, for pragmatists there is no sharp break between natural science and social science, nor between social science and politics, nor between politics, philosophy and literature. All areas of culture are parts of the same endeavour to make life better. There is no deep split between theory and practice, because on a pragmatist view all so-called "theory" which is not wordplay is always already practice. (1999, xxv)

Such a position, he contends, does not entail relativism, or irrationalism, or idealism. Rather, its point is that the representation-based notions of truth and realism at best serve no purpose; they are explanatorily and practically inert. The pragmatist is quite willing to grant that we (including our beliefs and desires and language) have been shaped by the environment(s) in which we live—in fact the pragmatist would insist on this. But "the world is out there" is not the same as "the truth is out there." What the pragmatist denies is any explanatory usefulness to claiming that truth is correspondence or that a belief or desire is what it is and has the properties it has because the world is "real." These concepts, Rorty says, just do no work. They certainly don't tell us how to proceed.

So, is pragmatism relativist? Certainly not, says Rorty, if what is meant by "relativist" is that any belief or desire is just as good as any other one. Some answers to questions are wrong, even if we can't say what the (or a) right answer is. "How many stars are in the Milky Way galaxy?" Who knows, but "seventeen" is a wrong answer. Simply saying that there is no ahistorical, noncontextual answer or standard does not entail that there are no answers or standards or that there aren't any more or less useful answers or standards.

Is pragmatism irrationalist? No, says Rorty, if what is meant by "irrationalist" is that there are no standards of rational inquiry. He takes rationality to be not adherence to ahistorical, noncontextual standards, but "the ability to cope with the environment by adjusting one's reactions to environmental stimuli in more complex and delicate ways" (1992, 581). Given certain stimuli, given certain goals, one course of action, X, can very well be more rational than an alternative course of action, Y. This does not mean that X is always the more rational course. In addition, rationality is not merely a cognitive state or capacity; it is intimately connected with practice, with action in the world.

Is pragmatism idealist? Not at all, says Rorty, if what is meant by "idealist" is that we create the world, notwithstanding his comment that the "causal independence of giraffes from humans does not mean that giraffes are what they are apart from human needs and interests" (see note 11 above). Standing firm that causation is not the same thing as explanation, Rorty remarks that not being able to compare a belief with something that isn't a belief, à la Kant, doesn't mean that there isn't something out there to have beliefs about. From the causal independence of those things about which we have beliefs and desires, we can't infer, or explain by appeal to, chosen objects stripped bare of human concerns, of things-in-themselves. The pragmatist agrees, for example, that there is such a thing as a brute physical resistance, such as the pressure of light waves on Galileo's eyeball or the stone on Dr. Johnson's boot. But "he sees no way of transferring this non-linguistic brutality to *facts*, to the truth of sentences. The way in which a blank takes on the form of the die which stamps it has no analogy to the relation between the truth of a sentence and the event which the sentence is about. When the die hits the blank something causal happens, but as many *facts* are brought into the world as there are languages for describing that causal transaction" (1991a, 81).

Nowhere does Rorty define or even attempt to define what he takes pragmatism to be, and this is no oversight. Less a set or even a constellation of doctrines or methods, pragmatism, for Rorty, is an attitude, a stance, a value. His characterizations of it, as noted above, tend to be in terms of what it is not (not relativism, etc.) or in "anti-" phrases (e.g., "antiessentialist"). Nevertheless, many other thinkers who are self-labeled as "pragmatist" or are sympathetic to pragmatism have been among the harshest critics of Rorty. For example, his own teacher, Charles Hartshorne (in Saatkamp 1995), has criticized Rorty's rejection of objectivity and realism, not merely in terms of ontological doctrine, but even in terms of underlying commitments for everyday inquiry. A crucial thing that makes us human, says Hartshorne, is that we think we can and ought to come to know, at least approximately, what things are. This applies to our religious interests as much as to our scientific interests. This desire and need to understand what makes up the world, so we can understand our place in it, is basic to being human. This desire and need is just what is meant by objectivity and realism. Likewise, Susan Haack (also in Saatkamp 1995) has objected that dropping truth is dropping inquiry, since the latter makes no sense without assuming the former, since to believe p is to accept p as true. Rather than detail the various pragmatists' criticisms of Rorty and provide his responses, I will focus on the objections that have come from the other two figures in this chapter, Putnam and Elgin.

First Elgin. Although she has not written extensively on Rorty, she has reviewed his *Consequences of Pragmatism* and written about his works in the context of her own antirealist (constructionalist) views. Her objections have been twofold. First, she likens his position's pure procedural approach to one of adjudication, one in which there is no criterion other than the procedure followed and the outcome that results for determining a correct outcome, much as the criterion for winning a race is simply running it and coming in first. Other than what a community decides in its edifying conversations or in its language-games, there is no independent standard or criterion for assessment. In spite of his insistence that his view is not relativist (in any "bad" sense) or subjectivist, Rorty does appear to be guilty of just those sins, says Elgin, as when he claims that Galileo "just lucked out" (Elgin 1996, 193) and cannot be said to have a better theory or terminology than Aristotle on any objective grounds. "Not only are there no transcendent standards," remarks Elgin, "there are no standards at all. There is only peer pressure" (Elgin 1984, 427).

Her second criticism of Rorty's position is that it probably really isn't a pragmatist one, for "it leads to a complacency that is alien to the pragmatist spirit" (Elgin 1984, 427). A defining trait of classical pragmatism, for Elgin, is its fallibilism, which entails not merely variability of beliefs and desires, but a means beyond social consensus for what counts as being wrong. So, again, in spite of his insistence that his view is not a relativist or subjectivist one, Rorty's position is just that, and hardly pragmatist.

Rorty has never spoken of Elgin in print. Still, her criticisms are related to those leveled by Putnam. And Rorty has responded numerous times to Putnam's numerous objections. For present purposes, I will focus on Putnam's objections from the early 1990s (appearing in his *Realism with a Human Face,* hereafter *RHF*) and his more recent criticisms, those that appear in Richard Brandom's *Rorty and His Critics* (2000). In *RHF*, Putnam states that, since both he and Rorty adopt the label "pragmatist" and both are critical of essentialism, realism, and the like, just where do they disagree? A major point of difference, he says, is that he (Putnam) feels the need to demonstrate that a position such as essentialism is mistaken while Rorty simply scorns it. There is a basic philosophical divide between refuting and ignoring. Underlying this divide is the commitment, or lack of it, that there is something to be gained by wrestling with a view and seeing what is worth keeping from it and worth jettisoning from it. As does Elgin, Putnam claims that philosophy has more to offer than simply joining into a conversation, a conversation in which, apparently, everyone else has a worthwhile perspective (as a politician or linguist or poet, etc.). And, like Elgin, Putnam sees, indeed, an underlying bad relativism in Rorty, despite his protestations.

In "Hilary Putnam and the Relativist Menace" (reprinted in Rorty 1998a), Rorty responds directly to these earlier objections. After acknowledging and highlighting the various points of similarity between their views, Rorty contends that he and Putnam have a basic disagreement about human nature. Relying on Dewey's and Darwin's naturalism, Rorty rejects talk of human nature, and instead sees humans as context-bound slightly-more-complicated animals, wherein their beliefs and desires are the product of their interactions with the changeable and changing world and nothing else. Citing Dewey's experimentalist teachings, Rorty claims:

We should see what happens if we (in Sartre's phrase) "attempt to draw the full conclusions from a consistently atheist position," one in which such phrases as "the nature of human life" no longer distract us from the absence of a God's-eye view. We can pursue this experiment by setting aside the subject–object, scheme–content, and reality–appearance distinctions and thinking of our relation to the rest of the universe in purely causal, as opposed to representationalist, terms (the same way we think of the anteater's and the bower-bird's relation to the rest of the universe). I suspect that many of my differences with Putnam come down, in the end, to his unhappiness with such a purely causal picture. (1998a, 49)

Another point of contention is that Putnam (when *RHF* came out, in 1990) took truth as idealized rational acceptability and not just as warranted acceptability, and so maintained some distance between truth and justification. Rorty responds that "idealized" doesn't seem to do any work and that Putnam's view either is like his (Rorty's) after all or collapses back into truth as correspondence. (Putnam has since retracted this idealized acceptability view.) But Rorty is unapologetic about demanding a dropping of the truth–justification distinction. Other than taking a realist stance, on what basis could we say that the entire community is mistaken about its beliefs or desires or goals? This is not to say, claims Rorty, that there aren't reasons for a community to abandon its beliefs or desires or goals, but these reasons will never be metaphysical ones, but only political ones (in the sense of being part of a "polis").

In his more recent criticisms of Rorty, Putnam argues that Rorty spends a lot of time denying that there is any correspondence between our words and elements of reality while at the same time denying that he is abandoning an independent world. He can't do both, says Putnam. Further, if the proper goal of inquiry is to help us cope with and in the world, how is this possible on Rorty's own terms, and why does saying that there is a reality outside ourselves that we act on help us cope? Rorty seems to argue that our causal interactions are real (we can kick a rock), but our descriptions are not; they are vocables that allow us to cope and nothing more. But, says Putnam, if my kicking a particular rock involves a particular (real, independent) rock, why doesn't describing that same particular rock involve a particular (real, independent) rock? Finally, Putnam claims that Rorty's view of justification has two aspects, a contextual one and a reformist one, both of which are suspect. The first is suspect, says Putnam, because it boils down to saying that justification is sociological; it is a matter of consensus. Citing the very discussion that occurred in Rorty's "Hilary Putnam and the Relativist Menace," Putnam asks how can a sociologist qua sociologist determine whether a community (or a majority within a community) is wrong, a possibility that Rorty allowed? Isn't the only way to fall back to commonsense realism? The second, reformist, aspect of Rorty's notion of justification is suspect because it fails to give any sort of account for what would constitute better or worse norms and standards, that is, reform, unless, again, there is a return to commonsense realism.

Is Rorty guilty as charged? First, does he deny that there is, or can be, any correspondence between our words and elements of reality? No. His criticism of correspondence is not that it is impossible. After all, we do share a public language and we do understand each other. Rorty's concern is that labeling something as correspondence does no work; it is epistemically and explanatorily inert. Words can correspond to objects, but nothing is explained by pointing this out. In addition, if correspondence is a commitment to the view that there is only one correct way in which words relate to objects, then Rorty disagrees, for much the same reasons that Elgin and Putnam (at least for much of his career) disagree. As for Rorty's view of justification, he rejects what he sees as Putnam's newly found direct perceptual realism. This view, for Rorty, privileges the Ordinary, in effect saying that Putnam's commonsense intuitions, apparently ones that all or most humans must share, constitute the one, correct picture of the world. But, says Rorty, preserving commonsense convictions are "merely a matter of not letting the fact that non-ordinary descriptions are available prevent us from using ordinary ones for ordinary purposes" (quoted in Putnam 2000, 88). Understanding ordinary convictions and descriptions, he says, is not at all the same thing as preserving realist convictions. What makes for reform is something we'll discover in the workings of our commitments. One view will be better than another if it allows us to cope better with and in the world, where "better" can only mean in light of those goals we envision worth pursuing. Those goals are no more given or static than our current theories are. Likewise, contexts change; a sociologist can say that a community or a majority is wrong, but only relative to some envisioned goal. And just as facts are value-laden, values are fact-laden. Our goals, our desires, are just as much a matter of our engagements with the world as our beliefs are.

The Future

We have to shift, Rorty tells us, from the kind of role that philosophers have shared in the past with priests and sages to one that has more in common with engineers and lawyers. Where priests and sages can set their own agendas, "philosophers, like engineers and lawyers, must find what their clients need" (Rorty 1995, 198). In particular, there is a persuasive power and value to philosophy. At the beginning of a new century, this power and value can especially be focused on certain political (in the broad sense of the term) goals. For example, there is the need to reconcile the moral intuitions that are clothed in the language of religion with the scientific world-picture that has proven to be so fecund and yet so dangerous. There is also the issue of mass democracy, an issue that could be fruitfully addressed by the power of philosophical analysis. Citing Putnam's lament that much contemporary philosophy has degenerated into quarrels between philosophers' competing intuitions, often on arcane topics, Rorty bemoans that the "desire to harmonize pre-existent intuitions has replaced the task of asking whether the vocabulary in which these intuitions are stated is a useful one" (1995, 202). As he says in his earlier *Contingency, Irony, Solidarity*, "a belief can still regulate action, can still be thought worth dying for, among people who are quite aware that this belief is caused by nothing deeper than contingent historical circumstance" (1989, 189). A belief can be grounding, even if not grounded, at least not grounded in Platonic soil.

6 Across the Pond: Eco, Apel, Habermas

"I have never doubted the truth of signs, Adso; they are the only things man has with which to orient himself in the world."

—Umberto Eco, *The Name of the Rose*

Umberto Eco

Known outside of academia primarily as the author of best-selling "intellectual" novels such as *The Name of the Rose* and *Foucault's Pendulum*, and known inside of academia primarily as the author of important works in semiotics such as *The Open Work* and *A Theory of Semiotics*, Umberto Eco has for decades addressed issues of reference and names and has done so from a perspective explicitly indebted to pragmatism generally and Peirce particularly. Drawing heavily, though not uncritically, on Peirce's semiotic writings, Eco has recently enunciated his notion of "contractual realism," a notion, he says, that is consistent with his previous attempts "to elaborate a theory of content featuring a blend of semantics and pragmatics" (2000, 5). A summary statement of this contractualist position involves four components: (1) referring is an action that speakers perform on the basis of a negotiation; (2) in principle the act of reference effected by using a term might have nothing to do with the knowledge of the meaning of the term or even with the existence of the referent—with which it has no causal relationship; (3) nevertheless, there is no designation definable as rigid that does not rest on an initial description ("label"), albeit a highly generic one; and (4) therefore, even apparent cases of absolutely rigid designation constitute the start of the referential contract, or the auroral moment of the relation, but never the final moment (2000, 295–296). What, then, are his reasons for maintaining these claims?

Interpretation and Unlimited Semiosis

From his earlier writings (e.g., 1979, 11) to his later works (e.g., 1995, 12), Eco has indicated an affinity to speech act theory. In particular, he has noted (2000, 280; 1990, 208) an acceptance of Strawson's (1950) proposal that referring is not something an expression does but something someone can use an expression to do. Speakers, not expressions, refer. Citing Strawson, Eco remarks that giving the meaning of an expression is to give general directions for its use to refer to particular objects or persons, and giving the meaning of a sentence (rather than of an expression) is to give general directions for its use in making true or false assertions. This emphasis on the "doings" of language, including referring expressions, is reminiscent not only of James's notion of "workings" and of Dewey's notion of "living behaviors," but also of Peirce's view that referring expressions are signs, involving both interpretation and unlimited semiosis, both aspects of language and reference that Eco repeatedly stresses.

These stresses have evolved over time, however. Though sometimes misunderstood as propounding an idealist, or a there-is-nothing-beyond-the-text, view, some of Eco's early writings on semiosis sounded just that way:

> Therefore the process of unlimited semiosis shows us how signification, by means of continual shiftings which refer a sign back to another sign or string of signs, circumscribes *cultural units* in an asymptotic fashion, without even allowing one to touch them directly, though making them accessible through other units. Thus one is never obliged to replace a cultural unit by means of something which is not a semiotic entity, and no cultural unit has to be explained by some platonic, psychic or objectal entity. Semiosis explains itself by itself: this continual circularity is the normal condition of signification and even allows communicational processes to use signs in order to mention things and states of the world. (1979, 198)

What Eco means by "unlimited semiosis" is drawn from Peirce's conception of a sign, or something that represents something to someone. Every sign involves an object (or thing represented), a sign (or that which does the representing), and an interpretant (or that by which the sign represents). An interpretant is not an interpreter (e.g., a person), and Peirce was purposefully omitting from a sign's conception that it must be intentionally emitted or artificially produced. Rather, an interpretant is that which guarantees the validity of the sign. With respect to the issue of unlimited semiosis, the point, for Eco, is that an interpretant is another representation. As he notes, "in order to establish what an interpretant is, it is necessary to name it by another sign and so on. At this point there begins a process of *unlimited semiosis"* (1976, 68). Interpretants can be varied: an (apparently) equivalent sign-vehicle in another semiotic system (e.g., a drawing of a dog to correspond to the word "dog"); an index directed to a single object (e.g., pointing); an emotive association that acquires the value of an established connotation (e.g., dog signifying fidelity), among others.

While Eco is insistent that "interpretation is indefinite" (1992, 32), he is equally insistent that "there are somewhere criteria for limiting interpretation" (1992, 40). As he phrases it, there is not only the intention of authors and audiences, but also of texts themselves. One example (among a number that he gives) of the limits of interpretation and of the constraints of a text is the following story, taken from John Wilkins's 1641 work, *Mercury; Or, the Secret and Swift Messenger:*

How strange a thing this Art of Writing did seem at its first Invention, we may guess by the late discovered Americans, who were amazed to see Men converse with Books, and could scarce make themselves believe that a Paper could speak. . . .

There is a pretty Relation to this Purpose, concerning an Indian Slave; who being sent by his Master with a Basket of Figs and a Letter, did by the Way eat up a great Part of his Carriage, conveying the Remainder unto the Person to whom he was directed; who when he had read the Letter, and not finding the Quantity of Figs answerable to what was spoken of, he accuses the Slave of eating them, telling him what the Letter said against him. But the Indian (notwithstanding this Proof) did confidently abjure the Fact, cursing the Paper, as being a false and lying Witness.

After this, being sent again with the like Carriage, and a Letter expressing the just Number of Figs, that were to be delivered, he did again, according to his former Practice, devour a great Part of them by the Way; but before he meddled with any, (to prevent all following Accusations) he first took the Letter, and hid that under a great Stone, assuring himself, that if it did not see him eating the Figs, it could never tell of him; but being now more strongly accused than before, he confesses the Fault, admiring the Divinity of the Paper, and for the future does promise his best Fidelity in every Employment.

Of course, says Eco, we could interpret this story in many ways, but it cannot be interpreted to mean anything whatsoever. If there is something to be interpreted, says Eco, the interpretation must speak of something that must be found somewhere, and in some way respected. Maintaining his commitment to the pragmatics of a speech act approach, Eco avoids saying that a given interpretation is false (though he does not deny this), but minimally points out that some interpretations are infelicitous. Even though there is a difference, for Eco, between interpreting a text and using a text, what and how a text (or, noted earlier, an expression) signifies has to do with what we do with it. This involves two related elements: purpose and coherence.

Citing Peirce again, that "the idea of meaning is such as to involve some reference to a purpose," Eco stresses that purpose connects interpretation and semiosis generally to something outside of language. Above I remarked that, by advocating unlimited semiosis, Eco had been misread as holding some form of idealism. Here he makes it clear that this is not his position. Speaking of purpose and interpretation, he claims: "Maybe it has nothing to do with a transcendental subject, but it has to do with referents, with the external world, and links the idea of interpretation to the idea of interpreting according to a given meaning" (1990, 38). Purpose, as related to interpretation, involves aspects of a text that are or can be pertinent to a coherent interpretation. On (at least) one interpretation of the fig story above, figs are in themselves not particularly relevant; the story could have mentioned apples. On (at least) one other interpretation, figs are particularly relevant, as they carry certain connotations (say, biblical). What determines the relevant aspects of what is important for interpretation is not given in isolation, but (1) is a matter of "checking upon the text as a coherent whole" (1992, 65). As will be seen below, this becomes especially important for the issue of reference, because Eco rejects the notion that expressions or sentences are taken in isolation.

Reference and Names

In his essay, "On Truth: A Fiction" (in Eco, Santambrogio, and Violi 1988, 41–59), Eco remarks that "in order to use a sentence referentially you must grasp its meaning, and in the process of grasping the meaning of *it eats meat* the use of *it* depends on a previous interpretation, not necessarily on a referent" (52). Likewise, in *The Open Work*, he states, "A sentence such as 'That man comes from Paris,' uttered in front of Napoleon during his exile on Saint Helena, must have awakened in him a variety of emotions such as we could not even imagine. In other words, each addressee will automatically complicate—that is to say, personalize—his or her understanding of a strictly referential proposition with a variety of conceptual or emotional references culled from his or her previous experience" (1989, 30). For the present, the point of these remarks is, as was noted above, that Eco rejects the notion that expressions or sentences are taken in isolation. This is not merely the claim that what a speaker refers to is contextualized, but what an expression or term refers to is contextualized. This is not to deny any distinction between speaker reference and semantic reference, but it is to insist that both are a matter of interpretation, interpretation that is ineliminably social: "Every attempt to establish what the referent of a sign is forces us to define the referent in terms of an abstract entity which moreover is only a cultural convention" (1976, 66). By insisting on the "cultural convention" nature of reference, and of signs generally, Eco—once again—is not advocating an idealist position, but rather the contractualist position identified earlier. Of particular concern here is how this contractualist position elucidates reference and names. Two aspects of these issues that have been especially highlighted in his writings are his take on rigid designators and his take on haecceities.

For quite some time, Eco has expressed reluctant "acceptance" of the notion of rigid designation. In *Semantics and the Philosophy of Language* (1984), he claimed that this notion, which he associates with both Kripke and Putnam, works not simply because there was an introductory event for the designator (e.g., a baptismal event), but "the encyclopedic set of more or less definite descriptions I was able to provide" (1984, 75). Not only is interpretation inextricable at the baptismal event, but also it is so throughout the intermediary links of speakers using the designator. It is the encyclopedic descriptions, not the baptismal events followed by causal chains of usages, that allow reference to occur, for Eco. He offers several arguments, or at least scenarios, to support this view. One (science fiction) example is the following: In order to avoid future world wars, the United Nations decides to establish a peace corps of ISCs (interspecies clones). These clones, being independent of national and ethnic heritage, would be fair and unbiased with respect to any conflicts. The UN Assembly, simply to come to some agreement, must speak about this new "natural kind" prior to them existing, indeed in order to make them exist. Eco claims that it is clear that what would be christened as an ISC would not be some original "thing" but an encyclopedic description of such a thing. Eco takes this science fiction example to show that it is evident that

we use linguistic expressions or other semiotic means to name "things" first met by our ancestors, but it is also evident that we frequently use linguistic expressions to describe and to call into life "things" that will exist only after and because of the utterance of our expressions. In these cases, at least, we are making recourse more to stereotypes and encyclopedic representations than to rigid designators. (1984, 76)

One can object that Eco has missed an important point of the causal view, namely that how the reference is fixed is unimportant. The point is that, once fixed, the designator is rigid; it always picks out the same thing in any possible world in which it picks out anything at all. But Eco thinks the attempt to separate out any purely semantic features of reference from pragmatic ones will not work. Insofar, he says, as the view of rigid designation proffers that names are directly linked to the essence of what they designate, and insofar as this view takes such an essence as a solid core of ontological properties "that survive any counterfactual menace" (1990, 209), it seems adamantly to exclude any kind of contextual knowledge. Such exclusion, for Eco, is illusory at best. As he puts it, in order to use the designator properly, a cultural chain is needed, a chain of *word-of-mouth information*. The only way to make this view understandable, or at least coherent, is to take the pragmatic dimension for granted, as it is what survives the process of transmission across usages that constitutes the identifiable essence of what is designated. For Eco,

> The causal theory of proper names could only work if one (i) takes for granted that it is possible to teach and to learn the name of an object *x* by direct ostension and (ii) the ostension takes place in face of an object that is able to survive its namer. . . . But what happens when one names a human individual, let us say, Parmenides? The causal chain is broken when Parmenides dies. From this point on, the speaker *w* telling the hearer *y* something about Parmenides must introduce into the picture some definite descriptions. . . . The speaker *y* must learn to use the name *Parmenides* according to the set of contextual instructions provided by *w* and is obliged to resort to contextual elements every time he wants to ascertain whether the name is used in the right sense: *Parmenides? Do you mean the philosopher?* It is true that the instructions provided by *w* "causes" the competence of *y*, but from this point of view every theory of language is a causal one. . . . It is exactly such a form of nonphysical and indirect causality that calls for a pragmatic explanation of the process. (1990, 209–210)

Reiterating that reference (i.e., referential usages) cannot be taken in isolation, Eco claims that designators, including names and definite descriptions, have the function of providing speakers and hearers with elements necessary for identification of a given thing. This identification is a process, one that is not only distinct from the presupposition of existence, but is dependent on pragmatic phenomena of cooperation and negotiation. In his more semiological mode of addressing this point, Eco claims, "The problem of proper names is similar to the problem of iconic signs, which are commonly supposed to refer to someone without there being a precise code to establish who this person is (for example, images of people). . . . The expression /Napoleon/ denotes a cultural unit which is well defined and which finds a place in a semantic field of historical entities" (1976, 86–87).[1]

Above it was remarked that Eco has expressed a reluctant acceptance of rigid designation. The sense of acceptance has to do with the fact that Eco acknowledges that at some level there can be acts of reference that do not presuppose an understanding of the meaning of the terms used for referring (i.e., we can use designators simply to designate, without knowing the meaning of the term or whether the referent even exists). Nevertheless, acts of referring involve an inherent semiological element of trust and reveal an ambiguity in the notion of rigid designation. The ambiguity is this: on the one hand, we are supposed to assume that the referent causes the "appropriateness" of the reference, while, on the other hand, we are to assume that the receiver of the name must intend to use it with the same reference as the person from whom the receiver learned it. This is not, says Eco, the same thing. The second assumption relates to what Eco means in speaking of the element of trust. In mundane communicative interaction, we accept a great number of references on trust. For example, if someone tells us that he must take urgent leave of absence because Virginia is ill, we accept that "Virginia" refers to someone who is in some way dependent upon the speaker for Virginia's well-being. "We collaborate in the act of reference, even when we know nothing of the referent and even when we do not know the meaning of the term used by the speaker" (Eco 2000, 292). Among the aspects of this communicative trust is the feature of names that they cannot be merely denotative. If proper names did not have content (i.e., if they were not to some extent connotative), not only could we not use antonomasia, such as "The Voice" for Frank Sinatra, but also we could not use individual names as the sum of properties, such as "He is a real Rambo." The point here for Eco is that designators, including names, have descriptive content, not merely accidentally, but inherently. This content is linked to the contractual, social nature of names and of reference generally. Rigid designation might have an introductory function, to get the contract started, so to speak, but it does only that. Names then take on a social life of their own.

A second concern that Eco raises about the causal view of names, besides general concerns about rigid designation, is the nature of the underlying commitment to haecceities. While acknowledging that a commitment to the "thisness" of some individual does not constitute a commitment to any necessary essence of that individual (at least if essence is taken in terms of properties), Eco still requires that there be some principle of individuation in order for haecceity—and, for that matter, the notion of rigid designation—to make sense. But it is just this notion of a principle of individuation that is very much a matter of negotiation within the contractual theory of meaning. As Eco phrases it, "the attribution of identity (or authenticity) depends on different parameters, negotiable or negotiated from one time to the next" (2000, 323). In supporting this claim, he provides several examples:

(1) The abbey of Saint Guinness was built in the twelfth century. Scrupulous abbots had it restored day by day, replacing stones and fixtures as they fell victim to wear and tear, and so from the point of view of materials the abbey we see today no longer has anything to do with the original (i.e., there are no original parts remaining). From the point of view of architectonic design it is the same one. If we favor the criterion of identity of form over identity of materials, and moreover, if we introduce the criterion of homolocality (the modern abbey stands in exactly the same place as did the original), from a tourist's point of view, we are led to say that this is the same abbey.

(2) Citizen Kane, who dreams of building the perfect residence, finds it in Europe in the abbey of Cognac, which has remained intact since the time of its construction. He buys it, has it dismantled, with the stones numbered before having it shipped back to Xanadu, and then reconstructed. Is this the same abbey? To Kane, yes, as his criterion is identity of materials (and perhaps form). But if the appropriate criterion (i.e., principle of individuation) is homolocality, then no.

The point, of course, is that there is a pragmatics of individuation and of haecceities; so to insist, as Kripke does, that we can make sense of rigid designators outside of the social, contractual nature of reference and names is simply mistaken.[2]

Inference and Evidence

In the context of a discussion of Peirce on concepts and sensations, Eco says that "to name is always to make a hypothesis" (2000, 62). In addition, he claims that "inferential processes (mainly under the form of Peircean *abduction*) stand at the basis of every semiotic phenomenon" (1984, 8). These remarks point to a crucial feature of Eco's conception of interpretation being at the core of reference and names. To see this, Peirce's notion of abduction (which he also at times calls "hypothesis") first needs to be explained.[3]

Peirce distinguished three types of inference: deduction, induction, and abduction. He outlines the difference between them in relation to what he calls a Rule, a Case, and a Result. Peirce illustrates these notions with an example of white beans selected from a bag of beans. A deductive inference is characterized as follows:

Rule: All the beans from this bag are white.
Case: These beans are from this bag.
Therefore
Result: These beans are white.

An inductive inference is characterized differently, as such:

Case: These beans are from this bag.
Result: These beans are white.
Therefore (probably)
Rule: All the beans from this bag are white.

Finally, an abductive inference has the form:

Rule: All the beans from this bag are white.
Result: These beans are white.
Therefore (probably)
Case: These beans are from this bag.

How this relates to reference and names is that the interpretation of signs is inescapably abductive. Eco draws an example from Augustine, pointing out the limitations and underlying presuppositions about ostension. Here Augustine asks Adeodatus how he would explain the meaning of the expression "to walk." Adeodatus states that he would simply start walking (with, we imagine, some sort of verbal clue such as "it's to do this!"). But what would he do to explain the expression if he were already walking, asks Augustine (i.e., if the action and "do this" didn't work). Adeodatus exclaims that he would just walk faster. Augustine, of course, notes that this would not distinguish "to walk" from "to hurry up," noting that ostensive signs do not provide or clarify meaning by means of simple induction. Eco insists that a frame of reference is necessary, a metalinguistic (or, rather, a metasemiotic) rule expressed in some way that prescribes what rule should be used in order to understand ostension. But at this point we have already arrived at the mechanism of abduction. Only via hypothesizing Adeodatus' behavior (Result) as a Case of a Rule will any sense be made. "Abduction," Eco states, "is, therefore, the tentative and hazardous tracing of a system of signification rules which will allow the sign to acquire its meaning" (Eco 1984, 40).

Names, of course, are a species of signs. Another example illustrates how this conception of abductive inference connects directly to reference and names. It is taken from Voltaire's *Zadig* and involves the character Zadig making reference to a dog and a horse he has never encountered. One day while walking near a wood, Zadig is approached by the Queen's Chief Eunuch who asks if Zadig has seen the Queen's dog. Though he hasn't, he replies that the dog was actually a bitch, a very small spaniel that had recently had puppies, that its left forefoot was lame and it had very long ears. Just at that moment, the Master of the King's Hounds comes by and asks Zadig if he has seen the king's horse pass by. Though he hasn't, he replies that the horse was the best galloper in the stable, it was fifteen hands high, with a very small hoof; as well, its tail was three-and-one-half feet long, the studs on its bit were of 23-carat gold and its shoes of eleven-scruple silver. The Chief Eunuch and the Master of the King's Hounds are astonished that Zadig could know these things about the animals, not having seen them. (Indeed, they did not believe he hadn't seen them.) Zadig then explains how he inferred these properties of the animals. For example, he saw animal tracks on the sand and judged them (based on past experience) to be dog prints; the sand was always less hollowed by one paw than by the other three; the marks of horse-shoes were all perfectly equally spaced; from the marks his hoofs made on certain pebbles he knew (based on past experience) the horse had been shod with eleven-scruple silver; and so on. Using certain designators as identity operators in the context of his discussions (e.g., *she* had recently had puppies, *its* tail was a certain length, *the* dog, etc.), Zadig engaged in abductive reasoning while making reference to the unseen animals. In Eco's "retelling" of this incident, as he incorporates it in his *The Name of the Rose*, Brother William (i.e., Zadig) even correctly uses the horse's name, Brunellus, though no name had been uttered in his presence. The point here is that Zadig is able to refer based on his abductive inferences of semiological information.

Closely connected to this feature of naming as hypothesis is the ineliminability of evidence in relation to reference. Zadig's ability to refer to the dog and horse (and his ability qua Brother William to use "Brunellus" to refer to the king's horse) is dependent upon evidence culled, in this case, from nonlinguistic signs. Clearly, what counts as evidence is signs carrying some recognized or enunciated similarity to other signs. Eco states three conditions on a sign's being so related: (1) it cannot be explained more economically; (2) it points to a single cause[4] (or very limited set); and (3) it fits in with other evidence. The importance here is not so much for "normal" cases of evidence, for example, clues leading to inferences about, say, a crime. Rather, the point about evidence relates to how even names can be used and understood, and the fact that they are so used and understood only against a background of inference and interpretation.

Appealing to Putnam's notion of using expressions successfully as part of a community of speakers, and relying on the use that is in some sense determined by "expert" speakers, Eco gives the following example:

> For example, faced with the sentence *Napoleon was born in Cambridge*, convinced as I am that *my* Napoleon was born in Ajaccio, by no means do I agree to use the name according to the intentions of the Community, because, out of the principle of charity at least, I immediately suspect that the speaker intends to refer to *another* Napoleon. Therefore I do my best to check the appropriateness of the reference, trying to induce my interlocutor to interpret the [nuclear content of the expression] that he makes correspond to the name *Napoleon*, to discover perhaps that his Napoleon is a used car salesman born in this century, and so I find myself faced with a banal case of homonymy. Or I realize that my interlocutor intends to refer to my Napoleon, and therefore intends to make a historical proposition that defies current encyclopedic notions (and therefore the Mind of the Community). In such a case I would proceed to ask him for convincing proof of his proposition. (2000, 300–301)

Just who has been referred to by the use of the name "Napoleon" here is in part a matter of interpretation and inference. As was noted in the earlier chapter on Wittgenstein, Steinman (1982) has forcefully argued for the interconnection of naming and evidence. And the larger point here is the inherent connection between names and our ability to refer (as well as their ability to refer), interpretation, and Eco's contractual view of reference.[5]

Karl-Otto Apel

At the Twentieth World Congress on Philosophy, which was held in Boston during August 1998 and was noted as the final such congress of the twentieth century, a special roundtable session was held, with six panel members addressing the question: "What has philosophy learned in the twentieth century?" Those six panelists were: Willard Van Orman Quine, Donald Davidson, Peter Strawson, Margorie Grene, Seyyed Nasr, and Karl-Otto Apel. Apel's inclusion in this select group was a tacit but clear acknowledgment of his status within the philosophical world. Known less widely to English-speaking philosophers than his long-time friend and colleague, Jürgen Habermas, Apel has nonetheless been a major voice and influence in German and European philosophy since the 1960s. He has been especially central in drawing connections between the work and concerns of critical theory and analytic philosophy of language as well as semiotics and pragmatism, particularly the work of Peirce.

Known primarily for advocating a view of transcendental semiotics and transcendental pragmatics, Apel has been explicit in both drawing from classical and contemporary pragmatists and extending (as well as correcting) their foci to epistemological, axiological, and methodological matters. As several commentators (e.g., Mendieta, Kettner, Gorner) have noted, a major concern for Apel over the years has been the elaboration of rationality in light of the linguistic turn in philosophy, as well as a subsequent development of discourse ethics. Although the latter emphasis on discourse ethics is beyond the scope of the present analysis of Apel's contribution to a pragmatic conception of reference, within the context of Apel's overall project, it is not unrelated. For example, Eduardo Mendieta has pointed out:

Apel develops a philosophy of language that does justice not just to the prepositional-descriptive but also to the performative, pragmatic dimension of language. Originally, Apel did so in terms of a mediation between the world-disclosing and world-coping functions of language. Later, as the question of ethics moves to the fore, Apel develops his philosophy of language in terms of the mediation between the constitution of meaning and the justification of validity. Language, for Apel, cannot be comprehensively and nonreductively analyzed if only one aspect of language is emphasized. Language remains irreducibly oriented to issues of meaning constitution while always raising issues of validity. (Mendieta 2002, 164–165)

Here, however, the focus will be on what Apel says about reference and how that flows from and displays his notion of transcendental pragmatics.

On Reference and Names

In 1981, Apel published an essay entitled "Intentions, Conventions, and Reference to Things: Meaning in Hermeneutics and the Analytic Philosophy of Language" (reprinted in Apel 1994, 51–82). Displaying an awareness of the disputes between the descriptivist account of meaning and reference on the one hand and the causal (direct reference) account on the other, Apel summarized his position:

> Thus, from the perspective of a *transcendental semiotics*, which includes *transcendental pragmatics and hermeneutics*, one may only come to the conclusion that the key notions of *subjective intention, linguistic convention* and *reference to things* (in a broad sense) are of equal importance for the understanding of meaning. They complement each other and restrict each other as regulative principles of inquiry within the context of the so-called hermeneutic circle of meaning-disclosure. For, in order to initiate the hermeneutic enterprise of understanding and explicating the meaning of utterances or of written texts, it is possible, in principle, to start out from each angle, so to speak, if a certain preliminary understanding of the language can be taken for granted. But it seems equally necessary in this enterprise to oscillate between the three viewpoints and regulative principles, in order to correct and deepen one's meaning-conjectures. (1994, 78)

This passage points to various aspects of Apel's overall philosophy and to aspects of his related view on reference: (1) there are three irreducible elements involved in meaning (subjective intention, linguistic convention, and reference to things); (2) each of these three is necessary for a complete understanding of meaning and each can be the point of entry into that understanding, but none is hierarchically prior to the others; and (3) each serves as a regulative principle of inquiry. These aspects need elaboration.

Apel begins with what appears to be obvious and rather trivial: we interact with the world and we use language to do so. The world of interaction includes things "out there" that we refer to, such as cabbages and kings; the world of interaction also includes our subjective perspectives and intentions (our interactions are purposive); linguistic interaction requires public language. But there is much beneath what seems obvious and trivial here. In his essay, "The 'Pragmatic Turn' and Transcendental Semiotics," Apel speaks of these three aspects as the "three angles of understanding meaning, namely extensionality [reference to things], intensionality [linguistic convention], and intentionality [subjective intention]" (Apel 1994, 139). Of course, speakers use language to communicate their intentions, but, says Apel, our ability to have such intentions, much less our ability to communicate them, is inseparable from public intensionality. As will be noted below, Apel finds much about Searle's speech-act theory to agree with, but he is consistently critical of what he sees as Searle's analysis of speech acts in terms of intentionality. Prelinguistic intentional consciousness, or states of mind, is what Apel sees as Searle's fundamental basis for linguistic meaning, and he rejects this. As he claims, "it is not possible to separate the notion of referential intentionality, say in perceptual identifying of something *as* something, from the notion of public meaning qua intensionality of (proper or general) names" (ibid.). Our very ability to recognize something as something underlies the claim of intentionality, a point Apel makes repeatedly.[6] As with others (e.g., Putnam), this is to deny that meaning is in the head. But it is not to deny, for Apel, that there is no intentionality or that there is no difference between intentionality and intensionality. It might very well be possible and even necessary to ascertain a difference between them. Indeed, the very distinction between speaker reference and semantic reference rests on such a difference. What is the significance of this, then? For Apel, we might very well want to make the sort of move that Frege did to de-psychologize meaning (and reference) by acknowledging the two (intentions and intensions) while focusing on the publicity of meaning. But, Apel says, epistemologically, the abstractive separation between public meaning-intensions and subjective meaning-intentions must be suspended. As he puts it:

the logical semantics of a Fregean or Carnapian type would lose its meaningful function if we did not suppose that the ideal, intersubjectively valid meanings of language-signs can be grasped, in principle, by every human being qua subject of meaning-intentions. Otherwise we could not understand that different people can agree, in principle, on the intersubjective validity of an argument. Furthermore, it must be possible for every subject of meaning-intention to contribute by his or her meaning-intentions to the public meaning-intensions. Otherwise we could not understand that human experience can constitute the content of public meaning-intensions of language-signs: only the human subject of meaning-intentions may realize the reference-dimension of public meanings by identifying real denotata. In short, what we have postulated before, an integration of abstract semantics by pragmatics, implies suspending the abstractive separation between public meaning-*intensions* and subjective meaning-*intentions*. (Ibid., 140)

More directly related to the specifics of Kripke and Searle (as representative of the received views of reference), Apel speaks to the third element, extensionality.[7] His remarks on "something *as* something" provide a hint—indeed, more than a hint—both to the necessary element of reference to things and to concerns about the causal view. Echoing Searle's comments that an external description of a causal chain of behavior (or uses of a name) can never ensure that the meaning-intention of a user of a name correctly refers to the name's denotatum, Apel claims that the pragmatics of identifying denotata must include an account of causal and intentional chains simultaneously. One should think, he notes, identification of real referents as denotata of signs is eventually a case of complete integration of all three elements (or dimensions) of the triadic sign-function, as enunciated by Peirce. Apel claims that "identifying a denotatum is a case of an encounter with the real world that is at the same time mediated by language and language-constitutive" (ibid., 138). While acknowledging the importance of a Kripkean treatment of reference ("especially the theory of the 'original baptism' of individuals and natural kinds by 'rigid designators'") (Apel 1998, 32), any value of this view would "have to be integrated into a transcendental semiotics of Peircean provenance" (ibid.). Kripke, says Apel, tries to detach the determination of the extension of names from the intensions and intentions by instead connecting the name with the indexical function that it takes on by the original baptism (in the case of individuals) or as an exemplar of a natural kind (in the case of kind terms). Highlighting the ineliminable extensional character of reference is all to the good, but Kripke does so at the expense of the other elements of reference. The very identity, and not merely the identification, of an entity being baptized requires, for Apel, the intensional and intentional elements of reference. About the right method of making use of a semantics of the indexical account of names, Apel says:

I think the first requirement of the method would be to make sure that the indexical definition that is connected with the "original baptism" can be remembered and transferred by communication. For as we have pointed out before in accordance with Searle, the "original baptism" and the communicative transfer of the name must not be confused with a causal reaction and its transfer, which could be the object of an external description of a "causal chain" of behavior. . . . In order, for example, to refer by baptism to an individual in such a way that the indexical definition can be remembered and transferred by communication, it would at least be necessary to determine the extension of the attached proper name by a phrase somehow like this: "the child that was baptized at the time *t* at place *p* by person *p*." . . . In the case of the "original baptism" of some (supposed) exemplar of a natural kind that cannot yet be subsumed under the head of a general concept—say by the name "baboo"—it would not even suffice to provide a definite description like: "the material that was baptized at time *t* and place *p* by person *p*," for this would not provide a sufficient determination of the extension of a (supposed) natural kind by indexical identification of its real essence. In order to achieve this, one either has to complement the indexical definition of "baboo" by some picture (say by a photograph) or to provide some description of the phenomenal qualities (and relations of qualities) that point to the structure of the given material. . . . But if this proposal should be relevant, then it would appear as if the intended detachment of the indexical definition of the *extension* of the name from its *intension* has already been proved impossible. (1994, 143–144)

Kripke, of course, accepts that descriptions or intensions might be used to *fix* reference, but once it is fixed, then such matters play no further role in reference. As he noted himself, the reference of the name "Neptune" was fixed via descriptions, as was the reference of the kind term "meter." Nevertheless, once fixed, the semantic reference became detached from any and all pragmatic dimensions (i.e., these are not needed for reference to succeed). They became rigid designators, independent of intensions or intentions that might be associated with them. But, as noted above, Apel disagrees, as the ability to transfer reference by communication requires that names are more than indices. Kripke's indexical-only view amounts to a Kantian view of an unknowable *Ding an sich*. On such a view, we could arrive at a situation in which users of a name might know nothing at all about that which they must define indexically. Although Kripke is content with this result (Nixon is Nixon! I can talk about *this* table!), Apel recoils from it, suggesting a Peircean opposition: "According to Charles Peirce, such a purely indexical definition is nonsensical because it cannot show, in principle, how the meaning of 'identical in essence with . . . this . . .' could be conceptually interpreted. Thus it reduces the meaning of the real to the limit case of a bumping (of the will of the I) against something in the night (the resistance of the non-I)" (1994, 148).

Apel's rejection of the implicit (or, perhaps, explicit) haecceitism of Kripke's view is part of his own Peircean semiotic view of the tridimensional nature of signs. Kripke, while making the case for the indexical nature of names, ignores their iconic and symbolic features. To explicate these features, and to provide a Peircean account of reference, Apel returns to his "baboo" case and offers the following scenario:

That thing over there—under the big tree in the foreground—looks so and so (to be specified by describing the perceptible qualities and relations of qualities that make up the phenomenal structure). On the basis of these perceptible qualities, I don't know how to determine *what* it is (i.e., under which general concept it could be subsumed). That is, I find it impossible at present to provide a conceptual subsumption of the given stuff on the basis of an abductive inference of the form: "This there is so and so; what is so and so might be an exemplar of 'A.'" Hence, in order to provide for the possibility of a later determination on the basis of a reidentification, I will give it a name: I hereby baptize the given stuff by the name of "baboo." I thereby define the extension of "baboo" as being everything that is the same as this over there which now causes my present experience by presenting the following phenomenal structure (to be specified by a picture or by a list of phenomenal qualities). (Ibid., 151)

Recourse of indexicals (indices) such as "this" and "over there" is integral for reference, or in this case naming, to occur. But, in addition, the use of icons is needed, whether in the form of physical icons such as a photograph or in the form of linguistic icons such as a list of phenomenal qualities. Finally, symbols, in the form of general concepts, are also required.

Transcendental Semiotics

As noted above, Apel enunciated the three elements of subjective intention, linguistic convention, and reference to things all within what he identified as a view of transcendental semiotics. That, in turn, he remarked, included transcendental pragmatics and hermeneutics. A fuller picture of his position on reference and names, then, demands a fleshing out of these notions. Related notions of community of interpretation and community of communication, as well as "futuro," also require discussion.

In his *Charles S. Peirce: From Pragmatism to Pragmaticism*, Apel cites one of Peirce's criticisms of nominalism: "Nominalism, up to that of Hegel, looks at reality retrospectively. What all modern Philosophy does is to deny that there is any *esse in futuro*" (1958, 8.292). The import of this remark for Apel is Peirce's insistence on turning away from causes of cognition in the past to the goals of cognition and inquiry in the future. This is part and parcel of Peirce's dictum of our conception of an object being a matter of what effects, which might conceivably have practical bearings, we conceive the object to have. This holds not simply for a conception of an object, but for the meaningfulness and truth of propositions as well. Indeed, this is, for Apel, the "pragmatic maxim." Possibility is integral to reality, and real possibility represents itself in the truth of general conditional sentences. For Apel:

Through those [general conditional] sentences, according to the "pragmatic maxim," the meaning of general concepts can be explicated in concepts of really possible actions and thereupon expectable experiences. . . . If the meaning of general concepts were dependable on *factual* actions and experiences, then, according to Peirce, the meaning of *reality* itself should depend on the factual results of our cognition [cf. *CP*, 5.457]. But as *recognizable* (in the sense of a modal concept) *reality* cannot depend on the *facts* of our cognition, but only—indeed—on the *real possibility* of its being cognized (in the long run). (Apel 2001, 460–461)

Not only is this pragmatic maxim future-oriented, but it is communal. That is, Apel takes it to be inherently and necessarily intersubjective. This intersubjectivity is exhibited by both his notion of a community of interpretation and a community of communication.

Drawing the term "community of interpretation" from Josiah Royce (1913, 146), Apel speaks of the progress from a discussion of the interpretation of signs to a discussion of the hermeneutic problem of the understanding of intended meanings. Where Peirce focused on the triadic structure of sign interpretation, Royce focused on the triadic structure of the mediation of tradition, thus situating semiotic understanding in historical and concrete housings. The subjects of the pragmatic dimension of the sign function, Apel insists, must be taken into account in "a very striking, anthropologically and socio-comprehensible sense as the precondition of the possibility for the perspectivistic interpretation of reality 'as something'" (1980, 99). Communication, then, between those subjects is not simply information exchange but an attempt to secure a preunderstanding as to how one can interpret the world. Peirce's "community of experimenters" (who will function as determining the *esse in futuro*) is just a concretization of the community of interpreters, one that "converts its understanding of symbols into real operative rules of behavior or habits" (Apel 1981, 29). Clearly, linguistic convention and communication require the interpretation of signs, and, as Apel insists, just interpretation is necessarily public and communal.

Not only is interpretation communal, but also, obviously, communication is. We participate not just in interpretation, but also in communication. Indeed, the former is inseparable from the latter. Interpretation does not happen by subjects in a vacuum. What is crucial for Apel, however, is not just the descriptive fact of a "community of communication," but also that this functions regulatively. With Peirce and others, Apel claims to have "fallen back upon the normative conception of an ideal consensus to be established within an ideal and unlimited communicative community" (1998, 151), that is, upon the conception of a regulative idea regarding the building up of a consensus concerning rule-following. As he elucidates:

> [There is] the undeniable historicity of meaning constitution [and also] the fact that, already on the level of communicative understanding of meaning of our utterances, a claim to universal validity of meaning is presupposed; a claim to the validity of meaning which can be definitively redeemed—if at all—only by the possible consensus of an indefinite, ideal community of communication and interpretation (as understood by Peirce and Royce). (Ibid., 117)

Validity Claims

"Reference to reality is all right," says Apel, "as long as it is *not* separated from, and even played off against the claim of every serious assertion to *universal intersubjective* validity and hence *acceptability*" (2001, 446). This reiterates the inherent and ineliminable sociality of language in general and of reference in particular. Like other pragmatists before him, Apel is not advocating or committed to an idealist metaphysics ("reference to reality is all right"), and, like pragmatists before him, he is adamant about acknowledging and highlighting both the intersubjective quality of language and the requirement of standards that transcend individual users of language ("acceptability"). As several commentators have noted, and as Apel has stated repeatedly, while language is used to denote and refer, it also has other functions, and its denotative function is neither more basic than these other functions nor possible without them.

Two fundamental functions of language that Apel speaks of are (1) its world-coping function and (2) its world-disclosing function. The notion of "world-coping" points to the referential function of language; we use language to cope with a world in which we find ourselves, in which we are situated. Again, Apel is no idealist. But the world in which we find ourselves is not a world of *Dingen an sich*; rather, we encounter situations and things *as* something, always mediated via signs. This sign-mediation is constitutive, not merely descriptive. That is, we engage always and only in a sign-mediated world.

This sign-mediated process is captured by Apel's criticisms, noted above, of Searle's emphasis on intentionality. As Mattias Kettner points out, Apel thinks that "even meaning-intentions should not be classified primarily as isolated psychological phenomena" (Kettner 1996, 262). Rather, they should be seen as meaning-claims, truth-claims, rightness-claims, and sincerity-claims, all in the context of communication. The emphasis here is on *claims*, that is, as saying something about something in the context of intersubjective understanding and communication. The recent emphasis on language as embedded in philosophy of mind (an emphasis Searle and many others are wont to make) is, for Apel, a return to the psychologizing of language and philosophy that was eschewed early in the twentieth century. But neither understanding nor communication can be psychologized, for Apel. Furthermore, the emphasis on claims is to be seen normatively as well as descriptively. Here, Apel speaks of *validity claims*.

In two essays in particular, Apel enunciates the notion of validity claims. These are part of his overall transcendental semiotics, in the sense that four conditions (identified below) are a priori conditions of communication and understanding in that they are necessary for communication and understanding to be possible (i.e., failure of any of them would involve performative contradiction). In "Regulative Ideas or Sense Events? An Attempt to Determine the *Logos* of Hermeneutics" (reprinted in Apel 1998, 160–182), he identifies four presuppositions as:

(1) the claim to verbally expressible and to that extent intersubjectively communicable sense;

(2) for prepositional statements, the assertorically raised claim to intersubjectively consensual truth;

(3) for the verbal expression of intentional states of subjects, the claim to truthfulness or sincerity (which cannot be assured through arguments but only through behavioral *praxis*); and

(4) for speech acts as communicative acts with appellative force, the claim—which is also always already implicitly raised for the assertive acts—to normative, finally ethically justifiable correctness or rightness.

In "The Self-recuperative Principle of a Critical-Hermeneutic Reconstruction of History" (reprinted in Apel 1998, 232–243), he identifies these transcendental validity claims as follows:

(1) a claim to linguistically articulated meaning, about which it must be possible, in principle, to reach a consensus between all possible discourse partners;

(2) a claim to truth, about which it must be possible as well to reach a consensus, in principle;

(3) a claim to veracity, which also must be capable of consensus, in principle; and

(4) a claim to moral rightness capable of consensus of the acts of arguing as acts of communication and interaction in an ideal argumentation community.

In both cases of enunciating validity claims, the points are the same. The first condition requires that claims have an intersubjective sense, so that the very semantic meaning requires sociality; the second condition points to the possibility of claims having truth-value, which itself requires the possibility of consensus. This is not the position that truth is convention; rather, it is the position that truth-value must be ascertainable. The third condition, of sincerity or veracity, necessitates the testability in action of claims. Finally, the fourth condition points to the ineliminable axiological aspect of claims. Claims never occur in isolation, but always in contexts, just as speakers and hearers never exist in isolation, but always in contexts.[8]

For Apel, then, there are transcendental conditions of meaning, and, for present purposes, of reference. These conditions apply to assertive speech acts as well as to, say, directive speech acts, though there are differences between them:

> At this point, it seems to me that an extension—or, if the reader prefers, a deepening—of the philosophical presuppositions of the possible *explication of meaning* is required—an extension which understands the *truth conditions* in the light of which the prepositional contents of speech acts or sentences can be explicated not as a special case of the *conditions of satisfaction* of *intentional states*, but as a special case of the *validity conditions* of *illocutionary acts*. In other words, we must take seriously the idea of the integration of semantics and pragmatics—as suggested by Austin and Searle I [Searle's early views as expressed in *Speech Acts*, as opposed to his later views emphasizing intentionality]—in the sense of an extension of the "linguistic turn." And insofar as the extension of the "linguistic turn" has to take into account all functions of language and all relations of language to the world, it ought to be possible to understand the *meaning* of speech acts—beyond the *intended proposition-related conditions of satisfaction* in terms of *validity conditions*. (1991, 46)

There is a difference between the conditions for assertive speech acts and directive speech acts. The legitimation of the validity claim of assertive speech acts is dependent upon the existence of facts that are independent in the external world of the speech act, whereas this is not necessarily the case for directive speech acts. In the case of the latter (i.e., directive speech acts), the validity claim, which contributes to the constitution of the illocutionary force, has nothing to do with the prepositional content or external facts in the world, but, first, has to do with the fact that a demand is made upon addressees to bring about some state of affairs, and, second, with the fact that for the appropriateness of the directive, grounds are claimed which might be binding (or at least motivating) for the addressees. Clearly, the speech act of referring is not the same as the speech act of commanding, and validity conditions for the two will be different, at least in some respects. Nevertheless, both are cases of speech acts, and both are to be understood in the context of semiosis. Coming back to the fact that, for Apel, reference involves three components—intention, intension, and extension—no one or two of which fully account for reference, he reiterates his Peircean semiotic position:

the orientation to *language-functions* can help toward an extended—or more profound—philosophical "architectonics"—an architectonics which overcomes the *one-dimensionality of the modern subject-object relation* (and with it also the one-dimensionality of the explication of linguistic meaning in terms of *truth*-conditions of propositions or conditions of satisfaction of intentional states of mind) in favor of the three-dimensionality of *linguistic meaning, validity claims, and relations to the world* as the possible conditions of redemption of validity claims. We might, therefore, in summary, say that in language an architectonics of meaning of validity dimensions is laid down which is a fitting basis for *theoretical* and also *practical* philosophy (in the dimension of sincere or authentic self-expression, it also seems that we see a *necessary* condition of *aesthetics* emerge). (1991, 51)

In summary, following Mendieta's overview of Apel,[9] several aspects of his transcendental semiotic philosophical view can be identified. First, Apel rejects what he calls "methodical solipsism" and affirms intersubjectivity. That is, intersubjective meaning cannot be reduced to subjective intentions. Likewise, it cannot be reduced to idealism. Second, Apel denounces what he sees as abstractive and reductive fallacies. Semiosis requires all three components of the Peircean analysis of the sign-relation, the sign, the object, and the interpretant. Third, language has an irreducible double structure. That is to say, neither the world-coping function nor the world-disclosing function can be reduced to the other. Both understanding and communication require the denotative and performative elements of language. Fourth, Apel emphasizes a normative hermeneutic. Understanding, communication, and interpretation all involve transcendent conditions of possibility, validity conditions. The point of the present look at Apel has been to suggest that these features are revealed in his analysis of reference.

Jürgen Habermas

Jürgen Habermas is regarded by many philosophers as one of the most important thinkers of the latter half of the twentieth century, in terms of both breadth and depth. His writings, especially the two-volume *Theory of Communicative Action*—considered by most as his magnum opus—display remarkable intellectual rigor and acuity over a range of philosophical concerns. Known most prominently as a social and political philosopher, Habermas has also written a great amount on philosophy of language and epistemology (or reason) as well. With Apel and Rorty, Habermas has not only incorporated into his own thinking positions and influences across the "analytic–continental" philosophical divide, but he has (also like Apel and Rorty) striven for decades to bridge that divide, engaging with the thought of Quine and Davidson with equal comfort and familiarity as with that of Heidegger and Lucaks. Though rarely, if ever, labeled a pragmatist, he has frequently acknowledged an intellectual debt and affinity with pragmatism, particularly with the works of Mead and Peirce. Along with his close colleague and friend, Apel, the overall emphasis of his work has not been on language, but on social and political emancipation. Nevertheless, much of what he has said about language resonates clearly with pragmatist views and concerns. It is this resonance that will be the focus here.

On Pragmatism

In 1985 Habermas remarked, "As a good pragmatist, I hold the view that a philosopher's capacity to create problems through intentionally inciting doubt is quite limited" (Habermas 1998, 409). No doubt, Habermas was speaking nonliterally in characterizing himself as a pragmatist. Nevertheless, he has openly acknowledged the impact of pragmatism on his own intellectual development, and, as will be seen, has much in common with pragmatism on a number of topics, including reference. The first and strongest influence, he has noted, is Peirce.[10] This influence goes back to *Knowledge and Human Interests*, published in the late 1960s, especially in areas of epistemology and a theory of truth. Here the value

of Peirce was his opposition to "the limited view of the logical empiri-
cists and their focus on the semantic dimension," as well as the positive
contribution that "reason and understanding were from the start embod-
ied in the research activities of a community of investigators" (Aboulafia,
Bookman, and Kemp 2002, 227). (Beyond the remarks here on epistemology, Habermas has also noted pragmatism as a corrective for the
deficiencies of democratic theory in Marxism. See Dews 1986, 192–193.)
The greatest strength of pragmatism, for Habermas, is the "combination of fallibilism with anti-skepticism, and a naturalist approach to the
human mind and its culture that refuses to yield to any kind of scientism"
(Aboulafia, Bookman, and Kemp 2002, 228). When asked about the most
lasting contribution of pragmatism in the tradition of Western philosophy
and social thought, Habermas remarked:

Peirce and Royce, James, Mead and Dewey felt the obligation to solve problems,
one by one, just in the local context where they actually faced them. But equally,
they would have objected to a false generalization of this honest attitude in terms
of a contextualization that cheers the local provincialism of our problem-solving
capacities. Alongside Marx and Kierkegaard, again, pragmatism emerges as the only
approach that embraces modernity in its most radical forms, and acknowledges
its contingencies, without sacrificing the very purpose of Western philosophy—
namely, to try out explanations of who we are and who we would like to be, as individuals, as members of our communities, and as person *überhaubt*—that is, as man.
(Aboulafia, Bookman, and Kemp 2002, 229)

His affiliation with much of pragmatism is seen also in his comments
on Dewey's *The Quest for Certainty* (L.W. 4.iii–307). Not only does Dewey
eschew the way in which classical theory withdraws from the world and,
instead, propagates a turn toward being engaged with the world, but also
he criticizes the empiricist "spectator-model of knowledge," according
to which elementary sensations provide a firm basis for experiences. As
opposed to this empiricist (scientistic) view, Dewey insists (and Habermas
agrees) that experiences are gained only in interaction with a reality
against which behavioral expectations may run aground. For this reason,
Habermas says, "reality is disclosed not through the receptivity of the
senses, but rather in a constructive manner in the context of projecting
and performing actions that succeed or fail. Objects are not 'conceived'
independently of the controlled outcome of deliberately performed
actions" (Aboulafia, Bookman, and Kemp 2002, 231). The influences of
these stances will become apparent below.

On Names and Reference

Though Habermas has written extensively on language, he has not said a great deal explicitly about reference or names. He has often commented on Searle, but has never written about Kripke in particular or directly about a causal view in general. Nevertheless, he has made some telling remarks about names and reference. In the mid-1970s he noted the function names, demonstrative pronouns, and other linguistic designations have for undertaking the identification of things and events (Habermas 1979, 106). Indeed, in his Gauss Lectures, given at Princeton University in 1971, he spoke to names and reference. It is worth quoting him at length:

In the case of organizing experiences of objects we conceive the primitive terms as cognitive schemata; in formulating beliefs about objects of experience we can represent them as logico-semantic categories. Evidently the connection between these two levels (of experience on the one hand and language on the other) is created by action: specifically, by either instrumental or communicative action. This can be seen if we examine the use of referential expressions. We denote objects by means of names or definite descriptions. To do this, we have to orient ourselves by characteristic features. That is why we can always replace a name with a definite description. If it is to function pragmatically, the definite description must contain an identifying description of the object. It generally depends on the context which feature is sufficiently characteristic for speakers and hearers to be able to pick out from all possible objects precisely that object which is being discussed. The less we can rely on contexts of pre-understanding, however, the more deictic expressions must bear the burden of denotation. Here we make use of specifying expressions (definite articles: the; demonstratives: this, that), quantifying expressions (numerals; indefinite quantifiers such as some, many, all), as well as spatial and temporal adverbs. At the linguistic level these expressions represent cognitive schemata, namely, substance, quantity, space, and time. These expressions, however, form a functioning denotative system only after they have been interpreted within the framework of a descriptive language (a thing-event language or an intentional language). The identifiable object is categorized in the first case as a moving body (or an aggregate of things, states, or events) and in the second as a person (or a structured web of persons, states, or utterances). These categories, in terms of which we perceive and understand the identified object, refer to alternative patterns of action. (Habermas 2001a, 79–80)

The significant details of this view will be identified and analyzed below, but first it must be noted that the overall view offered here is carried on in his later writings (see, e.g., *The Liberating Power of Symbols* [1995 in 2001b], 12–18). For example, a decade later, in the second volume of *The Theory of Communicative Action*, Habermas claims:

But the institution of giving names is such that a proper name functions as a guide-post by which we can orient ourselves in gathering the data that would be sufficient for identification: date and place of birth, family background, nationality, religious affiliation, and so forth. These are, as a rule, the criteria on the basis of which a person is identified—for instance, when he presents a passport. The usual identity criteria refer the questioner to those situations in which alone, *in the final analysis*, persons can be identified. They refer him virtually to those interactions in which the identity of the person in question was formed. . . . Since . . . persons acquire their identities through linguistically mediated interaction, they satisfy the conditions of identity for persons, and the basic criteria of identity for specific persons, not only for others but for themselves as well. . . . A person can ascribe to *himself* such prop-erties [ancestry, geography, religious affiliation, etc.] only by answering the ques-tion, *what kind of* a person he is, and not the question, *which* of all persons he is. A person satisfies the conditions and criteria of identity according to which he can be numerically distinguished from others only when he is in a position to ascribe to himself the relevant predicates. In this respect, the predicative self-identification of a person accomplished at an elementary level is a presupposition for that person's being identifiable by others as a person in general—that is, generically—and as a specific person—that is, numerically. (1987, 105)

There are several features of names (and of reference generally) that emerge from these two passages and must be explicated. First, Habermas clearly has strong reservations about objects or persons, or more broadly, referents, as mere haecceities. Though he does not use that term, he obvi-ously balks at the idea of noncategorized particulars (what kind of a person one is precedes which of all persons he is). Second, reference via names involves actions. These actions are not simply speech acts, though they are that (e.g., naming is a speech act); rather, they are housed in purposes and goal-oriented behaviors. More will be said on these two features momen-tarily. Before addressing them more fully, however, one potential (and, for some commentators, actual) infelicity must be pointed out.

At least two commentators, Barbara Fultner and John B. Thompson, have claimed that Habermas holds a descriptivist view of names and refer-ence.[11] One can see why, given that Habermas draws explicitly on Searle's speech-act theory and given his comment (quoted above) that: "We denote objects by means of names or definite descriptions. To do this, we have to orient ourselves by characteristic features. That is why we can always replace a name with a definite description." For example, in her introduc-tion to Habermas (2001), Fultner states: "When attributing a property to an object, [Habermas] claims, a speaker presupposes that the object exists and that the proposition she asserts is true. That is, she assumes that the subject expression has a referent and that the predicate can be correctly applied to it. Habermas here endorses a description theory of reference" (2001, xvi–xvii). Thompson says:

The languages in which sensory and communicative experiences are expressed contain terms which enable a speaker to identify particular objects. Such terms include proper names, but these in turn must embrace or entail predicative expressions. For in Habermas's view, "a properly functioning system of reference has to have a certain prepositional content" [Habermas 1973, 173], since reference presupposes some characterization, and in what sense the latter is presupposed, are questions which are not directly confronted by Habermas. However, a sympathetic footnote to Searle suggests that Habermas, like Ricoeur, endorses the cluster theory of reference. (Thompson 1981, 196–197)

Does Habermas endorse a descriptivist view of names and reference? Though he has never responded directly to these authors,[12] it is apparent from other things he has said that he does not, nor do his views commit him to such. For example, in identifying Searle's view as an intentionalist model of language, he likens it to the operation of an isolated brain in a vat, as such a view (i.e., intention has priority over meaning, or in this case reference) could be the case "only under the premise that communication within a community of speakers is secondary to the capacity for representation possessed by the individual mind or brain" (Habermas 1991, 21). Likewise, he has explicitly rejected any descriptivist view that identifies a referent with a description: "we would not be able to explain the possibility of learning processes without reference to the capacity for recognizing the same entities under different descriptions" (1998, 378n23). As will be shown below, Habermas insists on reference being understood within the context of intersubjective communication, which itself requires ineliminable validity claims. The inadequacy of the intentionalist model, he says, condemns the hearer to a peculiar passivity. Likewise, in volume 1 of *The Theory of Communicative Action*, he rejects any version of an intentionalist semantics:

Intentionalist semantics is based on the counterintuitive idea that understanding the meaning of a symbolic expression X can be traced back to understanding the intention of speaker S to give hearer H something to understand by means of a sign. . . . The attempt of intentionalist semantics to base the meaning of the symbolic expression X on what S means by X, or indirectly gives to understand by X, miscarries. For a hearer to understand what S means by X—that is, the meaning of X—and for him to be aware of the intention that S is pursuing in using X—that is, the purpose that S wants to accomplish with his action—are two different things. . . .

For a theory of communicative action only those analytic theories of meaning are instructive that start from the structure of linguistic expressions rather than from speakers' intentions. (1984, 274–275)

Such remarks demonstrate quite plainly that Habermas does not endorse a descriptivist view of names or reference. How, then, are we to understand his claim that we can always replace a name with a definite description? To answer this, we need to get a fuller sense of his conception of language, which is to say an understanding of his theory of communicative action.

Communicative Action

As a number of commentators (e.g., McCarthy, Gorner) have noted, Habermas has focused much of his attention on shifting philosophy, especially the social and political philosophical concerns of his fellow critical theorists, from a philosophy of the subject (or philosophy of consciousness) to a philosophy of communication. As well, he has argued for a shift from action theory, with its emphasis on means–ends (or instrumental) rationality to an understanding of action in terms of communicative rationality. Under the umbrella notion of communicative action, Habermas has striven to elucidate a universal (or formal) pragmatics as well as communicative rationality.

In his essay "What Is Universal Pragmatics?" (in Habermas 1979, pp. 1–68), he claims to start from the assumption that other forms of social action are derivatives of action oriented toward reaching understanding. Anyone acting communicatively must raise universal validity claims and suppose that they can be vindicated. There are four such presumed validity claims, identifiable as follows:

uttering something understandably

giving (a hearer) something to understand

making oneself understandable

coming to an understanding with another person

That is, there must be intelligibility (or comprehensibility) as well as truth or propositional content to the communicative act. In addition, there must be truthfulness (wanting to communicate so as to have the hearer believe the utterance) and rightness (acceptability between speaker and hearer so agreement, or understanding, can be achieved). Drawing on the thought of Karl Bühler, Habermas claims that communication takes place within three spheres: a subjective sphere of a person's intentions, an objective sphere of an external world of situations, and an intersubjective sphere of interaction and shared normative expectations with others. Like Apel, he sees each of these three spheres as real, as necessary for communication, and as irreducible to the other two.

Though relying heavily on the contributions of speech act theory, especially as enunciated by Austin and Searle, Habermas insists that universal pragmatics is not simply empirical (i.e., descriptive of language use). Rather, he says, it can be understood as semantic analysis, that is, analysis of meaning. However, it can be distinguished from other theories of meaning by requiring that the meanings of linguistic expressions are relevant only insofar as they contribute to speech acts that satisfy the four validity claims above. And it is distinguished from empirical pragmatics by requiring that the meaning of linguistic expressions comes under consideration only insofar as it is determined by formal properties of speech situations in general, and not by particular situations of use. In identifying what he calls the "double structure" of speech, that is, the illocutionary and the propositional, he states that the task of universal pragmatics is to be the rational reconstruction of this double structure. Quite simply, this is the attempt to identify universal presuppositions of everyday communication, with the clear commitment that by focusing on communication and not simply sentences, both the pragmatic and semantic elements of language are fundamental.

Earlier, before the discussion of whether or not Habermas's view is an endorsement of a descriptivist model, two features of his take on names and reference were identified, first, a strong reservation about haecceities and, second, the claim that reference via names involves action. These two features come out vividly in his essay, "Peirce and Communication" (in Habermas 1992, 88–112). Here he identifies six Peircean considerations that he embraces and that point to commitments of his universal pragmatics:

1. the methodological critique against introspection, which relies on the private evidence of so-called facts of consciousness;

2. the epistemological critique against intuitionism, which claims that our judgments are constructed from immediately given and absolutely certain data;

3. the critique of any view that confers a foundationalist distinction on self-consciousness;

4. the critique of any sort of Kantian construction of a "thing-in-itself";

5. the critique of any Cartesian doubt, or any conception of a worldless subject standing over and against the world; and

6. the critique against privileging a knowing subject over an acting agent.

We see here not only a rejection of an intentionalist focus and of haecceities (Kantian things-in-themselves), but also the insistence on action and agency. The emphasis, of course, is on language in Peirce's case, on an analysis of signs and semiosis. This leads Habermas to claim: "A sign can fulfill its representative function only if, along with the relation to the objective world of entities, it simultaneously establishes a relation to the intersubjective world of interpreters" (1992, 101).[13]

"Communicative rationality" is the term that Habermas uses to indicate the rational potential of action that is oriented toward understanding. The structural, formal characteristics of this is what he attempts to reveal and illuminate via his universal pragmatics. Maeve Cooke, in *Language and Reason*, has elaborated on the features and consequences of communicative rationality. First, communicative rationality is a procedural, not a substantive, account. It speaks primarily to the use of knowledge in language and action rather than a property of knowledge. Second, this knowledge is not foundationalist, but takes on the "task of a mediator" between specialized scientific knowledge and everyday communication. Third, reason (and understanding) is always situated historically, as are agents. The validity claims noted above are both context-bound and context-transcendent, in the sense that they transcend particular speakers and subjects while they are also not independent of all speakers and subjects. This is much of the point of Habermas's shift from subjective consciousness to intersubjective communication. In an interview in 1981, Habermas summarizes his conception of communicative rationality thus:

Here we find the three dimensions [of what is intended, what is said, and how it is used] in the concept of communicative rationality: first, the relation of the knowing subject to the world of events and facts; second, the relation to a social world of an acting, practical subject entwined in interaction with others; and finally, the relation of a suffering and passionate subject (in Feuerbach's sense) to its own inner nature, to its own subjectivity and the subjectivity of others. These are the three dimensions that come into view when one analyzes communication processes from the participants' perspective. To these should be added the life-world, however, which stands behind the back of each participant in communication and provides resources for the resolution of problems of understanding. Members of a social collective normally share a life-world. In communication, but also in processes of cognition, this only exists in the distinctive, pre-reflexive form of background assumptions, background receptivities or background relations. (Dews 1986, 108–109)

In the original essay on universal pragmatics (in Habermas 1979), Habermas summarizes his results as follows:

A speech act succeeds, that is, it brings about the interpersonal relation that S intends with it, if it is comprehensible and acceptable, and accepted by the hearer.

The acceptability of a speech act depends on (among other things) the fulfillment of two pragmatic presuppositions, namely, the existence of speech-act-typically restricted contexts and recognizable engagement of the speaker to enter into certain speech-act-typical obligations.

The illocutionary force of a speech act consists in its capacity to move a hearer to act under the premise that the engagement signaled by the speaker is seriously meant; in the case of institutionally bound speech acts, the speaker can borrow this force from the binding force of existing norms, while in the case of institutionally unbound speech acts, the speaker can develop this force by inducing the recognition of validity claims.

Speaker and hearer can reciprocally motivate one another to recognize validity claims because the content of the speaker's engagement is determined by a specific reference to a thematically stressed validity claim, whereby the speaker, in a cognitively testable way, assumes (1) with a truth claim, obligations to provide grounds, (2) with a rightness claim, obligations to provide justification, and (3) with a truthfulness claim, obligations to prove trustworthy.

Twenty years later, in 1996 (Habermas 1998, 338–341), he reiterates this view by stating that the conditions of communication require:

a speaker and an addressee who have command over a common language (or could establish such a command);

a speech situation that can be scrutinized by both parties;

an intersubjectively shared (or sufficiently "overlapping") background understanding; and a locally situated utterance of a speaker, with a "yes" or "no" position on it by an addressee.

These conditions, in turn, rest on two assumptions: (1) linguistic communication essentially exists in order for one person to reach understanding with another about something in the world; and (2) reaching understanding implies that the hearer recognizes a validity claim raised by the speaker for a proposition. What follows from all of this, says Habermas, is that to understand a linguistic expression is to know how one could use it in order to reach understanding with someone about something in the world.

This later statement of his view is not merely a reiteration, however, as he identifies two revisions to what he had said earlier. These are (1) to understand a speech act is to know the conditions for the illocutionary or perlocutionary success that the speaker can achieve with it, and (2) one knows the conditions for the illocutionary or perlocutionary success of a speech act when one knows the kinds of actor-independent or actor-relative reasons with which the speaker could vindicate her validity claim discursively. As he goes on to say, these revisions "take account of the fact that speech acts are illocutionary acts even when they are connected only with claims to truth and truthfulness [and not necessarily with rightness], and when these claims to the seriousness (and viability) of intentions and decisions can be justified only through reference to the preferences of the speakers in an attitude oriented toward success (and, thus, from their perspective)" (1998, 341). More to the concerns here, about Habermas's view of names and reference:

Naturally, understanding a linguistic expression is not the same as reaching an understanding about something with the help of an utterance held to be valid. Nonetheless, as has already been observed by truth-conditional semantics, in language the dimensions of meaning and validity are internally connected; moreover, they are connected in such a way that one understands a speech act when one knows the conditions under which it may be accepted as valid. An orientation toward the *possible* validity of utterances is part of the pragmatic understanding itself. (Incidentally, this explains why we can learn to speak only under conditions of communicative action, that is, in practices from which it *emerges* when the given linguistic community accepts what is valid.) (1998, 339)

Back to Reference

Earlier I showed that Habermas does not endorse a descriptivist (intentionalist) view of names and reference. Given his emphasis on speech acts, on the pragmatic dimension of language, on the fundamental aspect of understanding that informs his universal pragmatics and communicative action, it would also seem apparent that he does not endorse the causal view of names and reference, either. And, indeed, he does not. This is not to say that he disagrees with all aspects of a causal view, but what he says about semantics generally and about a semantic account of communication shows that he sees such an account as incomplete at best. On a number of occasions he speaks of the limitations, or faulty nature, of a semantics-focused account. In his essay, "Toward a Critique of a Theory of Meaning" (in Habermas 1992, 57–87), he remarks:

The relation of the signified (the meaning) to the signifier (the sign) was thought to be explicable in terms of the relation of the symbol (the meaningful sign) to the designatum (the object referred to). This basic semiotic notion was suitable for the object-centered theory of knowledge in the philosophy of consciousness. In fact, names or designators, indeed all referential terms that we use to identify objects, do as it were establish contact between language and reality. If, however, this part is taken for the whole, a false picture arises. (1992, 61)

This sentiment is reinforced in a recent analysis of Rorty ("Richard Rorty's Pragmatic Turn," in Habermas 1998, 343–382). Here he claims:

The truth-predicate belongs—though not exclusively—to the language game of argumentation. For this reason its meaning can be elucidated (at least partly) according to its functions in this language game, that is, in the *pragmatic dimension* of a particular employment of the predicate. Whoever confines herself to the semantic dimension of sentences and of metalinguistic commentaries on sentences comprehends only the reflection of a prior linguistic practice that . . . extends even into everyday practices. (1998, 362)

Maeve Cooke (1994, 97–98) identifies three abstractions of which Habermas claims traditional semantic views are guilty: a semanticist one, a cognitivist one, and an objectivist one. The semanticist abstraction is the belief that the analysis of linguistic meaning can confine itself to the analysis of sentences, abstracting from the pragmatic rules that affect the use of sentences. The cognitivist abstraction is the belief that all meaning can be led back to the propositional content of utterances, thus indirectly reducing meaning to the meaning of assertoric sentences. The objectivist abstraction is the conception that truth conditions are what make a sentence true, abstracting from the knowledge of truth conditions that can be ascribed to a speaker and hearer. The present point is that these concerns that are raised about semantics in general show that any view of names or reference that abstracts the semantic features of reference from the pragmatic features, as the causal view does, is faulty. Again, for any communicative speech act there is, for Habermas, what is intended, what is said, and how it is used. Each and all three are necessary and are irreducible. Semantic analysis focuses on what is said, but this is only one dimension of reference. As mentioned earlier, Habermas has never spoken of Kripke or the causal view directly, but it is clear that such a view, to the extent that it permits (indeed, requires) the omission of the pragmatic dimension, is not one he endorses.

7 Individuation and Similarity

Even the status of (nameable) things, perhaps the most elementary concept we have, depends crucially on such intricate matters as acts of human will.
—Noam Chomsky, *New Horizons in the Study of Language and Mind*

Like most "isms," pragmatism means many things to many people, both proponents and opponents. James is well known for claiming that it is a method for settling disputes, a method emphasizing the effects of holding to some conception. But he also spoke of a pragmatic theory of truth. Though infamously objecting to aspects of James's characterization of pragmatism, Peirce, too, spoke of a pragmatic method for conceptual clarity and subsequent action. He speaks of two pragmatic functions: "Namely, it ought, in the first place, to give us an expeditious riddance of all ideas essentially unclear. In the second place, it ought to lend support, and help to render distinct, ideas essentially clear, but more or less difficult of apprehension" (*CP*, 5.206). As was noted in chapter 5, Rorty provides a negative account of pragmatism in terms of what pragmatism rejects: it is antiessentialist, antirealist, anti-fact–value dichotomy, and it opposes the notion that there is any significant methodological difference between morality and science. Joseph Margolis specifies "characteristic pragmatic doctrines" as a denial of any foundationalist theory of knowledge, the claim that human inquiry is continuous with, and develops out of, the biological and precognitive interaction between organism and environment, and the affirmation of some form of empirical realism, "to the extent at least that human organisms are perceptually in contact with the external world, whatever the internal conditions on which their sentient capacities depend" (Margolis 1986, 259–260).

What of a pragmatist view of reference and names? What can be garnered from the survey of the nine philosophers over the previous three chapters? There are definite differences and even disagreements among them. Some differences and disagreements are explicit, such as Putnam's of Rorty (and vice versa)[1] as well as Putnam's (2002) of Apel and Peirce. Some differences are less disagreement and more alternative emphases. For example, Peirce's semiotic approach is considerably different from James's or Dewey's. Nevertheless, the family resemblance of views of these nine (as well as of Wittgenstein and Geach) reveals several features that I will elaborate on in this and the next chapter. I will speak of these features in terms of referring (1) as conferring, (2) as deferring, and (3) as inferring. These features will become clearer over the course of these final chapters, but for now, I will note some aspects that are evident from the previous philosophers. A common aspect was a rejection of the givenness of referents (or of haecceity). There is no identity–identification dichotomy. Likewise, there is no sharp boundary between the process of naming (or referring) and the "product," that is, the name (or other referring expression). In addition, successful reference involves present and future reception, or understanding. Names (and other referring expressions) are to be understood in terms of their functions, with "function" to be spelled out not merely as a semantic notion, but as a pragmatic one, as well. Indeed, a common aspect of these thinkers is their rejection of a sharp semantics–pragmatics split. In this chapter, then, I will address these features of reference and names, with an emphasis on what I take as underlying (or presupposed) metaphysical commitments about what is named and referred to.

On What Is Named

We have names for many types of "things." Not only do we use names to talk about particular actual individuals (e.g., "Nixon"), but also we have names for fictional individuals (e.g., "Santa Claus") as well as abstract objects (e.g., "two"). Besides names for objects, we have names for events (e.g., "the battle of Waterloo") as well as for interactions (e.g., "gravity"). These categories of object, event, interaction, and so on might not be sharply demarcated (e.g., does "Tuesday" name an event?). The point is that we use names to speak about a variety of metaphysical types and tokens. One element of views about reference and names, then, is what is named or referred to. Throughout this book I have indicated this aspect of reference and names (as well as of referring and naming) as the notion of haecceity, the "thisness" or givenness of what is named. I have claimed that it is a commitment to haecceities that is called into question by many of the pragmatists surveyed. It is just this issue that I now want to flesh out. I will argue that the notion of haecceity rests on commitments to views about individuation and similarity. In the next chapter I will further argue that a pragmatist view of individuation and similarity are at odds with the views of the descriptivist account of reference and names (at least in Searle) and the causalist account of reference and names (at least in Kripke).

Individuation and Similarity

Individuation and identity are two sides of the same coin. To ask what something is and to ask how something is individuated are not only inter-related, but are essentially to ask for the same information. Identity might be said to be a metaphysical issue and individuation an epistemic issue, but I do not think that characterizing them as such differentiates them in any significant way. Both are questions of partitioning the world. By saying, "This is what X is," we are individuating X from Y; by saying, "This is (an) X and that is (a) Y," we are saying what X is (e.g., minimally something that is not-Y). The significance of this with respect to reference is that reference only makes sense within the context of an underlying conception of individuation, since names attach to things, usually things treated as individuals of some sort. Our ability to refer to X by (the use of) "X" rests on there being a prior understanding of what X is. There must be (in some sense) an X for us to refer to X. We could not know whether we have referred to Glub by (the use of) "Glub" unless there was something that has been individuated as Glub. Indeed we could not refer to Glub if there were not an individuated Glub. (Again, this does not mean that Glub must exist; Glub could be fictional, "future," abstract, etc.) For reference to occur, individuation must already have occurred.

Similarity and sameness are also two sides of the same coin. To ask what makes this the same as that is the same as to ask what makes this similar to that. In both cases what is being asked for is a criterion (or some criteria) for identification. To say that X and Y have the same color is to say that they are similar with respect to color. With respect to ontology, sameness is the limiting case of similarity: to say that X is the same as Y is to say that X and Y are similar in all respects. But notice that there seems to be no difference between identity and sameness. X's identity with Y just is X being the same as Y. We are led, then, to the realization that individuation and similarity are conceptually interconnected (not an unwelcome result, as far as I am concerned).

What's the point of all this? I want to argue that the cluster and causal accounts of reference are committed to a particular view of individuation and the similarity relation. I want to show that they have a shared conception of these notions and it is at this fundamental level that they are more similar than different—they are two versions of a received account of reference. I then want to argue against their shared conception of individuation and similarity (and say more on why I take these notions to be so fundamental, not only to reference, but to many issues).

Individuation

In their discussions of reference, neither Searle nor Kripke speaks explicitly about individuation. Neither seems to indicate that there is any question about or problem with individuation. That is, although both might question whether this name picks out that individual, neither indicates any question or problem with a principle of individuation. Individuals are "out there" so to speak and reference is a matter of "the right" hookup of names to individuals. Searle speaks of picking out "an independently located object" as though there is no question or problem with (conceptually) locating such an object. The question of what name picks out what individual is different from, and rests on, what individuals there are and how they are individuated. About the latter Searle says nothing. About the former he makes claims such as the following:

In short, if none of the identifying descriptions believed to be true of some object by the users of the name of that object proved to be true of some independently located object, then that object could not be identical with the bearer of the name. (1969, 169)

Besides statements such as this one, Searle's commitment to private reference indicates that he sees individuation as a straightforward matter, and the "fact" about individuation is that individuals are given in the world, independent of our concerns or interpretations. For Searle, there may be a question as to whether "Gödel" refers to Gödel or to Schmidt, but there is no question as to Gödel and Schmidt being independently located (or at least locatable, in the sense of being capable of being located) objects.

Kripke's acceptance of the view that individuation is a straightforward matter, essentially one of simply seeing or coming to see what individuals there are "out there," can be seen in the context of his discussion of possible worlds. One of the issues connected with the postulation of possible worlds is that of transworld identity. That is, how do we identify the same thing across possible worlds? What properties must a thing have in different possible worlds in order for that thing to be the same thing (e.g., what properties must a thing have in different possible worlds for that thing to be, say, Nixon)? In rejecting the idea that questions about transworld identification make sense only in terms of questions about component parts of an object, Kripke says the following:

> Theorists have often said that we identify objects across possible worlds as objects resembling the given one in the most important respects. On the contrary, Nixon, had he decided to act otherwise, might have avoided politics like the plague, though privately harboring radical opinions. Most important, even when we can replace questions about an object by questions about its parts, we *need* not do so. We can refer to the object and ask what might have happened to *it*. So, we do not begin with worlds (which are supposed somehow to be real, and whose qualities, but not whose objects, are perceptible to us), and then ask about criteria of transworld identification; on the contrary, we begin with the objects, which we *have*, and can identify, in the actual world. We can then ask whether certain things might have been true of the objects. (1980, 53)

Kripke's commitment is obvious here. By saying that we can "refer to the object and ask what might have happened to *it*," and by saying that we begin with the objects "which we *have*, and can identify," Kripke is clearly implying that there is no problem of individuation in this world. His later discussion of natural kinds reiterates this view. Our understanding of what gold "really" is (or what tigers "really" are) might change over time, but that there are natural kinds, say, elements (or species), is not in question. Gold is gold, and whatever it "really" is, it's that way independently of us. So, says Kripke:

> When I refer to heat, I refer not to an internal sensation that someone may have, but to an external phenomenon which we perceive through the sense of feeling; it produces a characteristic sensation which we call the sensation of heat. Heat *is* the motion of molecules. (1980, 129)

So, both Searle and Kripke are clearly committed to a particular view of individuation, namely, one in which individuals are given in the world (i.e., are haecceities). I want to argue now that this conception of individuation is mistaken at least in the sense of being not appreciative of underlying complexities and commitments, and that consequently both the cluster and causal accounts of reference are weakened by their commitment to it.

Goodman (1965) has argued—correctly, I think—that the partitioning of the world is (at least in part) determined by our cognitive interests.[2] Specifically, his argument is about legitimate inductions based on lawlike generalizations, and hence about the partitioning of the world in the sense of reference classes. I want to extrapolate from Goodman and suggest that his argument applies to the partitioning of the world in the sense of individuals as well. That is, the point he makes about reference classes (which I will review below) can also be made about individuals, namely, which ones there are is (at least in part) determined by our cognitive interests.

An immediate reaction to a claim such as this, and one that pragmatists of all stripes have to face repeatedly, is that this smacks of idealism and denies a reality that is independent of our cognitive interests. But, as has been stated (more than once!) in previous chapters, such a reaction misses the point and force of this pragmatist position. As noted earlier, in discussing James on truth, where a correspondence view sees truth as a dyadic relation between a sentence or belief on the one hand and facts or states of affairs on the other, and a coherence view sees truth also as a dyadic relation between a sentence or belief on the one hand and a set of other sentences or beliefs on the other, a pragmatist view of truth is that it is a triadic relation between (1) a sentence or belief, (2) facts or states of affairs, and (3) a set of other beliefs. For some pragmatists, truth is a quadratic relation including the above three components plus (4) goals or aims. The problem with a straight correspondence view, for pragmatism, is not that it is false, but that, as a theory, it has little (if any) value. For example, one could be a Goodmanian and hold that the reason that the sentence "Grass is grue" is true is because grass is grue, just as readily as an English speaker might hold that "Grass is green" is true because grass is green. Likewise, a coherence view of truth fails. Even William James, (in)famous for declaring that truth is a form of expediency, insisted on established, "older" truths as crucial for the status of a given sentence as being true. Quite simply, for pragmatists, the correspondence and coherence views of truth are incomplete; at best they provide necessary conditions. For some pragmatists, then, truth is a triadic relation of sentence, facts, and other sentences. For other pragmatists, however, "true" carries a normative component. Rejecting a fact–value dichotomy, pragmatism identifies as involving this fourth aspect of evaluation. This is not identical to or even indicative of advocacy of idealism or a rejection of an objective world (though, some pragmatists, e.g., Rorty, question what work is done by postulating a "realist" metaphysics, with its accompanying metaphysical–epistemological dichotomy).

Individuals and Reference Classes

Goodman asks us to consider a predicate "grue," which he defines in the following way: the predicate "grue" "applies to all things examined before time t just in case they are green but to other things just in case they are blue" (1965, 74). For example, we would say that an emerald is grue iff it is examined before, say, January 1, 3000, and is green or it is not examined before that date and is blue. Up to time t we have evidence that emeralds are grue. Assuming that all emeralds so far examined have been green, then it follows that they have all been grue. Before t, then, an English speaker, knowing these facts about emeralds, would make the inductive generalization that all emeralds are green, and the English speaker's prediction that the next emerald examined (after t) will be green will be based on this lawlike statement. However, a "gruesome" speaker, knowing these facts about emeralds, would make the inductive generalization that all emeralds are grue, and the gruesome speaker's prediction that the next emerald examined (after t) will be grue will be based on this lawlike statement. The immediate point is that the same evidence (green emeralds examined before t) seems to confirm equally two different, and, in fact, contradictory predictions (because the English prediction is saying that the next emerald will be green, while the gruesome prediction is, in effect, saying that the next emerald will be blue). Says Goodman:

Thus although we are well aware which of the two incompatible predictions is genuinely confirmed, they are equally well confirmed according to our present definition [of confirmation]. Moreover, it is clear that if we simply choose an appropriate predicate, then on the basis of these same observations we shall have equal confirmation, by our definition, for any prediction whatever about other emeralds—or indeed about anything else. (1965, 74)

So, says Goodman, the original problem of justifying induction (in a way, attempting to answer the question, "Why does a positive instance of a hypothesis give any grounds for predicting further instances?") has been displaced by a new problem of defining confirmation (in a way, attempting to answer the question, "What is a positive instance of a hypothesis?") and distinguishing confirmable and nonconfirmable hypotheses (in a way, attempting to answer the question, "What hypotheses are confirmed by their positive instances?"). Past cases of green emeralds were used to confirm rival, mutually exclusive, hypotheses. Past regularities of green emeralds seem to confirm the prediction that the next emerald would be green, but the past regularities of grue emeralds doesn't seem (to us) to confirm the prediction that the next emerald would be grue. However, the point of Goodman's example is that saying that valid predictions rely on past regularities without saying *which* past regularities is completely unhelpful. "Regularities are where you find them, and you can find them anywhere" (1965, 82).[3]

The significance of Goodman's argument for the present concerns is that if he is right that regularities are where you find them and you can find them anywhere, then the conception of regularities (or reference classes) as being "out there" in the world is mistaken. We do not "bump into" regularities in the world, independently of categories and cognitive partitionings. Again, the claim is not that we make up regularities with no constraints coming from "the world." We find what we're looking for, in part at least, only after deciding what it is we're looking for.[4] *It is both the world and our cognitive interests* that shape what regularities (reference classes) there are, as the grue example points out.

There are other cases to illustrate the interest-dependence of partitionings. Our taxonomic divisions (kingdom, phylum, etc.) are made on various bases. For example, divisions are made on the basis of whether or not organisms are caryotic or not; divisions are made on the basis of whether or not organisms are warm-blooded; divisions are made on the basis of dentition; divisions are made on the basis of pigmentation. Even to argue that these features (procaryotic versus eucaryotic, warm-blooded versus cold-blooded) are really "out there" does not deny that our taxonomic categories are interest-dependent. We choose to consider, say, dentition as a basis for partitioning rather than, say, eye color. We choose to classify an organism as a bird not because it flies (bats are not birds, but they fly; ostriches are birds, but they do not fly). Instead, we choose to classify an organism as a bird on the basis of other criteria (say, being feathered). The point, of course, is that we choose to partition in certain ways and based on certain criteria, and those partitionings both reflect and are a function of our interests.

Another objection at this point is that the examples above have, at best, shown only that our partitionings are theory-dependent, not interest-dependent. It remains to be shown that theories are interest-dependent. This issue, it seems to me, has been at the heart of much (if not most) of the debates in the philosophy of science for quite some time (at least since Kuhn 1962). There are, of course, numerous historical cases that illustrate that theories have been proposed and accepted on the basis of particular interests (interests both in a cognitive sense and in a moral, social, political sense). For example, Gould (1981) has argued forcefully that theories in intelligence testing have a long history of being interest-based. Harding (1981) has offered considerable evidence and argumentation that various antithetical approaches to social science research have shared normative gendered assumptions. Examples could be extended ad nauseam to show that actual, historical cases support the contention that theories are interest-dependent (e.g., Lysenko, and Einstein's remark that his physical theories followed from his epistemic and metaphysical views).

Indeed, the view that theories are not interest-dependent seems to me to rest on the assumption that there is a sharp dichotomy between the context of discovery and the context of justification. That is, one might argue that it doesn't matter whence our theories come, what matters is whether or not they are good theories (whatever "goodness" means with respect to theories). The host of objections to and arguments against this distinction are well documented and don't need to be repeated here. I do, however, want to make the following point: it seems clear that theories are interest-dependent in the sense that our cognitive (or what McMullin [1983] calls "epistemic") values determine our theories. That is, features such as simplicity, generality, testability, and the like are features that we insist on in theories because we value them (in a cognitive or epistemic sense). To the extent that we demand reliability from theories, we demand features such as testability, and so on. (Cognitive, or epistemic, values are inherent in other aspects of science as well, for example, in the demand for replicability of experiments.) The necessary connection between theories and cognitive values seems uncontroversial.[5, 6]

Now, even if the case can be made (as I have just tried to do) that our partitionings are theory- and interest-dependent, this does not say anything with respect to individuation. That is, even if Goodman is right that reference classes are where we find them and we can find them anywhere, this says nothing about the individuals that make up the reference classes. They, it is generally held, are "out there." Whether grass is green or grue, so the claim goes, grass is out there and individual blades of grass are what they are. I now want to argue that this view is mistaken. I want to claim that individuals are where you find them and you can find them anywhere. Individuation, I want to say, is just as much theory- and interest-dependent as partitioning at the level of reference classes (or predicates) is.

One argument for the treatment of individuation in a nonrealist way can be extrapolated from Goodman's gruesome language and from Quine (1953). In a context of discussing nonreferring singular terms, Quine suggests that such terms can be translated into a description or even into a predicate. So, "Pegasus" can be translated into "the thing that pegasizes" or simply "pegasizes." If Quine is right, and if there is no reason to restrict his point to *nonreferring* singular terms (and I see no reason for such a restriction), then this result, coupled with Goodman's point of the interest-dependence of reference classes (which are identified by predicates), seems to support the claim that individuation, too, is interest-dependent.[7]

Another, perhaps more intuitive argument for a "nonrealist" (or pragmatist) treatment of individuation comes from the consideration of the individuation of events. We clearly individuate one event from another.[8] For example, we speak of "this coin toss" or "that die roll." Many events have even been named, "the battle of Waterloo," "the 1948 Presidential election," and so on. It also seems clear that the individuation of events is not merely a matter of finding them out there in the world; nor is it a matter of simply making them up. We decide what counts as an event and hence what events there are. This can be seen (somewhat, at least) on an intuitive level by considering the difficulty of saying what the parameters of a given event are. Exactly when was the 1948 Presidential election? When did it begin? On election day? On the day that the first candidate was nominated? In asking, "When did it begin?," to what does the *it* refer? (The answer cannot be: to the 1948 Presidential election, because that is circular and vacuous in this context.) Or, when was the battle of Waterloo? Did it start when the first shot was fired? When Napoleon advanced his troops past a certain point? The point of these examples and questions is that the individuation of events is not a clear-cut, straightforward notion even at an intuitive level.

At a more technical level, Hanna (1969, 1978) has made much the same point. He distinguishes generic experiments (or events) from specific experiments (or events). By a generic experiment he means "an empirical procedure which can be replicated by different experimenters at different spatio-temporal locations—each particular replication constituting a specific instance of the generic experiment" (1978, 533). Scientific predictability and explanation refer, says Hanna, not to specific experiments, but to generic ones. So, the scope of the prediction of Jones's specific experiment conducted at this place and time under these conditions is not limited to that specific experiment. It covers every specific replication of the generic experiment. The problem, though, is that it is not a straightforward matter as to what counts as a replication of that generic experiment. Since predictions cover a potential infinity of observations and predicting the outcome of a generic experiment involves a commitment to corresponding projections for all replications of the experiment, it follows that scientific predictions can never be established (or not) beyond question. Says Hanna:

The relevance of any specific experiment, e.g., as performed by Jones in laboratory X, to prediction (A) is to a great extent a theoretical issue. The outcome is relevant only if Jones has created the appropriate stimulus situation: i.e., only if Jones has replicated the generic experiment. But . . . this latter issue is not a straightforward matter of observation; on some occasions it involves highly theoretical considerations. (1969, 312)

Consider a simple coin-tossing experiment. A coin is tossed and the outcome is tails. A prediction about the outcome of this event makes sense only if the experiment can be replicated. The question, however, is: what is the generic experiment of which this is a specific instance? We need the generic experiment to be individuated before we can say what this specific instance is an instance of, and the individuation of the generic experiment is what's at issue here. I am arguing (as is Hanna) that the individuation of the generic experiment is not "out there." We decide what constitutes the generic experiment and that in turn determines what counts as an instance of it. To be able to replicate the experiment, we first need to know what it is we are attempting to replicate, and that depends on our cognitive interests and concerns. We decide what the parameters of the coin toss are (whether the toss begins, say, when the coin loses contact with an other object—like my hand—or when it reaches the apex of its ascent, or whatever). If indeed replication is (at least in part) "highly theoretical," then this strengthens the argument that the individuation of events is interest-dependent. (This point of replication as nonrealist is also relevant to the issue of similarity, discussed below.)[9] It seems, then, that the individuation of events, at least, is interest-dependent. Is it also the case that the individuation of other kinds of individuals is interest-dependent? I want to argue: yes. First, following Quine's notion of translating talk of individuals into talk of predicates, it seems that there is no reason to suggest that this doesn't apply to all individuals (whether they are events or other kinds of individuals). Although predicates such as "pegasizes" or "is-the-battle-of-Waterloo" sound a bit unusual (indeed, more gruesome than "grue"), there is no clear reason to forbid them. Furthermore, the distinction between objects and actions (i.e., between event-individuals and thing-individuals) is not so sharp. For example, storms seem intuitively to be events, not things, yet they are treated linguistically on a par with things (e.g., both storms and children can satisfy the sentence "x is savage"). Fists, too, seem to be actions (moving the hand into a particular formation), yet "fist" is a noun, a grammatical feature that we associate with things. (What is taken to be an event and what is taken to be an object varies among natural languages. See, e.g., Whorf 1956, on such differences between English and Hopi.)

This points to another argument for a pragmatist treatment of individuation. Formally, individuals are whatever can satisfy the values of individual variables (e.g., whatever can replace the variable x in "x is red"). Informally, individuals are whatever can be referred to by a noun (e.g., whatever can be the subject of a sentence [in English]). As noted in the paragraph above, the distinction between events and objects then becomes blurred. Not only can storms be referred to by nouns, but particularly severe storms can be (and are) named (e.g., Hurricane Diana). Also, actions, such as running, become individuals when they are referred to as gerunds (e.g., "Running is good for one's health" or "Overeating is unhealthy, but fun"). The significance of this is that if event-individuals are individuated based (at least in part) on our theories and interests, and if there is no sharp distinction between event-individuals and thing-individuals, then there may be good reason to adopt the view that thing-individuals are also individuated based on our theories and interests.

With respect to individuals being whatever can replace individual variables or whatever is referred to by a noun, consider the following example. "July," on these criteria, is an individual. For example, it is proper to say, "July is my favorite month." Clearly, however, July is not "out there." What July is depends on our theories and interests. July is nothing more than a set of temporal coordinates. But, of course, we determine what the extension of that set is. Are "natural" individuals any different? I see no reason to assume so. "Natural" individuals are also sets of space-time coordinates. But then, of course, we decide the extensions of those sets, too. We decide what set of space-time coordinates constitutes this bird (or, for that matter, all birds). We set the parameters for what counts as these sets of coordinates. (An objection here is that this confuses and conflates epistemic claims with metaphysical claims. That is, even though epistemically we decide the parameters of these sets, nonetheless, metaphysically, these sets are independent of us. Of course, much of the present argument is that this dichotomy between epistemic and metaphysical claims is unwarranted.)

I think, however, that another, stronger, case can be made that individuation per se is interest-dependent. Perhaps the most intuitive notion of individuation (and of individuals) is that of ostension. The use of demonstratives (e.g., "I mean *this* mess! Clean it up now!" or "Get a load of *that* guy!") often has been taken as a paradigm case of individuation. Which mess? *This* one. Which guy? *That* one. This mess and that guy are "out there" if anything is.

The trouble here, though, is that, as both Wittgenstein and Quine have argued, even ostension is interest-dependent. Wittgenstein offers several examples. Suppose, he says, that someone points to a pencil and says, "This is *tove*" or "This is called *tove*." Does ostension work here? No, he says, because this could mean a number of things: this is a pencil, this is round, this is wood, this is one, this is hard, and so on. Another example is "This is sosh." Wittgenstein states:

For example, from "This is sosh" you would not understand the use of the word "sosh," though from "This color is sosh" you would. That is, if a person is to learn the meaning of a word from such a definition he must already know what sort of thing it stands for. The word "color" already fixes the use of "sosh." The ostensive definition is of use if you need to fill in only one blank. (1979, 45)

Quine (1960, 1969) also criticizes the notion of ostension as providing a clear means of individuation. Suppose, he says, that a native points to an object and says, "Gavagai." A nonnative, on witnessing this, might believe that the native has pointed to a rabbit and hence that "gavagai" can be translated as "rabbit." But things are not so obvious for Quine. It could be that "gavagai" is more nearly translatable as "rabbithood" or perhaps "undetached rabbit parts" or even "rabbit stages." Says Quine:

> The only difference between rabbits, undetached rabbit parts, and rabbit stages is in their individuation. If you take the total scattered portion of the spatiotemporal world that is made up of rabbits, and that which is made up of undetached rabbit parts, and that which is made up of rabbit stages, you come out with the same scattered portion of the world each of the three times. The only difference is in how you slice it. And how to slice it is what ostension or simple conditioning, however persistently repeated, cannot teach. (1969, 32)

Where does this leave us? It leaves us with the conclusion that ostension, the paradigm of realist individuation, offers no principle of individuation after all; ostension works only after the world has been sliced up, and as Goodman and others have pointed out, how the world is sliced up is interest-dependent (just as, to repeat once again, it is also world-dependent).

Returning to the issue of reference, it is precisely this view of individuation that has been found to be unwarranted, namely, the realist view, which underlies both the cluster and the causal accounts of reference. When Searle speaks of his principle of identification as "giving me an ostensive presentation" of "some independently located object" (1969, 168, 169), his commitment to a realist view of ostension and individuation is clear. Kripke claims: "When you ask whether it is necessary or contingent that Nixon won the election, you are asking the intuitive question whether in some counterfactual situation, *this man* would in fact have lost the election" (1980, 41). But just who *this man* is is not a straightforward matter. Indeed, who *this* man is depends upon how we partition the world, and Kripke, along with Searle, is mistaken in taking that to be given (or at least not interest-dependent).[10] Devitt (1981), likewise, in his discussion of grounding as being dependent upon seeing an object as a member of a very general category talks as though these categories (or reference classes) are "out there."

Similarity

At the beginning of this chapter, I suggested that individuation and similarity are interrelated. I now want to turn to the notion of similarity and claim that many of the conclusions reached above concerning individuation are applicable to similarity as well, namely, similarity is not a straightforward matter, with objects being similar inherently; rather, similarity is a significant fact.[11]

What does it mean to say that two objects are similar? Intuitively, it means that they share some property or properties in common (or perhaps that they have some of the same properties). To say that an object is more similar to a second object than to a third means intuitively that the first and second share more properties (or a weighted more) in common than do the first and third. As it stands, of course, this will not do, because we need to know: similar in what respect(s). Everything is similar to everything else with respect, say, to existing or being capable of being thought of. On the other hand, nothing is similar to anything else with respect, say, to being at a given spatiotemporal location. We say, then, that a hot, dry, still day is similar to a hot, rainy, windy day with respect to temperature, but not with respect to humidity. But where similarity simpliciter is incoherent, does similarity relativized fare any better? Not, I want to say, if it is still assumed that similarity is independent of our cognitive interests. Consider the following "objects:"

e   c   E

The object on the left is, of course, similar to the object in the middle in a presumably denumerable number of respects (e.g., being printed on this page, being English letters, being a certain distance above *this* word). However, the object on the left is also similar to the object on the right in a presumably denumerable number of respects. In addition, the object on the left is *dissimilar* to the object in the middle in a presumably denumerable number of respects (e.g., being less than one mile to the left of it, being less than two miles to the left of it, etc.). Likewise for the object on the right.

These considerations seem to argue against similarity simpliciter, but what about similarity relativized? That, too, is in trouble, for, as these objects show, the very notion of similarity per se rests on the notion of individuation. One of the ways in which the left and middle objects are similar to each other and dissimilar to the right object is that they are both curved and it is not. One of the ways in which the left and right objects are similar to each other and dissimilar to the middle object is that they are both instances of the English letter "e." However, for these claims to be made, they rest on our acknowledgment of the existence of, say, English letters. That is, if our partitioning of the world did not include English letters, then it would make no sense to say that two objects are similar with respect to that or dissimilar with respect to that. What sense would it make to say that the left and middle objects are similar to each other with respect to glub but dissimilar to the right object with respect to glub? If glubness is not a recognized reference class, similarity (or dissimilarity) with respect to it is meaningless. And, of course, similarity—even relativized to certain respects—is incoherent if it is taken to be similarity independent of our theories and interests.[12]

Issues of sampling and replication I take to be subsumed within the issue of similarity and included in this conclusion. Goodman (1972, 1978) mentions sampling in the course of discussing similarity. Similarity, he says, does not account for our predictive and inductive practices (one of the points of the grue example). He relays the following incident:

Consider again an ordinary swatch of textile in a tailor's or upholsterer's sample book. . . . Mrs. Mary Tricias studied such a sample book, made her selection, and ordered from her favorite textile shop enough material for her overstuffed chair and sofa—insisting that it be exactly like the sample. When the bundle came she opened it eagerly and was dismayed when several hundred 2" x 3" pieces with zigzag edges exactly like the sample fluttered to the floor. When she called the shop, protesting loudly, the proprietor replied, injured and weary, "But Mrs. Tricias, you said the material must be exactly like the sample. When it arrived from the factory yesterday, I kept my assistants here half the night cutting it up to match the sample."

The incident was nearly forgotten some months later, when Mrs. Tricias, having sewed the pieces together and covered her furniture, decided to have a party. She went to the local bakery, selected a chocolate cupcake from those on display and ordered enough for fifty guests, to be delivered two weeks later. Just as the guests were beginning to arrive, a truck drove up with a single huge cake. The lady running the bake-shop was utterly discouraged by the complaint. "But Mrs. Tricias, you have no idea how much trouble we went to. My husband runs the textile shop and he warned me that your order would have to be in one piece." (1978, 63–64)

Replication, too, as Hanna pointed out, is related to similarity. To say that a given experiment is a replication of another (or, to say that one specific instance of a generic experiment is a replication of that generic experiment) is to say that they are similar in relevant respects. But, as we saw, what counts as relevant is determined by our cognitive interests and what generic events there are is a reflection of our partitioning of the world.

Natural Kinds

Where the issue of similarity most clearly touches base with reference is with respect to the notion of natural kinds. Natural kinds are sets (or classes or categories—groupings of some sort or other) of things that occur "in nature," that is, in the world, independent of speakers of a language. Examples abound: lions, tigers, oceans, cabbages. The particular members of a natural kind are members of that kind because of some similarity (or similarities) that they share with other members of that kind. If one is committed to essentialism, then to be a member of a given kind is to have a particular property (or properties) that is necessary and sufficient to attain membership in that kind. For instance, if one takes "having atomic number 79" as the defining property of something being gold, then all and only those things having that property of having atomic weight 79 are things that are gold. Or if being feathered is the necessary and sufficient condition for being a bird, then all and only those things that are feathered are birds. This property (or properties) that guarantees membership in a kind is, then, an essential property of that kind. (I will say more on essences and essentialism in the next chapter.)

The notion of a natural kind, however, does not necessarily depend upon the commitment to essential properties or essences. Another conception of a kind, or of shared similarity, is that of "family resemblances." This notion, originating with Wittgenstein (1953), suggests that some kinds might not have essences. The members of a kind, say, might all be similar to one another, but not necessarily because they all share any common properties. For instance (and this is where the term "family resemblance" comes from), the various members of a family might share certain features with one another, but not the same feature. A mother and son might have similarly shaped noses, but the son and father might have similarly colored eyes (although very different shaped noses); sister might "have mom's hair" and "have dad's chin," while only brother and sister might have no (obvious) features in common. They all have enough features in common with at least some other members of the family such that they have a family resemblance with each other. Wittgenstein's famous example to illustrate this notion is that of games. There is no essence, he claims, to what we consider games. He says: "we see a complicated network of similarities overlapping and criss-crossing: sometimes overall similarities, sometimes similarities in detail" (1953, para. 66). This notion of family resemblance is not antithetical to that of natural kinds. One can still be committed to the notion of (and existence of) natural kinds, even if one denies that these kinds have essences (or that the members of a kind have essential properties). The notion of family resemblance can be taken as either an epistemic notion or a metaphysical notion. That is, one might say that so far as we know a given kind has no essence, but maybe we just haven't found it yet, or one might say that in fact a given kind has no essence independently of our state of knowledge.

Some problems of similarity have been noted above. Others, in connection with kinds, have been explicated by Quine (1969). Treating similarity as a dyadic relation (e.g., a is similar to b) won't work, says Quine, because it dismisses considerations of degrees. For instance, if colored things comprise a kind, then red things will constitute a set of things too narrow to count as a kind, whereas if red things comprise a kind, then colored things will constitute a set of things too broad to count as a kind. But there seems to be no reason to deny that kinds can overlap (e.g., both mammals and tigers are kinds). Although viewing similarity as a triadic relation (e.g., a is more similar to b than to c) escapes the problem just noted, it results in a different problem, namely, almost any two things could count as members of some broad kind.

These problems of similarity are essentially problems encountered by trying to define similarity in terms of kinds. What of the converse, trying to define kinds in terms of similarity? This, too, won't work. In arguing why it won't, Quine introduces two notions: *paradigm* and *foil*. He states:

If without serious loss of accuracy we can assume that there are one or more actual things (*paradigm* cases) that nicely exemplify the desired norm, and one or more actual things (*foils*) that deviate just barely too much to be counted into the desired kind at all, then our definition is easy: the *kind with paradigm a and foil b* is the set of all things to which a is more similar than a is to b. More generally, then, a set may be said to be a kind if and only if there are a and b, known or unknown, such that the set is the kind with paradigm a and foil b. (1969, 119–120)

This definition, however, won't work. For example, if we take a particular shade of red as the paradigm for a kind, we find that objects in that shade can come in all sorts of shapes, weights, sizes, smells, and so on. So mere degree of *overall* similarity to any particular paradigm case (e.g., a certain apple) will afford little evidence of degree of redness, since it will depend also on shape, weight, size, smell, and so on. For Quine, the notions of kind and similarity are substantially one notion.

There are other, related, problems with the notion of natural kinds. For example, most people countenancing natural kinds would probably agree that birds are a natural kind. Not only are birds a kind, but they are natural; the grouping of birds *as* birds reflects objective, external similarities existing among birds and separate from our languages. Science, we believe, allows us to deal with what we intuitively might take as borderline cases, e.g., penguins or ostriches or bats. If we take birds as a natural kind, there seems no reason not to take, say, warblers as a natural kind, also. Indeed, one of the jobs and virtues of ornithology is that it has shown in what sense(s) warblers are a kind, distinguishable from other kinds of birds. Warblers are not hawks, and neither warblers nor hawks are ducks.

However, if we grant that warblers are a natural kind, it seems that problems arise, problems of a slippery slope sort. If warblers are a natural kind, what of Pine warblers? Or Cape May warblers? Or Wilson's warblers? Are these, too, natural kinds? There is no obvious reason to deny that they are, and in fact ornithologists classify them all as separate species. Ornithologists distinguish species of warblers on the basis, at least at one level, of numerous and various sorts of considerations, such as plumage color, shape, size, geographic location, song. But if Pine warblers are a natural kind, different from the natural kind of Cape May warblers, then, as I will now argue, I see no escape from the conclusion that this Pine warbler is a natural kind and that Pine warbler is another—separate—natural kind. For what is the basis for distinguishing Pine warblers from Cape May warblers? If the distinguishing criteria are phenomenal properties (or a property), then obviously every Pine warbler is distinct from every other Pine warbler at a specific enough level. If the distinguishing criteria are genetic, then the same conclusion is reached. If the distinguishing criteria are potential breeding and reproduction (as Mayr [1942] suggested), then, as Hull (1965) remarked, we carry a commitment to talk of potentiality, and moreover it rules out things like mules as a natural kind. Actual breeding and reproduction might fare better than potential breeding and reproduction. Whether potential or actual, reproductive isolation might be a (or the) distinguishing criterion of a natural kind. But if the distinguishing criterion is reproductive isolation, then mules seem to stand as a counterexample (not only because they are sterile, and so not reproductively isolated, but also because they are the offspring of horses and donkeys, each of which is taken as a species [natural kind] separate from the other [yet not reproductively isolated]). If the distinguishing criteria are ancestry or historical lineage, then, as Holsinger (1984) claims, the determination of natural kinds becomes somewhat arbitrary.

If we accept this definition of a reproductive community and this justification of the "morphological yardstick," however, we are left in a quandary. In any "sexual" species there will be a large set of nested and overlapping entities within a single interfertile unit corresponding to different family genealogies. Although we may be able to specify how far back we are to trace the ancestry for defining the reproductive community by using the morphological yardstick, there is no obvious reason for regarding that segment of genealogy as any more important or fundamental than the segment of genealogy shared by the members of a single population or group of populations, or even the segment of genealogy shared by members of what would usually be regarded as a genus. Indeed, depending on the processes that we were considering, any one of these levels might be the most important one. (Holsinger 1984, 301)

There is no clear reason, then, to rule out the slide down the slippery slope to the conclusion that individual entities are kinds. However, this conclusion would destroy the very notion of a kind, at least to the extent of making it superfluous. There seems no clear nonarbitrary distinction between kinds and individuals.[13]

Whether or not this slippery slope argument works, it highlights the problem of what kinds are, and Holsinger points to what I take to be an even more fundamental trouble with talk of natural kinds independent of our interests and theories. Echoing and supplementing Holsinger's claim, Elgin (1983) suggests that like individuation and similarity (i.e., what we take to be individuals and what we take to be similarities), natural kinds (i.e., what we take to be kinds) are dependent on our cognitive interests and our theories:

The dependence of our systems of kinds on our theories, and the dependence of these in turn on our interests, values, technology, and the like, make questionable at best the thesis that our predicates pick out real properties or natural kinds whose existence, extension, and metaphysical status are independent of any contribution of ours. And the claim that just these kinds or properties are required to answer scientific questions or provide scientific explanations supports that thesis only if backed by an account of why these questions or forms of explanation have priority—an account that does not in turn appeal to the practices or institutions of which they are a part, else all questions are begged. (1983, 35)

Natural Kinds and Reference

What is the significance of this view of natural kinds (and of similarity) with respect to issues of reference? Searle has said nothing about natural kinds in connection with reference. However, Kripke has said a great deal. Within the context of discussing identity statements (and his view that for rigid designators, if identity statements are true, then they are necessarily true), he summarizes his view on natural kinds (and natural kind terms) in the following five claims:

First, [Kripke's] argument implicitly concludes that certain general terms, those for natural kinds, have a greater kinship with proper names than is generally realized.

Second, [Kripke's] view asserts, in the case of species terms as in that of proper names, that one should bear in mind the contrast between the *apriori* but perhaps contingent properties carried with a term, given by the way its reference was fixed, and the analytic (and hence necessary) properties a term may carry, given by its meaning.

Third, in the case of natural kinds, certain properties, believed to be at least roughly characteristic of the kind and believed to apply to the original sample, are used to place new items, outside the original sample, in the kind.

Fourth, scientific investigation generally discovers characteristics of gold that are far better than the original set.

Fifth, and independently of the scientific investigations just mentioned, the "original sample" gets augmented by the discovery of new items. (1980, 134–139)

To get clearer on what Kripke is saying here and on what his commitments are with respect to natural kinds (and, so, with respect to similarity) each of these five claims will be inspected.

First, natural kind terms have a greater kinship with proper names than is generally realized. Kripke states that this holds "for certain for various species names" (1980, 134), including count terms (e.g., "tiger") and mass terms (e.g., "gold"). It holds for terms designating natural phenomena (e.g., "heat") and corresponding adjectives (e.g., "hot"). This claim is made clearer by and supported by the arguments put forward for the other four claims, so at this point I will only say that for Kripke this first claim is true because he sees natural kind terms, just as proper names, as rigid designators. Identity statements involving natural kind terms are, for

Kripke, necessarily true if true at all. The reasons for this will be seen as the remaining four claims are inspected.

Second, we must keep in mind the difference between the properties by which reference is fixed for a natural kind term and the properties that the term carries (which are given by its meaning). The reference-fixing properties are a priori and (perhaps) contingent, whereas the "carried" properties are analytic and (hence) necessary. Just as descriptions or ostension can establish a connection between an object and a proper name (e.g., the Neptune case), so, too can descriptions or ostension establish a connection between a kind and a term (e.g., "gold" designates the substance instantiated by the items over there, or at any rate, by almost all of them). To see why the reference fixing properties are a priori (and perhaps contingent) while the "carried" properties are necessary, consider the following example. Suppose gold has been defined as "a yellow metal" ("gold" means—perhaps among other things—"a yellow metal"). Could we discover that in fact gold is not yellow? Perhaps because of some peculiar atmospheric conditions or properties, we have always experienced an optical illusion in seeing gold as yellow; in fact, after rectifying those conditions, we come to see that gold is really blue. Would we then say that there is no gold (since gold is a yellow metal)? Kripke says, no; rather, we would say that gold is not really yellow. That stuff, gold, exists, but we were wrong to think it was yellow. Our designation of iron pyrite, which shares many of the phenomenal properties of gold, as fool's gold (not as gold), shows that we can change which descriptions we associate with a natural kind term, yet say that we are nonetheless talking about the same stuff (e.g., gold, even if it turns out to be blue). So the properties that are associated with a natural kind when reference is fixed might well be contingent properties (such as being yellow), but once they have been used in the fixing of reference, they are a priori properties (because we have stipulated, in the fixing of reference, that this property is true of the object, or kind). On the other hand, since we could discover at a later time that those reference-fixing properties do not, in fact, pick out the stuff we thought they did (e.g., gold turns out to be blue, not yellow), they are not necessarily true of the object, or kind. Rather, the properties carried by the term (i.e., the properties that the stuff "really" has) are the properties that are necessary.

Third, certain roughly characteristic properties, believed to apply to the original sample, are used to place new items in the kind. These properties, Kripke tells us, need not hold a priori of the kind; we could at a later time establish that some of the properties of the original sample were peculiarities of that sample, and not generalizable to the kind as a whole. So, an object might not have all the properties of the original sample, but nonetheless belong to the kind (e.g., if "being capable of flight" were the property that characterized the natural kind bird, then ostriches would not be birds, but they are). On the other hand, an object might possess the characteristics of the original sample by which the kind was established, yet not belong to the kind (e.g., if "being capable of flight" were the property that characterized the natural kind bird, then bats would be birds, but they aren't). It is an empirical matter, then, whether the properties originally associated with the kind are in fact defining properties of the kind. While the joint sufficiency of those properties might be true, they are not necessarily true. Universal applicability, however, is necessarily true, if true. Kripke claims: "'Cats are animals' has turned out to be a necessary truth. Indeed, of many such statements, especially those subsuming one species under another, we know *apriori* that, if they are true at all, they are necessarily true" (1980, 138).

Fourth, scientific investigation generally discovers characteristics of gold (or any kind) that are far better than the original set. The standard of goodness here is strict necessity, in the sense that identity statements that express necessary truths are "better" than those that don't. Kripke gives the example of gold being identified with the property "having atomic number 79." If it is true that chemists have established that (pure) gold has atomic number 79 (i.e., an object is (pure) gold iff it has atomic number 79), then this identity is stronger ("better") than one that is based on the phenomenal characteristics of the original sample (e.g., gold is a yellow metal). Kripke states:

In general, science attempts, by investigating basic structural traits, to find the nature, and thus the essence (in the philosophical sense) of the kind. . . . The type of property used in science seems to be associated with *necessity*, not with a prioricity, or analyticity. (1980, 138)

Fifth, the "original sample" gets augmented by the discovery of new items. Kripke doesn't say further what he means by "augmented" here, but

I take it that he means that the extension of the term increases to include new or different objects than just the original sample (e.g., we find more chunks of gold or discover birds that were not discovered before—if for no other reason than that some of these new birds were just born).

Just as with proper names, species names (or kind names) can be passed from link to link in a chain and their reference is determined by a causal (historical) chain, not by the use of any items. A slight difference between kind names and proper names is that for some natural kind terms, sensed phenomena, the way that the reference was fixed seems overwhelmingly important to us, which, for Kripke, is not the case with proper names. The fact that we identify light in a certain way, he says, "seems to us to be crucial, even though it is not necessary" (1980, 139).

What is to be made of Kripke's account of natural kinds? It is, I think, basically mistaken, and mistaken because it rests ultimately on realist notions of individuation and similarity. As we saw above, both notions are coherent only as interest- and theory-dependent notions. With respect to kinds, what I have argued above is that what "natural" kinds there are depends on what reference classes and similarities we recognize, and those are interest- and theory-dependent. Perhaps the best way to see Kripke's commitment to a realist view of kinds is to look at his five claims about natural kinds.

His first claim, as we noted, was simply that natural kind terms have a greater kinship with proper names than is generally recognized. This claim, I said, would be borne out with the other four claims, and so I turn to them.

His second claim was that we must keep in mind the difference between the properties by which reference is fixed for a natural kind term and the properties that the term "carries." As we saw, Kripke hypothesizes that the reference of a natural kind term (just like a proper name) can be fixed by ostension or association of certain descriptions. Both methods, I have argued above, are mistaken if taken in a realist way. As we saw, Wittgenstein and Quine showed ostension to be not a straightforward matter at all, but interest- and theory-dependent. The association of descriptions, we saw, depends on a conception of partitioning the world, and that was interest- and theory-dependent.[14]

Besides commitments to talk of ostension and reference fixing, Kripke's talk of properties that a term "carries" is, if meant in a realist way, also mistaken. That is, a term "carries" properties only because terms are part of public language, and although—because of being public—these properties are indeed "carried" by the term independently of any given speaker, what properties a term "carries" depends on how we partition the world.

Third, certain roughly characteristic properties, believed to apply to the original sample, are used to place new items in the kind. There are several problems here. First, Kripke uses the notion of an original sample as though it were a straightforward matter. However, as we saw above, Goodman has shown that the notion of a sample depends on the notion of similarity, and that is not straightforward. (My criticism here is with respect to Kripke's apparent conception of a sample. Later I will criticize his apparent conception of an original sample.) A second problem with this claim of Kripke's is his view of the peculiarities of the original sample. Those properties roughly characteristic of a kind that are believed to apply to the original sample, Kripke tells us, need not hold a priori of the kind. He says: "later empirical investigation may establish that some of the properties did not belong to the original sample, or that they were peculiarities of the original sample, not to be generalized to the kind as a whole" (1980, 137). The issue above was that what properties belong to the original sample (or to anything, for that matter) depends on our interests and theories; the issue here is the other side of the coin—what counts as peculiarities of the original sample (or of anything, for that matter) also depends on our interests and theories. As noted earlier, objects are both similar and dissimilar to other objects in a denumerable number of ways. So, too, there are denumerably many things that are peculiar and not peculiar to an object (or, a denumerable number of ways in which an object is both peculiar and not peculiar). Again, it depends on our partitioning of the world. Our interests (or partitioning) might change in the future, so that what is taken as peculiar to the original sample (or to anything) changes, but that makes the notion of peculiarity no less dependent. A third problem with Kripke's claim is that I think he overstates his contention that universal applicability, if true, is necessarily true. He remarks that "cats are animals" is a necessary truth for us. I am somewhat sympathetic to his view here, but I think that it is far from obvious. Consider the following example. I believe that all coal is hard, black, and rough until one day I read in the latest mineralogy journal that Professor X has uncovered coal with the exact characteristics of chocolate pudding. Coal is not always hard, black, and rough, states

Professor X, but some types are in fact oozy, brown, and velvety smooth. What would we make of such a claim? I suspect, like Kripke, that we would be more inclined to believe that (fantastically) Professor X had unearthed an underground vein of chocolate pudding than that some coal is oozy, brown, and smooth. However, unlike Kripke, I do not think that such an inclination is obvious. The thought of unearthing underground pudding is not much less fantastic than the thought of some types of coal being oozy. (I am not suggesting that Kripke is wrong here, but that his confidence that he is right might be a bit questionable.)

A less science-fiction sort of example, and one which also illustrates Putnam's point that we often defer to experts in addressing and settling such cases, is a case from the history of geology. In the early 1900s Alfred Wegener proposed what came to be known as continental drift theory, that is, the view that broad, global features of the earth's surface are the result of the horizontal drift of continents across the earth's crust. While such a theory could provide an explanation for many "problems" (such as continental contours, similar flora and fauna across separate continents, both in the fossil records and in present-day bioforms), it violated much of the received geological and geophysical understanding of the earth. The preferred solution to these problems was, in part, to suggest the presence of now-lost land bridges that spanned expanses of oceans. Although the land-bridges hypothesis seemed somewhat far-fetched to Wegener and his few supporters, the proponents of this hypothesis, who were the majority of the experts in the field, saw this hypothesis as less fantastic than that of entire continents plowing through the ocean floor, with no apparent mechanism or force that could propel them. In hindsight, we now see the mistaken assumptions of both Wegener and his opponents, but the point here is rejection (especially in the empirical sciences) of a sharp dichotomy between what is taken to be necessary and what is taken to be contingent, in this case the possibility of horizontal continental displacement.

Fourth, scientific investigation generally discovers characteristics of kinds that are far better than the original set. I will say more about this claim in the final chapter, and in fact argue against it, but for now I only want to remark that Kripke's assertion that the type of property identity used in science seems to be associated with necessity, and not with a prioricity or analyticity, is not so clear. Kripke takes great care in distinguishing epistemic and metaphysical issues, between analyticity and necessity.

However, I think that the distinction is not as clear as Kripke indicates. Using the coal example above, for Kripke, if it turns out that "coal is hard, black, and rough" is a true identity statement, then it is necessarily true. We do not recognize this oozy stuff as coal because it doesn't have the properties of coal. It might not be chocolate pudding, but, whatever it is, it definitely isn't coal. I see little difference between saying something like that (or, "cats are animals" is necessarily true) and saying that scientific identity statements are unfalsifiable (an epistemic notion). If "cats are animals" expresses a necessary truth, then it seems to me that it also expresses an unfalsifiable statement. Where, then, is the difference between the metaphysical and the epistemic with respect to these sorts of identity statements? It seems that all necessary truths are unfalsifiable statements (something, I take it, that we don't want as part of science). It may or may not be the case that all unfalsifiable statements are necessary truths, but whether they are or not, the distinction between metaphysical and epistemic issues is not so clear.

Fifth, the "original sample" gets augmented by the discovery of new items. In a footnote to this claim, Kripke admits some hesitation to its formulation. He states:

Obviously, there are artificialities in this whole account. For example, it may be hard to say which items constitute the original sample. Gold may have been discovered independently by various people at various times. I do not feel that any such complications will radically alter the picture. (1980, 139n70)

Kripke's commitment to ostension and a realist conception of similarity seems to me obvious here. Gold could not be discovered, I want to say, by anyone anywhere independently of our particular partitioning of the world. We partition the world into, say, metals and nonmetals, yellow and nonyellow, elements and nonelements, and so on, and *in that sense*, gold is as much stipulated as discovered. An objection to this is that whatever we call it (or don't call it), this stuff was discovered (perhaps by various people at various times). But, of course, I want to ask: what stuff? We are right back to ostension and the issue of similarity, and, as I have repeatedly said, Kripke is mistaken to see these issues as interest- and theory-independent.

At this point I would like to quickly summarize the main points I have tried to make so far in this (and the preceding) chapters. Both the cluster and the causal accounts of reference, I have argued, share fundamental commitments to conceptions of individuation and similarity, in particular realist commitments and conceptions. Those conceptions, I have urged, are mistaken, and so those commitments to those conceptions weaken the accounts. To the extent that both accounts share certain commitments and conceptions, I see them as more alike than different, and to the extent that they hold the commitments and conceptions that I say they do, they are both mistaken and faulty. A pragmatist account rejects these realist commitments not because pragmatism denies a reality, a world "out there," but because pragmatism denies any meaningfulness or informativeness of a world "out there" unrelated to epistemic concerns. What the facts are, what phenomena there are, is a function not of a "given" world but of a world that is mediated, known, and accessible only through our interests, theories, and conceptualizations. Far from an idealist metaphysics, this pragmatist view insists on an ineliminable interplay between phenomena and conceptualization. In the next chapter I want to show that the cluster and causal views are further committed to essentialism and haecceities, and to the extent they are, they are both mistaken and faulty.

8 Haecceities and Essentialism

Until now it has not occurred to Gogol that names die over time, that they perish just as people do.

—Jhumpa Lahiri, *The Namesake*

Having just argued for particular conceptions of individuation and similarity, and having argued that these underlie accounts of reference and names, in this chapter I will claim that the cluster and causal accounts of names and reference have commitments to essentialism and, in particular, to haecceities, commitments I find to be faulty.

Theseus' Ship and the Cleveland Browns

Consider the following scenario: Theseus owns a ship and dubs it with a name, "*Enterprise.*" Over the course of several years, as part of a regular maintenance regimen, Theseus replaces various parts of the ship with structurally and functionally similar parts. All the while, Theseus stores the original parts (now replaced) in a warehouse. On the day of the first part-replacement (say, replacing a screw on the steering wheel), Theseus was asked by a friend, Jason, the name of the ship. Theseus answers, "*Enterprise.*" The next day, after Theseus has replaced a small section of cloth on the mainsail with a different patch of cloth, another friend comes by and asks Theseus the name of the ship. Theseus again answers, "*Enterprise.*" This continues every day for several years. At the end of, say, three years, Theseus has replaced every original part of the original ship (one piece per day) until there are no original parts remaining. All the while, Theseus has stored all of the original parts in a warehouse. At time t_1, the first day of the making of the original ship, Theseus dubbed the ship *"Enterprise."* At time t_2, three years later, on the day of the final part-replacement, Theseus calls the ship *"Enterprise,"* as he has done every day over the intervening three years. Common sense, I take it, tells us that the name of the ship at t_2 is, indeed, *"Enterprise."* Although there are no original parts remaining of the ship that had been dubbed *"Enterprise"* three years earlier, the gradual replacement of parts, along with the assumption that no part was the essence of the ship, leads us to deny that the ship stopped being *Enterprise* as some point. The name "Enterprise" refers to the "same ship," even though the ship is structurally not the same ship as it was three years previously (i.e., there are no parts in common between times t_1 and t_2).

Now imagine that while Theseus was storing all of the original parts as he replaced them day by day, he was not merely storing them in a warehouse, but was, in fact, reconstructing a ship in that warehouse with those original parts. Over the course of three years, he (re)built a ship using all and only parts from the original *Enterprise*. After three years, then, Theseus owns two ships. Theseus' friend Jason visits him in the warehouse just after he has completed putting the final (original) part in the ship. Jason asks what the name of this ship is. Should Theseus answer, *"Enterprise"*?

I claim that for Kripke and the thesis that names are rigid designators, there is a real conundrum here. If the name *"Enterprise"* is a rigid designator, then it must refer to the same object in all possible worlds (and all possible situations) in which it refers at all. Does it refer then to the ship in the warehouse or to the ship docked in the bay? There appear to be several choices here, none of them pleasant. If it is said that *"Enterprise"* refers to the ship in the warehouse, then Theseus (and the rest of us) must have been mistaken to claim on the day before that the ship docked in the bay was *Enterprise*. But when did it stop being *Enterprise*? Was it on the first day, three years prior, when the screw from the wheel was replaced? Was it when one part more than 50 percent of the original parts was replaced? Had the pile of original parts that were stored in the warehouse been destroyed rather than reassembled, would the ship docked in the bay be *Enterprise*? What if those parts had not been destroyed, but simply stored in the warehouse and never reassembled? So, if *"Enterprise"* refers to the ship in the warehouse, when and how did that happen? On the other hand, if *"Enterprise"* refers to the ship docked in the bay, how can we make sense of *"Enterprise"* as a rigid designator? After all, there is an unbroken temporal line of *Enterprise* parts being disassembled and then reassembled. The lineage view of identity of an object that is part and parcel of Kripke's position is maintained here. Had Theseus simply taken *Enterprise* apart, say, to clean each part, and then reassembled those parts, we would not say that *Enterprise* was destroyed and some other ship was built. Rather, common sense would tell us that *Enterprise* had merely been taken apart, cleaned, and then put back together.

The point of this scenario is that there is a problem with the position of names as rigid designators, namely, that this thesis does not do any useful work in explicating or elucidating what names are or how they function. Nor is this case a philosopher's rhetorical trick, as this sort of example is an everyday occurrence, that is, a case in which there is an identifying name for an object but that object has no structural or functional essence. An example of this occurrence (and one that is reminiscent of Evans's Madagascar example noted in chapter 1) is the case of the Cleveland Browns professional football team.

The Cleveland Browns were originated by Arthur McBride as a member of the All-America Football Conference in 1946. Paul Brown was named coach and general manager. The team actually got its moniker because of its coach, Paul Brown. Team owner McBride held a newspaper contest to name the team. Most of the entries that were submitted wanted to name the team the Cleveland Browns, because of the extreme popularity of Paul Brown. Coach Brown himself thought it would not be proper to name the team after him and convinced McBride to call the team the Cleveland Panthers. McBride agreed, but a few weeks later, McBride was informed that during the 1920s there had been a semiprofessional team called the Cleveland Panthers and that the owner of that team still owned rights to the name. Subsequently, McBride settled on naming his new team the "Cleveland Browns."

In 1995, Art Modell, then-owner of the Cleveland Browns, announced that he was relocating the team to Baltimore, Maryland. The team concluded its 1995 season in Cleveland. In February 1996 the National Football League approved the franchise move to Baltimore. In March 1996 the Baltimore franchise was officially named the "Baltimore Ravens" and the Ravens began their first season in September 1996. Meanwhile, the City of Cleveland secured an agreement with the National Football League to return the Cleveland Browns to Cleveland in 1999. The agreement stipulated that the name, colors, and heritage of the Cleveland Browns would remain in Cleveland. In 1998 the NFL awarded the Cleveland Browns to new owner Alfred Lerner. Formal ownership was transferred to Lerner (and Carmen Policy) on October 23, 1998. The Cleveland Browns played an official game on August 21, 1999 and have remained a fully enfranchised NFL team ever since.

On September 26, 1999, the Cleveland Browns played a game against the Baltimore Ravens. To which team playing that day did the name "Cleveland Browns" refer? If "Cleveland Browns" is a rigid designator, it seems that the team hailing from Baltimore is the referent, not the team hailing from Cleveland. This is not a case of one named-entity expiring and then the "same" name being assigned to another entity. Instead, there was a clearly identified and understood historical link in the lifeline of the referent of "Cleveland Browns." "Baltimore Ravens" was another name assigned to an already existing entity, much like "Mrs. Clinton" being assigned to an already existing entity, Hillary Rodham. On the other hand, the NFL, and most everyone else, treated "Cleveland Browns" as refer- ring to the team hailing from Cleveland, not from Baltimore. Indeed, the Cleveland Browns and the NFL identify the history of the team as having a hiatus from 1995–1999 (that is the years of 1996–1998), not as the team's franchise ending after 1995, with another team beginning its franchise in 1999. Like the Theseus ship example, the point is that there is much pre- sumed and much implied by what entity is identified with a given name. As discussed above, principles of individuation and similarity relations are intimately connected to names. As will now be discussed, the Theseus ship and Cleveland Browns examples point to concerns with the notion of rigid designation and, as will be seen, essentialism.

Haecceities and Essentialism

In the previous section we saw that the received accounts of reference are committed to certain conceptions of individuation and similarity, con- ceptions that I argued were mistaken. An area of particular intercourse between issues of reference and issues of individuation and similarity is that of the notion of kinds, especially natural kinds. As we saw, in the discussion of natural kinds, the notion of essences (or essential proper- ties) was integral. Among Kripke's claims about natural kinds (natural kind terms) was his assertion that in general, science attempts, by investigating basic structural traits, to find the nature and thus the essence of kinds. In this chapter I want to look more closely at essences and essentialism. I will argue that conceptions of individuation and similarity carry with them conceptions of essences. Furthermore, I will argue that both Searle and Kripke, by being committed to mistaken conceptions of individuation and similarity, are committed to a mistaken conception of essences (i.e., to essentialism as it is usually interpreted).

One of the difficulties in talking about essences or essentialism is that philosophers are not always in agreement about how they state the issue. Depending on whom one reads, one gets a different statement of what essences (essential properties) are or what essentialism is. Brody (1980), for example, speaks of essential properties as those properties necessary for an object's existence:[1]

What is the basic idea behind the claim that there is a distinction between the properties that an object has essentially and the properties that an object has accidentally? It seems to be the following: on the one hand, there are some properties that an object must have; if the object didn't have them, it wouldn't exist at all. These are the properties that an object has essentially. On the other hand, there are some properties that an object has but that it might not have. The possession of these properties is not necessary for the object's existence. These are the properties that an object has accidentally. (Brody 1980, 84)

Plantinga (1974) offers several definitions of "essence" including the following:

E is an essence of [say] Socrates if and only if E is essential *to* Socrates and everything distinct from him has i (the complement of E) essentially. (1974, 70)

E is an essence if and only if there is a world W in which there exists an object x that (1) has E essentially, and (2) is such that there is no world W^* in which there exists an object distinct from x that has E. (Ibid., 72)

S is an essence if and only if S is a complete and consistent set of world-indexed properties. (Ibid., 77)

Flew defines "essence" as the "notion of a fixed and timeless possibility of existence" (1979, 111). Subsequently, he offers several conceptions of essentialism. One conception of essentialism is: a position holding that something can have an essential property in virtue of a definition, or as described in a certain way. Another conception of essentialism is: a view that maintains that some objects—no matter how described—have essences; that is, they have, essentially or necessarily, certain properties, without which they could not exist or be the things they are.

Hirsch (1971) characterizes essence in terms of spatiotemporal continuity of an object. He argues that among the properties that are true of an object, some play a special role in determining an object's identity. The terms that name those special properties (he calls them *E* terms) are, in a sense, necessary to the object's identity. All other terms that name properties true of an object but are not E terms he calls *A* terms. He capsulizes his position (with the insistence that this is only preliminary) as follows:

A term is an E term if it cannot possibly be true of an object temporarily; if it is true of an object at all, it is necessarily true of the object throughout the object's entire career. (1971, 34)

The point, of course, of all these citations is that one of the difficulties in talking about essences and essentialism is that philosophers speak in a multitude of ways when discussing these issues. When I speak of essences or essential properties I will mean the following: to say that an object has an essence (i.e., an essential property or properties) is to say that the object has some property or properties that are necessary for that object to be that object (i.e., for that object to be what it is). Essentialism I take to be the view that objects have essences or essential properties. (I take the following definition of essence to be simply a different characterization of the definition I have just given: an object has an essence [i.e. an essential property or properties] if that property or properties is true of the object in all possible worlds; or, the object has a certain property or properties in all possible worlds.[2] Another characterization of this position I am trying to elucidate is given by Slote: a property *p* is essential to an entity *e* if and only if *e* could not have failed to have *p*; essentialism is the view that various entities have certain of their properties essentially [Slote 1975, 1].)

As noted above, one objection to essentialism is that not all objects classified as the same kind necessarily have a shared essence. (Keep in mind here that, for the moment, I am accepting the distinction between individuals and kinds, and, for the moment, I am speaking about essences with respect to kinds.) The notion of family resemblances is meant to illustrate this point. Some kinds might have an essence; an object might need to have a particular property in order to be a member of a certain set (e.g., for an object to be a bachelor it must be unmarried). However, this requirement of having an essential property might not hold for all kinds (e.g., there might be no essence to games). The notion of family resemblance, of course, is not so much a direct criticism of the notion of essences as it is a criticism of the universality of the doctrine of essentialism. That is, even if the notion of family resemblance is true, it does not show (nor is it intended to show) that there are no essences or that essentialism is wrong; rather it shows that not all objects have essences (or that having an essence is not an essential property of objects!). This is not so much a direct criticism of essentialism as it is a challenging "indirect" criticism of essentialism. The challenging aspect of it is that, at least with respect to kinds, the doctrine of essentialism should not be assumed. It might not at all be the case that as science progresses it discovers the underlying traits, and hence the essences, of (some) things. There might simply be no non-arbitrary underlying trait to kinds.

There is a deeper challenge posed to the doctrine of essentialism by the notion of family resemblance. It is this: the notion of family resemblance calls into question the presumed sharp distinction between questions and issues of ontology and epistemology. Let me explain. The doctrine of essentialism presumes that if objects are considered to be members of the same kind (are called the same kind of thing; are in the extension of the same predicate) then they must share some property (or properties) in common. As science progresses, the shared properties by which we group objects into kinds (by which we call objects by a certain term) will be the underlying properties that we discover these objects (and kinds) to have. Ideally, science will result in the discovery of essential properties. But note that this view presumes that the ontological question of whether kinds have essences (and if so what they are) is separate from the epistemic question of how we (come to) know this. Likewise, the semantic question of what we call essential properties is presumed to be separate from the epistemic question of how we (come to) know this. The notion of family resemblance, however, calls this separation of questions into question. That is, if there is no compelling reason to believe that all games share a particular property (or properties) simply because they are called games, then there is no compelling reason to believe that kinds "really do" have essences or that there "really are" things which we call essential properties. After all, what sense does it make to claim that games "really do" have an essence even if we can't find it?[3]

Although the notion of family resemblance is, I think, a strong challenge to the doctrine of essentialism with respect to kinds, it is not so
clearly a strong challenge to the doctrine of essentialism with respect to
the identity of objects. The doctrine of essentialism pertains both to kinds
and to individuals. Not only is it claimed that for an object to belong to
a given kind, the object must have an essential property (or properties) of
that kind, it is also claimed that for an object to be what it is, rather than
being some other object, it must have some essential property (or properties). The notion of family resemblance challenges the doctrine of essentialism in the former case, but it seems irrelevant to the latter case; it seems
to make little sense to speak of an object having a family resemblance to
itself. (The only sense it might make is trivially—it resembles itself since it
is identical with itself. Indeed, if the doctrine of essentialism is true at all,
then, as Cartwright [1968] has said, it is true in this sense, since the attribute of being self-identical is essential to everything.)

It seems to me that the distinction between the essence of kinds and
the essence of individuals is not so obvious (in one sense), nor does the
doctrine of essentialism hold in either case. At this point I want to argue
for this claim and then indicate how I see both Searle and Kripke as being
committed to the doctrine of essentialism.

Individual Essence versus Kind Essence

Intuitively, the distinction between the essences of kinds and the essences
of individuals seems plausible. This is reinforced by the consideration
that the notion of family resemblance makes sense with respect to kinds
but not with respect to individuals. However, other than with regard to
the applicability of the notion of family resemblance, what is the basis of
the distinction? It seems to be this: it makes sense to speak of an object
being what it is independently of an object being an instance of a kind.
True, Nixon is a member of a denumerable number of kinds (e.g., former
presidents, Americans, males), but independently of all of those, Nixon
is Nixon. In some possible world, he is not a member of the kind: former
presidents, but in all possible worlds Nixon is Nixon. The essential property (or properties) that Nixon has such that he is Nixon in virtue of
having that property (or those properties) is different from the essential
property (or properties) that Nixon has such that he is a former presi-

dent in virtue of having that property (or those properties). For example, Nixon's essence as Nixon might be his particular genetic makeup, whereas Nixon's essence as a former president is his having been president at some time in the past. So the distinction between the essence of kinds and the essence of individuals is legitimate.

I want to suggest that the intuitive legitimacy of this distinction is mistaken, or at least not so clear. We cannot speak of, say, Nixon as Nixon outside of speaking of Nixon as a member of some kind. What sense does it make to say that Nixon is Nixon regardless of whether he is a former president or an American or . . . ? Speaking of Nixon as the object with such-and-such a genetic makeup won't help because that, too, places Nixon within a particular kind (e.g., biological organisms).[4] My point here is that we can never say who (or what) Nixon is without individuating Nixon. But the process of individuating Nixon is also to place Nixon within kinds. To say that Nixon is this individual is to say that Nixon is not that individual (or anything else). This requires some principle of individuation. After all, we must use some criterion to individuate Nixon. But as I argued in the previous chapter, individuation is interest-dependent. This, I take it, is much of the point and the force of Quine's opposition to essentialism:

Mathematicians may conceivably be said to be necessarily rational and not necessarily two legged; and cyclists necessarily two-legged and not necessarily rational. But what of an Individual who counts among his eccentricities both mathematics and cycling? Is this concrete individual necessarily rational and contingently two-legged or vice versa? Just insofar as we are talking referentially of the object, with no special bias toward a background grouping of mathematicians as against cyclists or vice versa, there is no semblance of sense in rating some of his attributes as necessary and others as contingent. Some of his attributes count as important and others as unimportant, yes; some as enduring and some as fleeting; but none as necessary or contingent. (Quine 1960, 199)

The gist of Quine's example, I believe, is that it makes no sense to speak of essential (or accidental) properties without the presumption of some "background grouping." Although Quine does not address the issue directly, I take his point as pertaining to both individuals and kinds. It makes no sense to say that a particular property is essential to an object unless it is clear what kind of object the object is. In addition, it makes no sense to say that a particular property is essential to an object unless it is clear what object is being referred to and that the object is this object, not that object. This, however, presupposes the process of individuation, which in turn presupposes a principle of individuation. We cannot separate the issue of Nixon as an individual from the issue of Nixon as the member of kinds. Such a separation, though, is vital to the distinction between the essence of kinds and the essence of individuals.

At this point one might object that my claim is false that we cannot separate the issue of Nixon as an individual from the issue of Nixon as a member of kinds. The objection is that something must be some thing in order for it to be a member of some kind. To be a member of some kind is to be a member, that is, to be an (identifiable) individual. Individuation, then, precedes membership (and partitioning). However, I think that this objection fails. It fails because, as I argued in the previous chapter, individuation (and partitioning) is theory- and interest-dependent. Individuals are not "out there" waiting to be given membership into various kinds. Individuation requires a principle of individuation, which rests on some conception of similarity. As we saw, the paradigm case for supposed objective individuation is ostension. But, as we saw, ostension makes sense only when the objects referred to are partitioned into kinds (e.g., "sosh" makes sense, and objects can be identifiable as being sosh, only when we know that, say, sosh is a color). Although it is true that similarity makes sense only when there are individuals that we can call similar or dissimilar (and, so, individuation precedes membership and partitioning), it is also true that individuation makes sense only when there is a principle of individuation (i.e., some similarity relation so that we can determine that an object is what it is and not something else). Partitioning, then, precedes individuation. I do not see this result as contradictory. Rather, it seems to me that it points to the interdependence between individuals and kinds, between a principle of individuation and a similarity relation. To ask which comes first conceptually is like asking which comes first, the chicken or the egg. With respect to the particular point at issue, I think that the objection fails which says that because individuals precede membership the distinction between essences of kinds and essences of individuals is not blurred.

Earlier I claimed that the notion of family resemblances was a strong criticism of essences of kinds but that it seemed irrelevant to essences of individuals. I then argued that the distinction between essences of kinds and essences of individuals is blurred. These two claims might seem to entail that the notion of family resemblances is relevant, after all, to the issue of the essences of individuals (since we cannot sharply distinguish kinds and individuals). However, it is still not clear how family resemblances could be relevant to individuals. The reason this is not clear, it seems to me, is that it rests on an underlying conception of individuals as simple, indivisible entities. That is, family resemblance makes sense for comparing different entities, but it doesn't make sense when "comparing" a single entity to itself; the notion of comparison requires two or more entities being compared. This underlying conception, though, is questionable for two reasons. First, if Ghiselin (1974) and Hull (1978) are right, some individuals are not simple, indivisible entities (e.g., they argue that species can be considered individuals). I will return to their proposal at the end of this chapter. Second, as argued above, we cannot treat individuals as simple, indivisible entities outside of the context of treating individuals as members of kinds. Individuals are not just "out there" as simple, indivisible entities. I take talk of possible world individuals and cross-world identity to be an illustration of this. We speak of the same individual in different possible worlds (or in different counterfactual situations) and speak of identifying this individual in these various possible worlds. Criteria for cross-world identification might be the presence of some essential property (*pace* Kripke), but there is nothing incoherent with suggesting family resemblance as a criterion for cross-world identification. Kripke is a philosopher in this world, but he might be a plumber or an exotic dancer in other possible worlds, and there is nothing incoherent in claiming that we use family resemblance criteria for identifying him in these various possible worlds. Although this does not show the necessity of family resemblance criteria, it is not intended to. The notion of family resemblance was never intended to deny the existence or plausibility of essences; rather it was intended to deny the necessity of the existence or plausibility of essences.

Above I remarked that the separation of the issue of, say, Nixon as an individual from the issue of, say, Nixon as the member of kinds was vital to the distinction between essences of individuals and essences of kinds. In addition, it seems to me that it is vital to the essentialism to which both Searle and Kripke are committed. I want, then, to turn to them. I want to show in what sense they are both committed to essentialism and show how their commitment is based on this mistaken distinction and ultimately on their mistaken conceptions of individuation and similarity.

Reference and Essence

Searle does not directly address the issue of essentialism in his discussion
of reference; nevertheless, his view of reference does, I want to say, commit
him to essentialism. As noted in chapter 1, Searle states that it is "a necessary truth that Aristotle has the logical sum [inclusive disjunction] of
the properties commonly attributed to him" (1969, 173). It is a necessary
condition for an object to be Aristotle that it satisfy at least some of the
descriptions that speakers associate with the name "Aristotle." This sort
of claim strikes me as a clear commitment to essentialism. There is some
description (property) affiliated with Aristotle such that for an object to
be Aristotle, it must satisfy this description (have this property). Granted,
we might not know exactly what that description (property) is; nonetheless, within the disjunctive set of descriptions (properties) associated with
"Aristotle," it is necessary that for an object to be Aristotle it must satisfy
that disjunctive set.[5]

Searle makes other essentialist claims. For example, with respect to the
issue of whether or not proper names have senses, Searle interprets the
question "Do proper names have senses?" in two forms, a weaker and a
stronger form. The weaker interpretation of the question "Do proper names
have senses?" is: "Are any propositions where the subject is a proper name
and the predicate a descriptive expression analytic?" To answer this question, for Searle, we need to be clear on the identity of the object referred
to; we need to know that we are talking about the same object on different
occasions. We need to know that a particular name names the same mountain, person, river, and so on, on different occasions. So, he says, this gives
an affirmative answer to the weaker version of the question of whether or
not any propositions where the subject is a proper name and the predicate
is a descriptive expression are analytic. Says Searle:

Some general term is analytically tied to any proper name: Everest is a mountain,
the Mississippi is a river, de Gaulle is a person. Anything which was not a mountain
could not be Everest, etc., for to secure continuity of reference we need a criterion of
identity, and the general term associated with the name provides the criterion. Even
for those people who would want to assert that de Gaulle could turn into a tree or a
horse and still be de Gaulle, there must be some identity criterion. De Gaulle could
not turn into anything whatever, e.g., a prime number, and still remain de Gaulle,
and to say this is to say that some term or range of terms is analytically tied to the
name "de Gaulle." (1969, 167)

It seems to me that Searle is explicitly stating here that being a mountain is a necessary condition (an essential property) for being Everest, being a person is a necessary condition (an essential property) for being de Gaulle, and so on. There are several points here that are worth noting. First, Searle does not seem (at least in this quotation) to acknowledge a difference in kind between essence of kinds and essence of individuals. What is essential for an object to be de Gaulle is for the object to be an instance of a certain kind, namely, a person. Of course, this particular quotation does not rule out that Searle accepts a distinction between essences of kinds and essences of individuals, but I have found nothing to indicate that he notes such a distinction. And, as seen in the above quote, when considering what is essential to de Gaulle, Searle first suggests that it is his personhood, not, say, his genetic makeup or historical origin.

A second point worth noting with regard to Searle's position is that he insists that a criterion of identity is necessary for continuity of reference. That is, we need to be assured that we are referring to the *same thing* when we refer on different occasions. With this I agree, but where I think Searle goes wrong is that he seems to think that this is a fairly straightforward matter; a thing's sameness is given to us. Our ordinary language apparently provides us with no difficulty here because it reflects the thing's given sameness. Even if we grant Searle his claim that Everest or de Gaulle couldn't turn into just anything, still, he makes no comment that Everest's mountainhood or de Gaulle's personhood is problematic. His lack of comment here is, I want to say, indicative of his acceptance of his conception of individuation and similarity. Searle is right, I think, in pointing out that we need to consider a thing's identity in terms of its sameness, but he is wrong in failing to question the "givenness" of this identity and sameness. That is, Searle fails to note the interest-dependence of issues of individuation and similarity. Consequently, in discussing reference to an object, he stresses a conception of the object's essence, since that is ultimately how its identity will be assured (and, so, proper reference will be assured).[6]

As opposed to Searle, Kripke speaks frequently of essences and essentialism. He seems careful to avoid making any explicit commitment to essentialism, and Salmon (1981) has argued that the causal account of reference is not committed to any nontrivial version of essentialism; but, I want to argue, Kripke is committed to essentialism all the same.

As we saw earlier, Kripke suggests that as science progresses it discovers underlying traits, and hence essences, of natural kinds. And, as we saw earlier, Kripke ties natural kind terms to proper names by considering them both as rigid designators. It is with respect to this notion of rigid designation that I see Kripke's commitment to essentialism, particularly the dependence of this notion on a "realist" conception of individuation and similarity. To this end, we must look at Kripke's discussion of the necessary conditions for the identity of an object.[7]

Kripke offers several examples that, he says, suggest essentialist principles. One example is that of trying to imagine "this very woman" as having different parents than she did. He asks:

How could a person originating from different parents, from a totally different sperm and egg, be this very woman? One can imagine, *given* the woman, that various things in her life could have changed: that she should have become a pauper; that her royal blood should have been unknown, and so on. . . . But what is harder to imagine is her being born of different parents. It seems to me that anything coming from a different origin would not be this object. (1980, 113)

Another example is that of the origin of "this table." Kripke asks:

Now could *this table* have been made from a completely *different* block of wood, or even of water cleverly hardened into ice-water taken from the Thames River? We could conceivably discover that, contrary to what we now think, this table is indeed made from the river. But let us suppose that it is not. Then, though we can imagine making a table out of another block of wood or even from ice, identical in appearance with this one, and though we could have put it in this very position in the room, it seems to me that this is not to imagine this table as made of wood or ice, but rather it is to imagine another table, *resembling* this one in all external details, made of another block of wood, or even of ice. (1980, 113–114)

In footnotes to these examples, Kripke remarks that two principles are suggested. First, an "origin" principle is suggested, namely, if a material object has its origin from a certain hunk of matter, it could not have had its origin in any other matter. Second, a "substance" principle is suggested, namely, an object's substance, not its origin, is what is essential to it. Although Kripke does not explicitly endorse either principle, and although he claims that a full discussion of the problem of essential properties of particulars is impossible here, he offers several (obtuse) points for consideration. The first point is that ordinarily when we ask whether something might have happened to a given object, we ask whether the universe could have gone on as it actually did up to a certain time, but diverge in its history from that point forward "so that the vicissitudes of that object would have been different from that time forth" (1980, 115n57). Perhaps, he says, this feature (the history of the object?) should be erected into a general principle about essence. The second point that Kripke makes is that he is not suggesting that only origin and substantial makeup are essential. For example, had the very block of wood from which this table was made been used instead to make a vase, then the table would never have existed. So, says Kripke, being a table seems to be an essential property of the table.[8] The third point is that the question of whether an object essentially has a certain property can be vague (!). The fourth point is that Kripke is not convinced by the counterexamples to the origin principle that appear in ordinary parlance. The exact analysis of those counterexamples, he says, is difficult and he cannot discuss them here.

It seems to me that although Kripke is careful not to claim explicitly that he is committed to essences, he nonetheless is committed to them. If we take an essential property of an object to be a property that it is necessary for an object to have to be that object, then clearly Kripke is committed to essentialism. His remarks that "anything coming from a different origin would not be this object" and that this table must have come from the block of wood which it did, seem, despite his hesitance, to indicate that a particular historical origin is at least a necessary condition for this object to be this object. Likewise, Kripke's belief that science discovers the essence of kinds (at least ideally) is also an obvious commitment to essentialism. The connection between these cases, and the underlying source of the commitment to essentialism, is in Kripke's conception of rigid designation. As noted in chapter 2, for Kripke, a rigid designator refers to the same object in all possible worlds in which that thing exists. What I want to argue, and what I have been indicating in both this chapter and the previous chapter, is that Kripke takes "the same object" as given and unproblematic. In the previous chapter I argued that this is not the case; individuation and similarity are not given and unproblematic, but are interest-dependent. I now want to argue, and have been trying to indicate in this chapter, that it is at this point where Kripke's commitment to essentialism comes in. That is, I want to argue that Kripke's notion of rigid designation commits him to essentialism.

Devitt takes a similar view. He spends several pages commenting on the doctrine of essentialism and suggesting that Kripke has made such a doctrine "both intelligible and plausible" (Devitt 1981, 209). Devitt remarks that Kripke suggests that "a person has such [nontrivial] essential properties as coming from a certain sperm and egg, being human, being of a certain sex, and being of a certain race" (ibid., 208). It is only after mentioning the doctrine of essentialism that Devitt talks about rigid designation. He does so, I believe, because the latter notion rests on the former one. He asks, in virtue of what is a name a rigid designator, and answers in the following way:

> Suppose we take "name" here to refer to designational names only. Such a name designates whatever is causally linked to it in the appropriate way. It can only be causally linked to an object in the actual world. So it designates an object in another possible world simply in virtue of that object being the same as the object to which it is causally linked in the actual world. It is this that makes the name rigid. (Ibid., 212)

It should be noted that for Devitt the important point here is that of the scope of the modal operator and the roles of singular terms. He believes that the Kripkean account is suspect because it rests on the metaphor of possible worlds. He rejects this metaphor and instead suggests that the differing roles of names and descriptions can be accounted for in the following way: names do not give rise to ambiguities of scope because they are designational, whereas descriptions do give rise to ambiguities of scope because they are attributive (in the Donnellan sense of designational and attributive). My interest here is different from Devitt's, and his rejection of Kripke's possible world talk is irrelevant to my point. I am not trying to make Devitt sound as if he interprets Kripke as I do, but rather to indicate that even he sees Kripke's notion of rigid designation as resting on the prior conception of *the same object* being referred to across possible worlds. From my perspective, Devitt's reliance on the designational–attributive distinction does not get him (or Kripke) away from the essentialist commitment of the very notion of rigid designation.

Kripke introduces the notion of rigid designation and then immediately discusses another, related, notion: transworld identity. He spends several pages arguing against the objection that rigid designation rests on criteria of transworld identity. He claims that it is because we can refer (rigidly) to, say, Nixon, and stipulate that we are speaking of what might have happened to him that transworld identifications are unproblematic (in those cases). I think Kripke is right here—at least to the extent that rigid designation precedes transworld identification and that if actual world identification is unproblematic (for rigid designators) then so, too, is transworld identification. Where I think Kripke is wrong is in thinking that actual world identification is unproblematic, as I argued in the previous chapter. It is also clear from this that rigid designation rests on a commitment to essentialism. Rigid designation rests on the possibility of being able to refer to the same object on different occasions and on a name referring to the same object on all occasions. As we saw, for Kripke, for something to be "this object," and for us to speak of "the same object," requires (at least for names) some essential property (or properties), such as genetic makeup or historical origin. For Kripke, Nixon is Nixon and "Nixon" refers to Nixon regardless of the myriad of properties associated with him which could have been otherwise; but what makes Nixon Nixon and assures that "Nixon" refers to Nixon is that there is (in principle) a clearly identifiable object that is Nixon and nothing else is that object.[9] There must be some property (or properties) common to Nixon in all possible worlds such that "Nixon" refers to that object in all of those worlds. That property (or properties) is what is essential to Nixon. What else could guarantee that Nixon is referred to by "Nixon" in all possible worlds?[10]

"Legitimate" Essence

I have tried to show that Kripke's notion of rigid designation rests on a prior conception of sameness (i.e., of individuation) and on the identification of the same object in virtue of some essential property (or properties).[11] Let me review the context in which I have made this claim. I have argued (*pace* Quine) that the doctrine of essentialism rests on a particular conception of individuation and similarity. Furthermore, both essences of kinds and essences of individuals rest on these prior conceptions. As I argued in the previous chapter these conceptions of individuation and similarity are mistaken, and, consequently, views of essentialism that are based on them are also mistaken. I then argued that both Searle and Kripke are committed to essentialism, and indeed, given their positions on individuation and similarity, they are committed to a particular version of essentialism. (To me, they are doubly wrong.)

Before turning to those issues, however, I want to make good on my promise earlier in this chapter to explain what I see as correct about Searle's and Kripke's views of essences. Although I hold that for the most part they are mistaken, I do think that they touch on particular cases that are correct. The particular cases (and the general cases that these examples instantiate) are the following. For Searle, Aristotle can't be just anything. An object must have some property, say, personhood, in order for it to be Aristotle. That is, Aristotle cannot be a mountain or a prime number even though there may be many properties that we associate with Aristotle (many descriptions that we associate with the name "Aristotle") that turn out to be false. For example, Aristotle might not have been the teacher of Alexander, but for "Aristotle" to refer to Aristotle there must be some property (description) that an object must have to be Aristotle. That property (description) might be personhood.

The Kripke example was that a particular person, to be that person, must have come from the parents that she did. As Kripke put it, *this very woman* could not have come from a totally different sperm and egg. Likewise, *this* table could not have come from a completely different origin than it did and still be *this table*.

Although I maintain that both Searle and Kripke are mistaken for the reasons that I outlined above in this chapter, I do share their intuitions somewhat. I will explain the sense in which I think they are correct by discussing the examples. What I see as correct about Searle's example (and view) is his insistence that there must be some property (description) associated with an object (a name) in order for it to be what it is (refer to what it does) and not something else. As I mentioned above, I think he is right that we need a criterion of identity to have continuity of reference. However, I insist that this is true only in a public sense (i.e., within a public language). That is, Searle is wrong to claim that a speaker must have some description associated with a name be true of an object for that name to refer to that object. Kripke's counterexamples have shown that that view is troublesome. What I want to claim is that the language community (not necessarily any individual speaker) must have some description associated with a name in order for that name to be the name of a particular object. For example, if none of the descriptions associated with "Aristotle" by the entire language community was true of Aristotle, then, I insist, reference has not occurred. Kripke rightly points out that language (and reference) is public. Indeed, I think that Kripke's notion of semantic reference is meant in large part to capture what I am claiming here (although he dissociates it completely from talk of descriptions associated with a name). This ties in with Searle's discussion of essences in the sense that there must be some property (description) that the language community—not an individual speaker—associates with an object (name). If the entire language community were willing to give up personhood as a necessary property for something to have in order for it to be Aristotle, then, I want to argue, being a person is not essential to Aristotle. (For example, this could be the case for Homer. It might turn out that there was no person Homer. If the language community were to come to this conclusion, then being a person would not be essential to Homer.) A crucial point connected with what I am claiming here is that what properties turn out to be essential (if any) are a function of both the world and the language community. This is to deny the realist, metaphysical sense of essences and essentialism. If Aristotle has an essence, it is not because Aristotle *has an essence*; rather it is because the language community agrees that some property is necessary for something to be Aristotle. Searle is right, then, but only to the extent that essences are public, linguistic (and ultimately epistemic) entities.

This insistence on publicity also underlies my assessment of Kripke's examples (and view). My intuitions are, with Kripke, that *this very woman* could not have come from a different sperm and egg, or *this table* from a different block of wood. However, I maintain that this is the case only within the context of publicly determined individuals. That is, given that language is public and given that individuation is linguistically determined (i.e., given that the language community determines who *this very* woman is and what *this table* is), then, yes, *this very woman* could not have come from a different sperm and egg. Again, however, what is being abandoned is any commitment to a realist, metaphysical conception of essences. A possible (and, I think, plausible) objection to what I have said here is that how we, as the language community, determine who *this very woman* is is by appeal to her origin, that is, to what particular sperm and egg she came from. Consequently, so the objection goes, it makes no difference in the analysis to insist on a publicly, linguistically determined individuation (and essence). The objection fails, though, because it rests on the assumption that what counts as the origin of *this very woman* is given "out there" in the world (i.e., it rests on a realist view of origins). Such an assumption is untenable for the reasons that I claimed in the previous chapter concerning individuation and similarity. That is, histories are no more "out there" than are individuals or kinds. As I argued, what counts as a particular event-individual is not simply "out there," but is also a function of our theories and interests. For example, we decide what counts as *this coin* toss (or as the 1948 Presidential election, etc.). If this is true, then we cannot appeal to the history (origin) of an individual (e.g., *this very woman*) or a kind as though the history is not determined by our theories and interests. Past event-individuals and thing-individuals are just as theory- and interest-dependent as are present or future event-individuals and thing-individuals (e.g., the 1948 Presidential election). Hence, the objection fails to the extent that it relies on a realist conception of history (origins). Again, given that we, as the language community, have determined what the origin of *this very woman* is, then we can appeal to her origin to individuate her. This point, I believe, is similar to the question that Maurice Mandelbrot (1982) raised in introducing the mathematical notion of fractals. He asked, "How long is the coast of England?" His answer was: it depends on how it is measured. For Mandelbrot, there is no single correct answer; rather, given the measurement scale, the "actual" length will vary, because in one scale particularities of the coastline (indeed, what even counts as part of the coast) will be salient whereas in another scale, they won't. Nor is this an epistemic matter. The point, for Mandelbrot, is that there simply is no single "correct" length. This does not mean that any answer to the question is as good as any other or that there are no incorrect answers. Nor does it entail that there is no coastline "out there." Instead, there are multiple correct accounts.

I want to make one final point in connection with what I have just said. Earlier I commented that the distinction between individuals and kinds (and the essences of each) might not be so sharp. I mentioned that recent debate in the philosophy of biology has included the consideration that species can be treated as individuals. This debate is related to the present discussion of the origin (and essence) of individuals because in large part the argument for treating species as individuals rests on looking at the history of given species. That is, an argument for considering species as individuals runs along the following lines. Just as for "normal" individuals, for which spatiotemporal continuity tends to be the criterion (or, at least, one criterion) for individuation, so, too, for species, spatiotemporal continuity should be the (or a) criterion of individuation. Phenotypic features, even phenotypic similarity, is irrelevant for individuation. For example, identical twins might be phenotypically identical, but they are, nonetheless, separate individuals. On the other hand, an individual can change (drastically) phenotypically yet remain the same individual (e.g., a caterpillar/butterfly). What does, or should, matter for individuation is historical origin and spatiotemporal continuity. As Hull puts it: "Organisms are not included in the same species *because* they are similar to the type specimen or to each other but because they are part of the same chunk of the genealogical nexus" (Hull 1978, 353). Just as we treat mass terms (such as "gold" or "water") as naming individuals, so we can and should treat species as individuals. In both cases, just as with "normal" individuals, particular hunks of gold or particular organisms are part of the whole (the individual) because of sameness of origin, not sameness of properties. This sounds as though it supports a Kripkean-like analysis of individuals and essences (because having a particular historical origin can serve as the essential property). However, it does so only under the constraints noted above concerning the public language–dependence of individuation both synchronically and diachronically. Although a fuller treatment of the issue of species as individuals would shed some light on the issue of essentialism, the point I have just made concerning it will suffice for the present purposes.

9   Neptune and Nemesis

Then, Hermogenes, I should say that this giving of names can be no such light matter as you fancy, or the work of light or chance persons.
—Plato, *Cratylus*

The previous chapter looked at "the signified," what is named or referred to. The case was made that both the cluster and causal accounts of reference and names rest on underlying assumptions about individuation and partitioning. In particular, forms of essentialism, especially as played out via the notion of haecceity, was challenged and dismissed. Paraphrasing Nelson Goodman, individuals are where you find them and you can find them anywhere. To reject the view that individuals (and kinds) are "ready made" and, consequently, that there is only one way the world is, is not thereby to be committed to idealist metaphysics. By emphasizing the interest-ladenness of our principles of individuation and our similarity relations, pragmatists are not denying that there is a world "out there" and are not claiming that any account of what is real is as good as any other account. Pragmatism is neither identical with nor committed to idealism, solipsism, subjectivism, or unfalsifiable relativism.

As was seen in previous chapters, pragmatists, from the classical American "Big Three" through Putnam, Apel, and the others who have been summarized, reject a sharp separation of semantic and pragmatic features of meaning and reference, including how names refer and what they refer to. This chapter focuses on "the signifier," in particular, names. Here I argue that the cluster and causal accounts of reference and names are committed to "private" reference. That is, I claim that they omit a fundamental public aspect of what names are. In critiquing theses two accounts, I offer a pragmatist alternative.

Neptune

What makes "*X*" a name (of *X*)? How does "*X*" get to be a name? When is "*X*" a name? Who gets to name? These are questions that will be addressed now and which, I will argue, demonstrate that the cluster and causal accounts of the nature of names are mistaken (beyond the commitment to haecceity noted in chapter 8). In previous chapters, it was noted that Kripke allows and acknowledges that speakers use descriptions to *fix* reference, that is, to assign a name to some object. Of course, once reference is fixed, he says, the semantic reference of the name is completely independent of the speaker reference. It no longer matters how or why some object is assigned the name it has; the name designates rigidly. So, although the initial act of naming could involve associated descriptions, the relevance of those descriptions immediately evaporates with respect to what the name now refers to. A specific case (what he says is "a good example of a baptism whose reference was fixed by means of a description") that Kripke mentions is the name "Neptune." Kripke remarks:

An even better case of determining the reference of a name by description, as opposed to ostension, is the discovery of the planet Neptune. Neptune was hypothesized as the planet which caused such and such discrepancies in the orbits of certain other planets. If Leverrier indeed gave the name "Neptune" to the planet before it was ever seen, then he fixed the reference of "Neptune" by means of the description just mentioned. (1980, 79n33)

A fuller look at the case of the naming of Neptune will, I believe, point to deficiencies in Kripke's account of names and point to features of names and naming that pragmatists from the previous chapters emphasize.

How did Neptune come to be named? In answering this question, it is instructive first to look at how the planet Uranus was named. In March 1781, William Herschel spotted what he noted as "a curious either nebulous star or perhaps a comet." Within a few days he found that this "fuzzy object" had moved and, so, he identified it as a comet. Further observation revealed no tail or cloudlike coma, leading Nevil Maskelyne, from the Royal Greenwich Observatory, to suspect this might actually be a planet (a remarkable find, if true, as it would be the first "new" planet known since recorded human history). By November 1781 astronomers around the world had become convinced that Herschel's find was indeed a planet and not a comet. (Herschel was not the first to take note of this "fuzzy object"; in 1690, John Flamsteed made mention of it and even assigned it a designation, "34 Tauri," thinking it was a star.)

When it came to assigning a name to this newly discovered planet, a number of suggestions were made. The French astronomer, Joseph-Jérome Lalande suggested that it be named after Herschel himself. The German astronomer Georg Lichtenberg argued for the name "Astrea," after the Greek goddess of justice. The Swedish astronomer Erik Prosperin recommended the name "Neptune" (!), honoring the brother of Jupiter and son of Saturn. Other suggestions were "Cybele" (wife of Saturn), "Hypercronius" (being above Saturn), "Minerva" (Roman goddess of wisdom), "Oceanus" (a mythical river said to surround the Earth), even "Neptune of George III" and "Neptune of Great Britain." Herschel weighed in with the proposal "Georgium Sidus" ("the Georgian star"). Finally, Johann Elert Bode, who published the *Astronomical Yearbook*, an annual publication of astronomical tables, proposed the name "Uranus" (father of Saturn and grandfather of Jupiter). Abbé Maximilian Hell, director of the Vienna Observatory, commended this choice and immediately included it in his published astronomical tables. While the newly discovered planet was for a short time referred to as "Georgian" in England and as "Herschel" in France, the name "Uranus" quickly became widespread and eventually was the only name used.

Within several decades of the identification of Uranus as a planet, peculiarities in its orbit led astronomers to postulate the existence of an even more distant planet. Nationalistic competition, especially between French and British astronomers, resulted in a race to discover this presumed planet observationally. On the French side were François Arago and Urbain Jean-Joseph Le Verrier, while on the British side were George Biddell Airy, John Couch Adams, and James Challis. Armed with Newtonian theory and detailed astronomical tables, astronomers made specific predictions of where this new planet should be observed. Based on measured calculations of where the planet should be, it was finally Johann Gottfried Galle, of the Berlin Observatory, who made the initial sighting that was affirmed by other astronomers, in September 1846.

As in the case of Uranus, multiple names were proffered for *this* newly discovered planet. Galle at first suggested "Janus," saying that the double face would be appropriate for this planet's position on the frontier of the solar system. In a letter only a week later, Le Verrier stated to Galle that the

French Bureau of Longitudes had decided on the name "Neptune" (and, indeed, rejected "Janus" because it implied that there were no further undiscovered planets in the solar system). Within a few days, however, Le Verrier retracted the suggestion of "Neptune" and declared that the planet should be named after himself. Arago, claiming that Le Verrier was the actual discoverer of this planet (with Galle's sighting being but the confirmation of that discovery) and claiming that Le Verrier had delegated the task and choice of dubbing the planet, announced that he would indeed name it after Le Verrier. (Arago then went on to announce that he also refused to refer to Uranus by any other name than "Herschel".) While among the French the appellation "Le Verrier's Planet" became commonplace, in Britain "Neptune" had taken hold. As could be expected, other names were proposed. Challis suggested "Oceanus" and this was endorsed, though somewhat mildly, by Airy. This was followed by a plethora of proposals: "Chronos," "Hyperion," "Atlas," "Atreus," "Gravia," "Minerva." (Rejecting the suggestion that this planet should be named after Le Verrier, British Admiral W. H. Smyth wrote to Airy: "Mythology is neutral ground. Herschel is a good enough name. Le Verrier somehow or other suggests a Fabriquant and is therefore not so good. But just think how awkward it would be if the next planet should be discovered by a German, by a Bugge, a Funk, or your hirsute friend Boguslawski?" [Standage 2000, 147].) As with Uranus, very quickly, except for pockets of opposition in France, "Neptune" was accepted as the name.

What is the significance of this episode of the naming of Neptune (and the episode of the naming of Uranus)? It points to the nonsemantic features of naming and indicates answers to the questions posed above: What makes "X" a name (of X)? How does "X" get to be a name? When is "X" a name? Who gets to decide on the name? The causal account of names might treat these cases as interesting stories of *fixing* reference—and nothing more—but I think this view is mistaken. The act of initial naming can be complex and can reveal, as I believe the Neptune case does, the ineliminable sociality of naming and names.[1]

How do things come to be named? In many ways, often simply by a speaker announcing that some object is named thus-and-so. For example, as noted in chapter 2, Devitt claimed, "Consider the case of our late cat. We acquired her as a kitten. My wife said, 'Let's call her "Nana" after Zola's courtesan.' I agreed. Thus Nana was named" (1981, 26). It *seems* that simple. Of course, not every case of naming is so straightforward. The naming of a public building, for example, can involve layers of bureaucratic over-sight, scrutiny, and approval. Not just anyone can dub someone to be a knight; this requires the appropriate figure of royalty. Likewise, dubbing a newly launched ship, even if "named" by someone prior to an appropriate ceremony, can be done only by someone with appropriate acknowledged authority in an appropriate context. Even Devitt's mundane example of naming his cat is possible only against a background of social, pragmatic features of naming and referring. As the cases of Uranus and Neptune show, assignation can indeed be fairly complex. Neither Herschel, the "dis-coverer" of Uranus, nor Galle, the first to "observe" Neptune, had their respective dubbings accepted. Uranus is not named "Georgium Sidus" and Neptune is not named "Janus," even though they were so dubbed by their respective "discoverers."

As mentioned above, Kripke and others have argued that how an object gets its name is philosophically unimportant; dubbing and baptizing are simply acts that *fix* reference. What matters, they claim, is that once refer-ence is fixed, for names it is fixed forever; names designate rigidly. I dis-agree. Kripke and others do not explain, or even address, how reference is secured the first time a name is introduced, Devitt's cavalier example notwithstanding. How is it that we can refer to an object when introduc-ing a name? What is it that, in Kripke's terms, makes that name pick out and adhere, as it were, to that object? And if it can be done one time (at an initial dubbing) why is it any different the second time the name is used? What is missing in the cluster and causal accounts is what Peirce saw as the interpretant, what James called the "workings" of reference and names. Although both the cluster and causal accounts speak of both inten-tion and convention as necessary elements, neither of these capture the sociality of reference and names that is found in a pragmatist account. To help make the case for this claim, I will, in the next section, show how the cluster and causal accounts allow, and because of that allowance are com-mitted to, "private" reference, that is, reference that does not require this feature of sociality.

"Private" Reference

What I mean by "private" reference will, I hope, become clear in the ensuing discussion. Initially, what is meant here by the notion of private reference is that a speaker can refer to an object without any necessary conceptual or linguistic link to other speakers. So, a speaker can refer to X (e.g., Neptune) simply by, say, uttering a designating expression (e.g., "the object that caused such and such discrepancies in the orbits of certain planets") and having the intent to pick out X.

I want to offer two arguments showing that Searle and Kripke are both committed to private reference. The first argument involves the nature of the examples and counterexamples that they employ; the second argument involves the inclusion of intentionality as a (necessary) component of reference for both accounts.[2]

The very examples and counterexamples that both Searle and Kripke employ, I want to claim, show their commitment to private reference. Consider Searle's discussion of reference to Aristotle and his insistence that at least one description in the disjunctive set of descriptions associated *by the speaker* must be true of an object for the name to refer to that object. As Kripke argues, this view is clearly mistaken, for there are many cases in which the descriptions in the disjunctive set all seem to fail, yet our intuitions are that reference has successfully occurred. Although Searle's primary–secondary aspect distinction may well work as a defense in some cases, I think that it, too, fails because the problem is simply moved back one step. Reference at the level of the primary aspect can still suffer the Kripkesque problems. The important point here for my concerns is that Searle's original position stresses the descriptions associated by a single, given speaker, and his countermove to Kripke's objection is still at the level of reference made by a single speaker without any apparent need to appeal to the language community. This is not a definitive argument showing that Searle is committed to private reference, but it is, I think, a fairly reasonable indication.

On the other hand, for all his talk of the publicity of (semantic) reference, Kripke, I think, also shows an affinity to private reference. Consider his Feynman example. The example works against Searle only to the extent that Searle is not allowed to appeal to other speakers in the community for reference to successfully occur, as I mentioned in chapter 1. That is, Kripke thinks that *a given speaker* might still refer to Feynman even though none of the descriptions associated by *that speaker* with the name "Feynman" is true of Feynman. This strikes me as a clear indication that Kripke (implicitly, at least) sees reference as something that can be done by a single, given speaker independent of a language community. Although his example works against Searle, it fails if we allow the speaker to appeal to the language community for reference to occur. I agree with Kripke that one might refer even though all of the descriptions one associates with a name might fail to pick out the intended object of reference. However, I disagree with Kripke if he thinks that one might refer even though all of the descriptions that the entire language community associates with a name fail to pick out the intended object of reference. Quite simply, we cannot all be wrong and still have reference occur. Both Searle and Kripke offer examples that presume the plausibility of private reference (and this, I suggest, weakens both their views). I now want to turn to the second major argument that Searle and Kripke are both committed to private reference: the appeal to intentionality.

Intentionality

The very inclusion of intentionality as a (necessary) component of reference seems to be a commitment to private reference, as it is obviously something that a speaker can do by "going into the privacy of his room." That is, the ability to stipulate that a name refers to an object by, at least in a baptismal event, uttering the name and intending to pick out a unique object seems to be something that can be done by a linguistically isolated speaker. I will discuss, at the end of this chapter, whether intentionality is necessarily private. That is, I will consider the objection to my claims above that the inclusion of intentionality is not a commitment to privacy because there is a sense in which intentionality can be public. My immediate concern is to show that both the cluster account and the causal account are committed to intentionality as a necessary component of reference. First Searle:

The capacity of speech acts to represent objects and states of affairs in the world is an extension of the more biologically fundamental capacities of the mind (or brain) to relate the organism to the world by way of such mental states as belief and desire, and especially through action and perception. (1983, vii)

Searle seems to be saying here that reference (as a kind of speech act) is successful—when it is—in virtue of underlying mental (or brain) capacities. This is just another way of saying that for reference to occur, (the "proper") intention must be present, and this is borne out in the seven rules of reference that he enunciates. Furthermore, by couching reference in these terms it seems clear that reference can be and is a private matter. That is, because it is related to the individual organism's mental (brain) states, there is no necessary connection with it and other organisms, or, in the case of reference, other speakers. There is nothing in Searle's account of reference to prevent speakers from, as Kripke says, giving "ourselves some properties which somehow qualitatively uniquely pick out an object and determine our reference in that manner" (Kripke 1980, 94). A further elaboration of Searle's view of intentionality will help corroborate this claim.

According to Searle, intentionality (intending, intentions) is one form of Intentionality (with a capital "I"). Other forms include believing, hoping, fearing, loving. The commonality here is that Intentionality is a property of (many) mental states and events by which these mental states and events are directed at (or about, or of) objects and states of affairs in the world. Every Intentional state (including intending) consists of a representative content in a certain psychological mode. So, if a speaker intends to refer to Aristotle by using the name "Aristotle" in the statement "Aristotle taught Alexander," then the representative content of the Intentional state is the state of affairs of Aristotle having taught Alexander and the psychological mode is intending (rather than, say, wishing). Where the Intentional content (i.e., representational content) is a whole proposition and where there is a direction of fit (i.e., the Intention must "match" the world), the Intentional content determines the "conditions of satisfaction" (i.e., those conditions that, as determined by the Intentional content, must obtain if the state is to be satisfied). In the example above, Aristotle must have taught Alexander for the state to be satisfied.

With regard to reference, for Searle, there must be some Intentional content associated with the name for the speaker in order for reference to occur. Also, as mentioned in chapter 1, Searle allows the Intentional content to be nonlinguistic. One can refer by way of "names, descriptions, indexicals, tags, labels, pictures, or whatever" (Searle 1983, 259). The crucial point is that a certain mental (brain) state is directed toward the world (so that animals, too, have Intentional states). The important point for the present discussion on private reference is that Searle associates Intentional states (including intentions) with the mental (brain) states of individual organisms. This, coupled with the claim that the Intentional content can be nonlinguistic, seems clearly to commit Searle to private reference. For, under his view, a speaker can refer by having certain conditions of satisfaction satisfied by a certain Intentional content. The resulting Intentional state is identifiable with a particular brain state of the organism. Where this commits Searle to private reference is exhibited in the following example (see Anscombe 1957). Suppose that a particular mental (brain) state could be created in an aborigine (or even, say, in a cat) by stimulating a certain area of the brain. The particular resulting mental (brain) state is the intention to go to the bank and withdraw money from the person's (organism's) account. Under Searle's view, it seems that the aborigine (cat) does have the intention to withdraw money from the bank account because the appropriate mental (brain) state is realized. Or, similarly, an intention to refer to Aristotle by "Aristotle" could be induced. Intentionality, and subsequently reference, under Searle's view, then, allows private reference.

In fairness to Searle, he insists that his view of Intentionality does not allow Intentional contents to determine their conditions of satisfaction in isolation:

Rather, Intentional contents in general and experiences in particular are internally related in a holistic way to other Intentional contents (the Network) and to nonrepresentational capacities (the Background). They are internally related in the sense that they could not have the conditions of satisfaction that they do except in relation to the rest of the Network and the Background. (1983, 66)

At first glance this might seem to rescue Searle from a commitment to private intentionality (and private reference), but on further examination, it is evident that the commitment is still there. There is nothing in the introduction of a Network or Background that demands publicity. The Network and Background can still be restricted to a single organism, unrelated to any linguistic community or public "form of life." For example, the Background only requires that there be a non-Intentional capacity to identify the object in the world, and the Network only requires internal coherence, both of which are consistent with the aborigine (cat) having an entire Network of Intentional states induced by electrodes in the brain. (The aborigine [cat] could be a brain in a vat!) Nothing about the requirement of a Network or Background rules out the possibility of an aborigine (cat) intending to withdraw money from the bank account (or intending to refer to Aristotle by "Aristotle").

Not only is Searle committed to private reference, but to the extent that Kripke allows a cluster theory view of reference-fixing descriptions (as in the Neptune case), he, too, is committed to private reference. In spite of his insistence that reference depends not on just what we think ourselves, "but on other people in the community, the history of how the name reached one, and things like that" (1980, 95), he does allow private reference at the baptismal point. There is nothing in Kripke's account of reference to prevent speakers from intending to pick out an object by (the use of) a name when a name is being introduced (where this intending is in the sense just discussed). The aborigine (cat) just as easily could be a speaker in Kripke's view as in Searle's.

This is especially true of Devitt's conception of the causal account of reference. In fact his discussion of grounding thoughts sounds very much like Searle's portrayal of reference as an ability based on mental (brain) states. Devitt explicitly allows for private reference:

I see no reason to deny that beings which do not speak public languages could have grounding thoughts. If they do have them, then they must have appropriate mental representations. Call all these representations of the object in grounding beliefs "demonstrative representations." The act of perception leading to these representations defines a mode of presenting the object. It leads to an ability to designate made up of these grounding thoughts. Underlying the demonstrative representations in those thoughts is a d-chain grounded in the object in virtue of which they designate the object. (1981, 133)

Both the cluster and causal accounts of reference, then, are committed to the possibility of private reference. What is the significance of this? Two points are important. First, as I will argue now, to the extent that they are so committed, the accounts are weakened. Second, the issue of private reference points to a deeper underlying commitment of the accounts, a commitment to a particular view of the similarity relation and of individuation (which I explicated in the previous two chapters).

In criticizing the notion of private reference, I want now to focus on two points: (1) the plausibility of a private language (within which private reference is possible) and (2) the role of intention in private reference.[3]

Contra "Private" Intentionality

The issue of the plausibility of a private language is an old one and I will not engage in a thorough analysis of it. I agree with Putnam (1981) that the notion of a private language is a self-refuting one and that

Wittgenstein (1953) gave conclusive arguments against the possibility of a private language.

What is Wittgenstein's objection to the possibility of a private language? In a sentence, it is that the notion of rule-governance makes no sense within a private language, and, since all language must be rule-governed, there can be no private language. Wittgenstein is talking about the possibility of making reference to one's inner experiences, one's private sensations. He is not denying that we have sensations or feelings or even that we can name them (see Wittgenstein 1967, para. 487; 1953, para. 244). Rather, he is claiming that naming, even naming feelings, presupposes a context, or stage-setting, which is possible only within a public language: "'To give a sensation a name' means nothing unless I already know in what sort of game this name is to be used" (1968, 291; see also Wittgenstein 1953, paras. 257, 290, 1958, 69; 1967, para. 428; 1969, para. 472). So, naming presupposes a stage-setting, which presupposes a public language. Why the presupposition of a public language? Because naming (and referring) stand in need of agreement and outward criteria, or rule obedience. (Wittgenstein speaks of this in terms of language-games.) The "game" we play with "toothache," for instance, entirely depends on there being a behavior (or behaviors) that we call the expression of toothache. If someone claimed to have an unbearable toothache and yet exhibited none of the behavior that we have learned to associate with having a toothache, we would wonder whether the person was telling the truth or whether he understood what having a toothache is. We would, after a while, wonder if the person knew what "toothache" means or refers to. Behind this insistence on public, behavioral criteria is the demand for rule obedience in order for understanding and communication to be possible:

And hence also "obeying a rule" is a practice. And to *think* one is obeying a rule is not to obey a rule. Hence it is not possible to obey a rule "privately": otherwise thinking one was obeying a rule would be the same as obeying it. (1953, para. 202)

If one could in fact have a private language, one could not know whether or not one was following a rule, for the concept of rule-following involves publicity. Without rules of application, one cannot have a language, if for no other reason than simply because one would not know from one time to another whether one was giving the same name to whatever one was naming or whether one was referring to the same thing from one time to another.[4] A private language, then, is no language at all, and to the extent to which the received accounts of reference permit it and are committed to it, those theories are weakened.

I said before that there are two points about private reference that demand attention. The first is that private reference in the sense of reference in a private language is impossible. The second point involves the role of intention in reference. This point was raised earlier in explicating Peirce's conception of names and reference, and it is to this point that I now return.

As was noted in the discussion of Peirce in chapter 4, Putnam (1981) gives an "abbreviated version" of a Wittgensteinian argument that there is no necessary connection between names and objects and that intentionality does not enable reference to succeed or occur. Suppose, Putnam says, that in its crawling across the sand an ant traces a particular pattern of lines, which we depict as a recognizable caricature of Winston Churchill (or that the ant traces a particular pattern of lines which we depict as a recognizable shape resembling the name "Winston Churchill"). Would we say that the ant has referred to Winston Churchill? Putnam says: no. What may seem to be missing for reference to have occurred is the element of intention. However, this will not do:

But to have the intention that *anything* . . . should *represent* Churchill, I must have been able to *think about* Churchill in the first place. If lines in the sand, noises, etc., cannot "in themselves" represent anything, then how is it that thought forms can "in themselves" represent anything? (1981, 2)

Just as physical representations (e.g., lines in the sand) have no necessary connection to objects, so mental representations also have no necessary connection to objects. Words are included here; a discourse might seem to be, say, a description of a tree, but if it was produced by monkeys randomly hitting keys on a typewriter for millions of years, then the words would not refer. And—importantly—it's not just that the monkeys would not refer in this case, but the words would not refer. Or: it's not just that speaker reference would fail, but semantic reference would fail. Intentionality does not yield the ability to refer, but rather presupposes the ability to refer. To intend to withdraw money from a bank account (or to refer to Aristotle by "Aristotle") requires the ability to refer to those objects or actions or capacities that are the objects of the intentions. This is because, as Putnam puts it, to have the intention that something happen (e.g., money being withdrawn) or be represented (e.g., "Aristotle" refers to Aristotle), one must already have the ability to think about the event or object in the first place. Furthermore, the very ability to intend depends on a public "form of life," as I will argue at the end of this chapter. This bears on the question of whether there is any sense of intentionality that is not private, and subsequently, bears on the role of intention in reference. If Putnam is right, and I think that he is, this is a telling criticism of both the cluster and the causal accounts of reference, since, as we saw above, they are both committed to intention as a necessary component of reference.

Another criticism, already raised in the discussion of Peirce, of the role of intentionality in reference comes from Elgin (1983). She argues that the notion of intentionality is conceptually intermingled with that of interpretation and that this requires publicity. Says Elgin:

intending to produce an effect by getting one's audience to recognize one's intention to produce that effect is not, or at least is not always, required for reference. Someone talking in his sleep or under the influence of anesthesia or, for that matter, someone who is unconsciously "thinking out loud" may have no such intention. Whether to say that such a person refers depends on how his words are interpreted. If we can make no sense of his utterances we put them down to inchoate ramblings. If their interpretation is straightforward, we take his utterances to be sentences, and the terms in them to refer. It is the availability of a reasonable interpretation rather than the intention with which they were produced that is crucial in deciding whether his words refer. (1983, 17)[5]

Elgin's comments clearly are directed against Searle's theory (especially his rules 5 and 6) of reference as a speech act that is based on intentionality. She reiterates Kripke's speaker reference–semantic reference distinction by repeating that we can distinguish between what a speaker intends to refer to and what a speaker actually refers to (or: what a speaker refers to and what the words refer to). However, the same point can be directed against the causal theory as well, since, as seen above, it, too, incorporates intentionality. Nor can the causal account be defended by claiming that this criticism is appropriate to speaker reference only and not to semantic reference. This move does not work because, as Putnam's criticism points out, words have no more necessary connection to objects than do physical or mental representations. Yes, words (names) hook up to objects, but not by themselves. What counts as a name, and the fact that something functions as a name, is not inherent in the name (or in the object). Interpretation is

required. Another way of putting this is that reference, even semantic reference, is not a dyadic relation between word and object, but a triadic relation between word and object and interpretant.

   To extrapolate Elgin's point, interpretation not only determines (at least
in part) what is conceptually legitimate about intention (and indeed what
counts as intention), but also determines (at least in part) what is conceptually legitimate about naming (and indeed what counts as naming). It
is true that naming and referring are public, but the causal theory's treatment of semantic reference and of reference in general does not capture
the proper sense of publicity to account for successful reference.

Nemesis and AIDS

Having shown (I hope) that both the cluster and causal accounts of reference and names are deficient because of their commitment to "private"
reference, I want now to return to the lessons about names that were
taught by the Uranus and Neptune cases, namely, that initial and subsequent uses of names are not reducible to intention or to causal chains.
Rather, referring is a matter of conferring, deferring, and inferring. It is
a matter of conferring in the sense that there is an inherent sociality to
referring; it is not simply a private act (or: what appears to be a private act
of naming and referring, such as Devitt naming his cat, rests on and presupposes background publicity not just of the object, but of how names
themselves function). For much the same reasons, referring is a matter of
deferring, that is, deferring to subsequent public usage, what James spoke
of as "workings" and Apel's notion of "futuro." In many cases of names we
very much explicitly defer to recognized authorities for the establishment
of names and for successful reference of later uses of that name. Referring
is inferring in the sense of requiring interpretation, as Elgin demonstrated.
All of these inherent features of names are reflected in the Uranus and
Neptune cases. To make the case that these features are not only present
in the initial dubbing and use of names, but even once reference has been
"fixed," I want to end this chapter with two contemporary cases. With
these two cases I want to show that all cases of names—whether they pick
out "real" individuals such as Winston Churchill, fictional ones such as
"Sherlock Holmes," abstract ones such as "two," or any others—function
as names because they exhibit these features against a background of

public language. The first example is that of an ongoing debate about the cause(s) of the mass extinction of life on earth sixty-five million years ago (what is called the End Cretaceous extinction). The second example is that of the controversy concerning the discovery of the cause(s) of acquired immune deficiency syndrome (AIDS).

In 1977, Alfred Fischer and Michael Arthur suggested that a periodic interval of about 32 million years elapsed between mass extinctions of life on the earth. Included in the series of extinctions is the End Cretaceous extinction, approximately 65 million years ago (which included the death of the dinosaurs). Numerous proposed explanations for the extinction of dinosaurs had been advanced, including oncoming major climatic changes and early mammalian predation of dinosaur eggs. However, more than 75 percent of species on the earth were extinguished at the End Cretaceous extinction event, so predation seemed unlikely as an adequate explanation. Drastic climatic change also was questioned, given recent claims and evidence that dinosaurs were in fact warm-blooded and less susceptible to such change. In June 1980, the research team led by Louis Alvarez published its famous paper (Alvarez, Alvarez, Asaro, Michel 1980) suggesting an extraterrestrial impact as the cause of the extinctions at the K-T boundary (i.e., the geological boundary between the Cretaceous and Tertiary eras). The predominant evidence was the pronounced levels of iridium at the boundary. (By the end of 1983, the Alvarez team reported at least 22 sites, scattered around the world, exhibiting the iridium anomaly at the K-T boundary.) The initial Alvarez paper was immediately criticized in terms of its evidence and its conclusions. Challenges included whether the iridium anomaly was a true anomaly, whether it entails an extraterrestrial cause, where the impact crater is, and whether a single catastrophic event could account for late Cretaceous extinctions (which apparently span numbers of centuries).

In early 1984, David Raup and John Sepkoski announced a periodicity of mass extinctions of 26 million years, based on computer simulations producing a "best fit" analysis of family extinctions. This analysis was immediately criticized (and continues to be). In April 1984 two causes were proposed to account for a 26-million-year periodicity. First, two independent teams of researchers suggested that periodicity is caused by our solar system's oscillation with respect to the galactic plane. Second, both Whitmire and Jackson (1984) and Davis, Hut, and Muller (1984) suggested an unseen companion to our sun. This yet-to-be-found star was baptized "Nemesis." The presence of Nemesis, it is claimed, disturbs material in the Oort Cloud, resulting in some of it striking the earth so as to have caused intense volcanic activity and prolonged darkness on the earth's surface, leading to the mass extinction of life. The orbit of Nemesis is said to bring it within the crucial proximity every 26 million years. Since its postulation, Nemesis has not been observed. In January 1985, a third proposal was offered, that the cause of the periodicity is an unseen tenth planet in our solar system, which they dubbed "Planet X." Meanwhile, by the beginning of 1985, corroborating evidence for the Alvarez claim of impact included evidence of anomalous levels of osmium isotope ratios at the K-T boundary, findings of shocked quartz at the K-T boundary sites, as well as reports of worldwide distribution of iridium anomalies at the K-T boundary. The three proposals—galactic oscillation, a tenth planet, a companion star—all met with criticisms. The galactic oscillation view, while requiring no new or mysterious ontological objects, suffered the fate of not being in sync with the purported mass extinctions. As the solar system bobs up and down relative to the galactic plane, the mass extinctions should have occurred when the solar system was approaching the galactic plane, but that has not happened. The Planet X view received little attention, and suffered the fate of the planet not having been found. This is true as well for Nemesis (i.e., not having been found), but its defenders claim it is less likely that we would have missed a planet in our solar system than a (very likely dim) star that is not within our solar system, but only approaches it enough to have its gravitational field affect the Oort Cloud (a halo of comets and matter on the fringes of the solar system).

For present concerns, what is important is the name "Nemesis" and how it functions as a name. There are several points that I believe emerge and are highlighted by this case. First, the introduction of the name "Nemesis" was done within the larger context of proposing a scientific hypothesis. Naming Nemesis was not done privately, external to any other epistemic concerns, but as part of a larger practice and activity. Prior to the particular scientific context, established by various public publications and various espoused positions, the naming of Nemesis would have made no sense. Even with questions and criticisms about the hypothesis and the existence of Nemesis, the introduction of the name "Nemesis" was plausible (including the choice of that name) and conceptually coherent. The conceivability of a proposal to introduce this name for a companion star prior to the introduction of a reasonable hypothesis that could serve as a background context for the name would have been doubtful.

This leads to a second point that emerges from this case, namely, it is the acceptance by the community of researchers that secures (or will secure) reference, not any intentions by a particular speaker or any specific causal chain. The name "Nemesis" has, in a sense, stuck, and even critics of the hypothesis use the name. Scientists, both in favor of and in opposition to the hypothesis, use the name "Nemesis" in discussing the merits and demerits of the hypothesis. The simple introduction of the name did not (and does not) suffice for naming to take place. Rather the communal acceptance and adoption of the name that is introduced are necessary for naming to genuinely occur. Naming, as a social, linguistic practice, requires social, linguistic adoption.

A third point is that naming (and reference) is intimately tied up with epistemic issues. Whether "Nemesis" actually names anything, whether it continues to function as a name, is not determined by any a prior set of conditions, but by the subsequent actions of the scientific community. If it turns out that Nemesis is never found, whether because it doesn't exist or researchers just stop looking for it or for some other reason, then the name will, I suggest, drift out of the scientific vocabulary, except perhaps in an anecdotal way (like "Vulcan" as the suggested name of a planet between the Sun and Mercury). Without some verifiable evidence adding credence to the existence of Nemesis, "Nemesis" will fade from serious scientific discussion and will not be used as a name. The causal view of names, of course, must hold that if the appropriate causal chain is there, then reference is made. In such a case, we would indeed refer to Nemesis by the use of "Nemesis" even if, because of the lack of corroborating evidence, we reject the hypothesis that Nemesis exists. On the causal view, we might really be referring even if we (individually or collectively) aren't aware of it and believe that we aren't referring.

I take this Nemesis example to nicely illustrate the strength of the pragmatist (and Wittgensteinian) account of names and reference. The linguistic issue is not whether or not Nemesis exists, but whether or not the name "Nemesis" is accepted and adopted by the scientific community (and later by larger communities). Only with public, verifiable corroborating evidence granting support for the individuation of Nemesis will the name

"Nemesis" continue to be used and accepted. The claim that "Nemesis" caused the End Cretaceous extinction event" must cohere with other and future claims or we will not accept Nemesis as an object or "Nemesis" as a name of an object. At present "Nemesis" is a theoretical term for the scientific community and whether it remains so or becomes an observational term or is discarded altogether depends finally on the coherence of claims within the scientific community and the acceptance of these claims by that community. The determination of reference is made by a public, verifiable process, not by a given speaker or by a temporal causal chain. The dubbing by Davis, Muller, and Hut of "Nemesis" to the theoretical object Nemesis did not establish any baptism or any causal chain to an object, nor did it establish a name to then be used by the community of researchers. "Nemesis" became a name not by a dubbing (accompanied by intentions or mental representations), but by the gradual adoption by the scientific community of a linguistic label to an "object" whose existence was the question. While the Nemesis example illustrates the semiotic character of a name of an individual object, the following example of AIDS does likewise with the semiotic elements of partitionings and reference to a kind.

AIDS supposedly first appeared in 1981. Efforts to uncover a (or the) cause led to two independent announcements of such a discovery. In the spring of 1983, French scientists at the Institut Pasteur announced that they had discovered the cause of AIDS. The cause, they claimed, was a virus, which they dubbed LAV (lymphadenopathy-associated virus). Several months before this announcement, scientists reported that SAIDS (simian acquired immune deficiency syndrome) appeared to be caused by a virus. SAIDS, a disease held to be similar to AIDS in symptoms and pathology, having a viral-infectious agent, led researchers to look for a similar cause for AIDS. The viral organism responsible for AIDS, according to the French team, was so named because of its initial discovery in a patient with the swollen lymph glands and flu-like symptoms often associated with AIDS.

Almost a year later, in April 1984, American scientists announced that they had discovered the cause of AIDS. The virus that these scientists claimed was responsible was dubbed HTLV-3 (human lymphotrophic retrovirus-3). At the public announcement of the American researchers' discovery, it was claimed that HTLV-3 was probably the same organism as that identified as LAV, but genetic analysis and immunological comparisons would be necessary to determine this. It was suggested that both HTLV-3 and LAV belong to a class of retroviruses that use RNA rather than DNA as their basic genetic material. The American scientists dubbed the culprit organism as HTLV-3 because they linked it to another retrovirus called HTLV-1, which is associated with a rare form of human leukemia. According to published reports, the French researchers were not sure whether or not the virus they construed as the causal agent was a member of the HTLV family. When the American announcement was made, however, the French team claimed, "We are very happy that another team has found the same thing" (*Science News* 125 [1984]: 285). "From its effect, and the description of it, it can only be the same one [virus]" (ibid.). LAV, they said, was only a "provisional name."

Several interesting events occurred over the course of the year following the American announcement. The first was that the scientific community continued to use both "LAV" and "HTLV-3" to designate the virus that they investigated and studied. For example, in the science newsmagazine *Science News*, fourteen articles appeared on AIDS between July 7, 1984, and April 27, 1985. In five of those articles, both "LAV" and "HTLV-3" were cited as two names for the (probable) same virus. In four articles, HTLV-3 was cited as the viral cause and LAV was not mentioned. In no articles was LAV cited as the cause and HTLV-3 not mentioned. In the five remaining articles on AIDS, neither was cited as the cause. Meanwhile, another American researcher, Jay Levy, opted for a third name, ARV (AIDS-associated retrovirus). Levy and his colleagues isolated a virus from an AIDS patient and cloned the entire genome while trying to develop a screening test and, potentially, a vaccine. Pending a comparison of LAV and HTLV-3, Levy called his isolates ARV.

Another event related to this issue of naming and referring, following the identification of LAV/HTLV-3, was the effort to look for a (or the) historical cause of AIDS. In March 1985 it was reported that AIDS "or something very like it" existed in Africa in 1972. Scientists thawed frozen blood samples from Uganda taken in 1972 and 1973. They looked for the presence of antibodies to HTLV-3 and found it in two-thirds of the samples, suggesting that "the virus detected may have been a predecessor of HTLV-3 or HTLV-3 itself but existing in a population acclimated to its presence" (*Science News* 127 [1985]: 173). What is significant is that, *given the apparent identification of HTLV-3* as the cause of AIDS, researchers then looked for earlier instances of AIDS and, in effect, located, or determined, a different historical nexus for the disease.

What are the lessons of this case for naming and reference? First, as with the Nemesis case, the identification of a natural kind (or, in the case of Nemesis, an individual) was a social, diachronic process. Although two groups of researchers dubbed some virus type as the cause of the disease, the name that actually became accepted and used was one that depended not on the intentions of any particular speaker but on the agreement and subsequent use by the community. Nor was the name established by some appropriate causal chain, initiated by a speaker's perceptually caused hookup to an object (conjoined with the appropriate mental representation), because much of the debate itself concerned just what the causal hookup was. Much of what was at issue was in fact determining what "object" was there to be causally hooked up. Reference is a public matter, and how a name functions is a public matter—not in the simple "linear" manner associated with the causal account, but in a language-community consensus sense. That is, the communal agreement that is necessary for the name to function is not merely that once reference has been established (via a baptism), then future reference is parasitic upon that initial naming, but that communal agreement is the sense of the community as a whole over time comes to adopt a name (as well as the object or kind).

Conclusion

What, finally, is to be said about and for a pragmatist account—or, at least, approach—to reference and names? Such an account, I believe, displays a fuller understanding of these issues in large part because it places the underlying emphasis on what reference and names *do*, not simply what they *are* as part only of a conceptual analysis. We do many things when we name and refer, in many different sorts of contexts and for many purposes. Naming and referring function for us in a multitude of ways. The various accounts of reference and names that philosophers have proposed and considered are reminiscent of the fable of the blind men who encounter an elephant and then proceed to tell the others what the elephant is like. One of them, feeling the elephant's ears, says that an elephant is like a sail. Another, feeling its trunk, insists that an elephant is like a snake.

A third, feeling the elephant's tail, claims an elephant is like a rope. Yet a fourth, feeling the elephant's leg, says an elephant is like a tree. Well, we see the problem: each one is correct to an extent, but each is also mistaken. A strength of Searle's cluster account, for instance, is the insistence that reference must be understood as a speech act that it is intimately tied up with our extrasemantic concerns. One of the strengths of Kripke's causal account is the insistence that reference is public and diachronic, that we do not (successfully) refer simply because we intend to. Of course, as the bulk of this book has tried to show, both accounts at best elucidate necessary features of reference and names. Each account has provided telling criticisms of the other. In addition, Wittgenstein and the pragmatist philosophers surveyed in this book have critiqued these two accounts "from the outside," that is, by arguing for a larger view of language and what is missing with these accounts.

Given the survey of the pragmatist philosophers presented here, just what is the pragmatist account of reference and names? Although there is not a set of necessary and sufficient conditions provided, definite features emerge, indicated above as conferring, deferring, and inferring. Peirce's semiotic analysis of language generally, as well as reference and names more specifically, demonstrates that besides signifiers and signifieds, interpretants—the "effect of the sign"—is fundamental to all signs, including names. As he put it, naming is possible because Thirds are real, that is, because particulars are never bare particulars, but always instances of kinds. This is reiterated in James's "skrkl" example. Also from James, with his criticisms of Russell's "vicious abstractionism" and the treatment of names as having no content and no context, we get the notion of "workings," which, much like Peirce's requirement of effects, is future oriented. Names are names and they refer not because of a chain of past events, but because of what they allow us to do in the future, and this transcends any given speaker's personal, private intentions. Like Peirce and James, Dewey emphasized the lived nature of names and reference. Stressing naming as a process and names as tools, his rejection of mere logical name-letters as presupposing that "something has already been done to recognize and constitute A, B, C as individuals" applies equally to mundane names. There is no mere given-ness to names or to the individuals named. Like Peirce and James, he challenges the underlying commitment to haecceities that is found in the cluster and causal accounts.

With contemporary pragmatist philosophers, we see these themes and issues carried further. Putnam's famous rejection of "private" reference ("meanings ain't in the head") as well as his contextualized realism both reflect and reinforce positions seen in the classical pragmatists. In addition, he has been a forceful critic of a linguistic semantic–pragmatic dichotomy, something found in the current received accounts. Elgin, too, rejects both intention and convention as being sufficient for a full account of reference and names. Her focus on interpretation and on understanding emphasizes the dynamic features of reference and names, much like the classical pragmatists. Her insistence that we fit our interpretations *into* working categories and not simply *onto* a given world is reflected in her rejection of "inherently individuated" individuals (i.e., haecceities). Rorty also challenges the linguistic, epistemic, and metaphysical assumptions of the received accounts. Further, in language that is very reminiscent of James and Dewey, he stresses the axiological and teleological features that underlie reference and names and our accounts of reference and names.

Across the pond, contemporary continental pragmatic philosophers have argued for much the same conclusions as their American counterparts. Eco reveals his commitment to Jamesian-like "workings" with his view that referring is an act of negotiation. It is diachronic, encyclopedic descriptions, not causal chains, that allow reference to occur and succeed. For Eco, the problem of proper names is very much the problem of iconic signs in general, and these are to be understood only in the context of purpose and coherence. Apel's focus on intersubjectivity and future-oriented acceptability are two sides of the same coin in his treatment of language as lived interaction. Reference and names are a matter of coping with and in the world; this coping is not just a matter of functioning in the world but also a matter of changing the world. Effects of names are part of the very nature and function of names. Habermas, too, emphasizes the activity-like nature of reference. We do not merely bump into a world, but we act, and that process of action in large part shapes and constructs the future world in which we act. Communication is basic, not simply reflection or description. Communication, though, occurs in three spheres: subjective, intersubjective, and objective. Those elements involved in communication and action, including reference and names, function in all of those spheres and are understandable only when seen in the context of all of them. And last, in the final three chapters of this book, I have, following these nine pragmatist philosophers, argued against the cluster and causal views by trying to show their faulty underlying commitments with respect to similarity, individuation, haecceities, and privacy.

In the *Tao Te Ching*, Lao tzu states that "a journey of a thousand miles begins with a single step." This book is one step in several journeys, one being the journey of gaining a fuller understanding of the nature and function of names, a second being the journey of gaining a fuller appreciation of the fecundity of pragmatism as an approach to philosophical concerns. My hope is that the views and positions and arguments given here will be stimuli for further, better work by others on these issues.

Notes

Introduction

1. In this book I will not directly discuss differences between a "causal" account of reference and a "direct reference" view, though I recognize they are not identical (see, e.g., Devitt 1989, 1998; Luntley 1999; Recanati 1993; Williamson 1996, Soames 2002). Rather, the focus will be on a pragmatist alternative to the received accounts. I believe this pragmatist view is also an alternative to a direct reference view for many, though not all, of the same reasons it is an alternative to the causal account. Nor will I discuss more recent developments such as arguments for and against two-dimensionalism (e.g., Soames 2005), as I see these arguments as further elaborations on the received accounts, not significant alternatives.

1 The Descriptivist/Cluster Account

1. A few pages later Searle reemphasizes this point of reference as a speech act: "The term 'referring expression' is not meant to imply that expressions refer. On the contrary, as previously emphasized, reference is a speech act, and speech acts are performed by speakers in uttering words, not by words. To say that an expression refers (predicates, asserts, etc.) in my terminology is either senseless or is shorthand for saying that the expression is used by speakers to refer (predicate, assert, etc.); this is a shorthand I shall frequently employ" (1969, 28).

2. By "normal input and output" Searle simply means to cover such things as: both the speaker and the hearer understand the language, there are no physical impediments (such as laryngitis or deafness), both are aware of what they are doing, they are not acting or telling a joke, etc.

3. Searle's point here is to rule out gibberish.

4. This condition is meant to capture the axioms and the principle mentioned above.

5. This condition, says Searle, enables us to distinguish referring to an object from other ways of calling attention to it (such as hitting the hearer over the head with it).

6. A few pages later he reiterates this: it is a necessary truth that Aristotle has the logical sum (inclusive disjunction) of the properties commonly attributed to him.

7. Kripke adds a condition (C): For any successful theory, the account must not be circular. The properties that are used in the vote must themselves not involve the notion of reference in such a way that is ultimately impossible to eliminate. That is, among the properties associated with the reference of a term "X" cannot be the property "is called 'X.'" The motivation for this condition is obvious—to prevent a theory that does not lead to any independent determination of reference. Searle makes the same point: "we are only justified in calling [an object] 'Everest' if we can give a reason for supposing it to be identical with what we used to call 'Everest' and to give as that reason that it is called 'Everest' would be circular" (1969, 167).

8. While the Gödel–Schmidt example might seem a bit cooked up, Kripke provides other, more natural, examples. For instance, it is believed by some people that Columbus was the first man to realize that the Earth is round and that he was the first European to land in the western hemisphere. Neither of these beliefs is true. If thesis (3) is correct, then when people use the term "Columbus" they really refer to some Greek (?) if they use the roundness of the Earth, or to some Norseman (?) if they use the discovery of America. But they don't, says Kripke; they refer to Columbus.

9. Kripke never states in *Naming and Necessity* just what a priori knowledge is. He argues against its conflation with necessity. He says that "the notion of a prioricity is a concept of epistemology" (1980, 34). Beyond that, however, he says only what it is not (e.g., it is not the metaphysical concept of necessity). Since he is reticent about meanings and argues against a prioricity as knowledge that *can* be known prior to or independent of experience (because such a definition includes the modal notion of possibility, which is metaphysical rather than epistemological), it is not clear to me what Kripke takes a prioricity to be.

10. Kripke claims that there are two ways in which the cluster account (or even the single description account) can be viewed. One is that of saying that the cluster (or the single description) actually gives the meaning of the name (e.g., "Aristotle" *means* "the most famous student of Plato" or "the teacher of Alexander," and the like). Another is that of saying that the cluster (or single description) *determines the reference* (e.g., "the teacher of Alexander" is used to determine to whom someone is referring when someone says "Aristotle"). Apparently thesis (6) is a thesis of the cluster theory only if the descriptive referring expressions are used to give the meaning of "X."

11. McKinsey (1978) has done a somewhat similar critique and found Kripke's arguments lacking credibility. Other attempts have been made to defend the cluster account, e.g., by Boer (1972) and Ingber (1979).

12. Whether or not Searle succeeds in showing Donnellan's distinction to be bogus is not the main concern here. It should also be noted that Kripke (1977) criticizes Donnellan's distinction.

13. It is not clear if Kripke thinks that for the cluster theory the property (or set of properties) that the speaker believes uniquely picks out the object being referred to must be the same property (or set of properties) that in fact uniquely picks out the object being referred to. This, however, is a minor point.

14. Another argument as to the motivation for insisting that reference has occurred (to Einstein) is that the name "Einstein" refers to Einstein even if the speaker did not (intend to) refer to Einstein. This notion of semantic reference versus speaker's reference will be taken up later. In addition, in chapter 9, I will explore, and reject, the view that reference is a dyadic relation between word and object (which I take as an assumption of Kripke's criticisms).

15. Actually, for reasons seen later, I will clarify this claim and assert that in the second case Searle may well think that reference *does* occur. For now, though, I want to portray him as a "pure" cluster theorist, such that having the appropriate associated descriptions is necessary and sufficient for reference to occur.

16. I believe what I am suggesting here is very much Putnam's (1973) notion of reference borrowing and linguistic division of labor. Though he did not offer this notion in defense of the cluster account, I do not see it as antithetical to the account.

2 The Causal Account

1. It is noteworthy that at the "initial baptism" stage the description theory, for Kripke, might be feasible. He states in a footnote: "the primary applicability of the description theory is to cases of initial baptism" (1980, 96n42). Two things, however, must be emphasized. First, the description used in not synonymous with the name it introduces but rather fixes its reference. Second, most cases of initial baptism are not of the sort that originally inspired the description theory. Usually a baptizer is acquainted in some sense, according to Kripke, with the object he names and is able to name it ostensively. (In a later addendum, Kripke remarks that these brief comments on initial baptism give a somewhat oversimplified picture. He stresses here that "there need not always be an identifiable initial baptism" [1980, 162], though cases of such a lack of identifiable initial baptism are rarer for proper names than for other cases, such as natural kind terms.) Others (e.g., Fodor [2006]) have expressed concerns with the baptismal account, though I will not discuss them further here.

2. Devitt is somewhat vague here, perhaps unavoidably. He states: "we insist only that the object be in the same *very general* category as it is taken to be. There is an element of arbitrariness in our determination of these categories" (1981, 63). I find this quite unhelpful. Devitt claims that if we believe that we are referring to a cat, but the "cat" is in fact a mongoose, then we have referred to a mongoose, whereas if the "cat" is a shadow, then we have referred to nothing. Devitt strikes me as being rather cavalier about this issue, and it is one that I see as important. I will return to it later when discussing the underlying commitments of the alternative accounts of reference.

3. Others, e.g., Evans (1973) and Steinman (1982), have made similar criticisms. Kripke himself acknowledges that in his "better picture" one might never reach a set of necessary and sufficient conditions. Nevertheless, other proponents of the causal account, e.g., Devitt, seem more enamored with establishing such conditions.

4. Searle does not need abstract or "future" objects to show that the necessary condition is faulty. He gives another example: "I can, for example, refer to M Street in Washington [D.C.] simply because I know that there is in that city an alphabetical sequence of street names, 'A,' 'B,' 'C,' etc. I needn't have any causal connection with M Street to do that" (1983, 239). (Of course, we must also assume that Searle knows the English alphabet and that he knows that the street names go up to, at least, M Street, say, by knowing that there is an N Street.)

5. To my knowledge no one has responded in print directly to Searle, though, as noted below, causal account advocates have considered some of the criticisms in some form or other.

6. Donnellan considers several objections to rule (R), which are not essential to the present point, namely, to show how Donnellan could respond to Searle's criticism. Suffice it to say that Donnellan considers himself to have successfully defended rule (R) and his position from the objections that he himself raises.

7. For Devitt, a sentence is true if and only if it is m-true for every structure that corresponds to it (i.e., for every structure in which each of the sentence's designational terms partially designates the object it m-designates and applies to the objects it m-applies to).

8. I should say that although I think Kripke is right on this point, I don't think he has said anything to refute Searle's "infinity of descriptions" objection. The force of Kripke's point and of Searle's objection lies in their respective notions of intention. Kripke makes use of the notion, but, I think, does not flesh it out. A major difference between Searle and Kripke, it seems to me, is that Searle places far more explicit emphasis on the role of intention in reference than does Kripke.

9. There are many cases of reference being fixed by a description, especially for "theoretical" entities. For example, fairly recently scientists at CERN claimed to

"see" the top quark, although it had been dubbed as such, predicted to exist, and sought after for years.

10. This statement should be tempered somewhat. Searle does see differences between the descriptivist account and the causal account. To the extent that Kripke's view works, says Searle, it works because it is descriptivist. Among the differences, Searle lists three that he sees as noteworthy: (1) for the causalists the transfer of intentionality in the reference chain is essential for proper names, for the descriptivists it is incidental; (2) for the causalists the only intentionality that secures reference is that each speaker intends to refer to the same object as the previous speaker, for the descriptivists this is not the case, as other "intentionalities" are important; (3) for the causalists parasitic identifying descriptions are paramount, for the descriptivists they are not. Whether or not Searle is correct in his assessment here is not important for the present concerns.

11. This point, just as some earlier ones related to criticisms of Searle's view, involves the issue of private reference versus public reference, which will be discussed later.

12. The fact that in this first case the name "Gödel" is mentioned rather than used should be irrelevant to a "pure" causal account, since the historical, causal chain is the same. Indeed, it would seem that for a "pure" causal account any mention of a name, as well as any use of a name, would refer as long as the utterance of it is causally connected to previous utterances of the name.

13. Notice the philosophical gymnastics in which Devitt engages in order to avoid talk of intentions. As noted above in this chapter, designation involves three types of links in the designating-chain: (1) groundings, (2) abilities to designate, and (3) communication situations in which abilities are passed on or reinforced. The grounding consists in the person coming to have "grounding thoughts" about that object as a result of the act of perceiving the object. "A grounding thought about an object includes a mental representation of that object brought about by an act of perception. The thought is one which a speaker of a public language would express using a *demonstrative* from that language" (1981, 133). About the ability to designate, Devitt states that his strategy is to tie an ability to an object and a term in virtue of their role in bringing about the relevant mental representations. We have (at least) two abilities: abilities in thought (which are basic) and abilities in speech (or writing, etc.). An ability to designate an object in thought is to have thoughts including tokens that are grounded in the object. If, as Devitt claims, the notion of intention is in as much need of explanation as is the notion of designation, then I want to say likewise for mental representation and his conception of thoughts. Although he never gives an analysis of what a mental representation is, he does say the following about thoughts:

A thought consists of an attitude to a sentence in the language of thought. I continue my former practice of ignoring the fact that most of the thoughts we have we never entertain; also of using the word "thought" to refer to the sentence only. . . . Now a thought token will be "about our cat" in the appropriate sense if it includes a token—a mental representation—that designates her. That token in thought will designate her if she is in fact the object in which the token is grounded. (1981, 131)

I, for one, do not find this a great improvement over talk of intentions. As it turns out, Devitt's prohibitions against talk of intentions is later relaxed, or forgotten, in his discussion of fictional discourse. He introduces an "F operator" to indicate sentences that "can be true even though the contained singular terms are empty" (1981, 130). What determines whether a given sentence token is or is not an F-sentence (i.e., one with an F-operator)? Devitt says: "That is determined by what the speaker had in mind, meant, or intended" (1981, 181).

3   A Wittgensteinian Account

1. In fact, Wittgenstein made this very point toward the end of paragraph 79, that part of the paragraph that Kripke neglected to quote when identifying Wittgenstein as a cluster advocate. It is worth noting that Linsky (1977) did recognize this difference between Wittgenstein and Searle:

[Wittgenstein and Searle] say that the main difficulty with [Russell's] theory is that it ignores a certain looseness in our use of proper names. Proper names, they say, are not, in general, associated by their users with unique descriptions as Russell's theory requires. Here Searle and Wittgenstein part company. Searle thinks that in place of the unique description required by Russell there are a cluster of descriptions which the users of a name associate with it. He thinks that it is a necessary truth that some "sufficiently large" (but indefinite) number of the open sentences on which these descriptions are built are uniquely satisfied by the referent of the name. Wittgenstein's correction to Russell's theory is rather different. He thinks proper names are characteristically used without any fixed meaning; there is neither a unique description nor a cluster of them which fixes the sense of our names. We can use these names without a fixed sense. (1977, 93)

2. This insistence that we often use names without any fixed meaning is tied up with Wittgenstein's notions of language games and rule-following, and his rejection of the distinction between contexts of discovery and contexts of justification. This is not to say that no names have a fixed meaning. What is important in connection with the fixing of meaning when it does occur is that it is done as part of an activity (within a language game), for certain purposes (see Linsky 1977, 104–105). In other words, a word is a name only when it is used as one (as opposed to being used as, say, a demonstrative; see Kripke 1977, 272n9). To be used as a name means that we employ it in calling for, asking about, saying something about, etc., the object being named. See also Canfield 1977, 108–109, where he considers Kripke's case in which a speaker mistakenly says that Jones is raking leaves (but actually Smith is):

It is correct to say that either he'd attribute the predicate ["is raking leaves"] to Jones or to Smith depending on how we take the question. How we take the question is something we have to learn to do. We can take the question in a way that will give only the results that Donnellan intends. But then the right thing to say is that it is the series of examples he gives that teaches us how to take the question. In Wittgensteinian terms Donnellan teaches us a certain language game, one of establishing the speech act referent by answering a certain question in a certain way.

3. Cf. Ishiguro 1969, 23: "Throughout his later works, Wittgenstein discusses the temptation to look in the wrong direction for a mark which would tell us why a word refers to a certain object. We look for mental processes that go on as we utter the words rather than the rule governing the use of the words that we can come to grasp. And similarly in the *Tractatus* Wittgenstein is anxious to stress that we cannot see how the name refers to an object except by understanding the role it plays in propositions."

4. Quine (1969, 31) makes an analogous point (limited to count terms) by arguing that the use of a term like "rabbit" cannot be mastered by pure ostension.

4 The Big Three: Peirce, James, Dewey

1. Unless otherwise noted, all Peirce citations are from the *Collected Papers of Charles Sanders Peirce* (CP) (1931–1935) and (1958). Numbered citations refer to volume number followed by page number. For example, 2.329 refers to volume 2, page 329.

2. One does not need abstract or "future" objects to show that the necessary condition is faulty. Searle gives an example: "I can, for example, refer to M Street in Washington [D.C.] simply because I know that there is in that city an alphabetical sequence of street names, 'A,' 'B,' 'C,' etc. I needn't have any causal connection with M Street to do that" (Searle 1983, 239). (Of course, we must also assume that Searle knows the English alphabet and that he knows that the street names go up to, at least, M Street, say, by knowing that there is an N Street.)

3. However, in some passages, Peirce appears less emphatic that a proper name is uncontroversially an index. For example, shortly before the original passage cited above, he says: "But the proper name so nearly approximates to the nature of an Index, that this might suffice to give an idea of an informational Index" (2.320).

4. All of the discussion in this chapter has focused on names as indices. As was noted, Peirce saw them as genuine indices only when we meet them for the first time. After that, they take on the status of icons and symbols. If Peirce's understanding of names and reference is superior to the causal theory even at the level of indices, it is a fortiori superior at the level of icons and symbols.

5. There are questions about Peirce's views on names yet to be raised. To this point, I have tried to differentiate his views from those of Kripke et al. and I have taken Peirce's semiotic approach to names and reference as being distinct from and superior to the causal account. I am left, however, with several questions.

(1) I take it that it is true for each and every person that a proper name is a genuine index for that person when he or she meets it for the first time. Does this mean that the sign's status changes each time it is met for the first time? When I first encounter the name "Nixon" it is a genuine index *for me*. Tomorrow, when you encounter it for the first time, it is a genuine index *for you*, but now it is an *icon for me*. For Devitt, the name is grounded only once. Is this the case for Peirce? Does the sign itself have a status independent of each of us? How can its status be as variable as it seems to be?

(2) Don't we sometimes "meet" a name for the first time and it is attached, so to speak, to descriptions? ("Come and meet Max the Wonder Dog!") *Must* it be an index on that occasion? Indeed, how is it even recognized as a name (as opposed to, say, a nonsense word or a description or a title or something else)? Is "Max the Wonder Dog" a complex-sounding name or is it a name plus a description? How do I even know, when I first meet it, that it is a name at all rather than gibberish? (The old children's name game could very well be confusing to listeners: e.g., Charles, Charles Bo-barles; Banana-fana Fo-farles; Fi-fie Mo-marles.) Perhaps another way of expressing my concern is: for it to function as a name, must I recognize a sign as a name? (This is related to the problems attached to ostension that many philosophers have wrestled with.)

(3) When Peirce says that after that first encounter we have with a name, we later regard it as an Icon of that Index, how does this happen? Is it by simply recognizing the similarity of phonemes or morphemes? (Surely not, as more than one object can "have the same name," at least same in a common-sense notion of two people named "John Smith.")

(4) When even later a name takes on the status of a Symbol, *must* the Interpretant represent it as an Icon of the Index? What is presupposed here? Does this presuppose recognition that there is the same object and even the same representamen at issue?

6. All references to Dewey's works are from *John Dewey: Collected Works, 1882–1953* (37 volumes), edited by J. A. Boydston, Carbondale: Southern Illinois University Press, 1976–1990. Specific references are to the Early Works (EW), Middle Works (MW), or Later Works (LW). So, for example, LW.16.266 stands for volume 16, page 266 of the later works.

7. There are numerous examples of Dewey's emphasis on language as being primarily communicative: EW.5.226, MW.6.321, MW.7.266, LW.1.141, LW.8.308, LW.17.236.

5 Contemporary Americans: Putnam, Elgin, and Rorty

1. Mark Quentin Gardiner (2000) has suggested that there have been "two Putnams," Putnam the Elder (pre-1976) and Putnam the Younger (post-1976). Perhaps he would acknowledge an even younger Putnam (post-1990). Whereas

in the 1990s, Putnam somewhat shied away from identifying himself with pragmatism, in his most recent work, e.g., *Ethics without Ontology* (2004), he reiterates his appreciation of American pragmatism and speaks of his position as "pragmatic pluralism."

2. Two essays published in 1973, "Explanation and Reference" (reprinted in Putnam 1975b, 196–214) and "Meaning and Reference," present abbreviated versions of what is expanded much more fully in "The Meaning of 'Meaning.'"(reprinted in Putnam 1975b, 215–271). Even more important is his 1970 essay, "Is Semantics Possible?" (reprinted in Putnam 1975a).

3. It is worth noting that in spite of the many affinities and similarities between Kripke and Putnam, Kripke does not embrace Putnam's linguistic division of labor notion. In his essay, "A Problem in the Theory of Reference: The Linguistic Division of Labor and the Social Character of Naming," Kripke calls Putnam's notion a *suggestio falsi*. Kripke says:

It is of course true that the experts have a special capacity that we don't have for telling whether something is or is not gold. That is among other things what makes them experts. So far, I don't see that one has to refer to linguistic division of labor here or to any special linguistic capacity of the experts. . . . There is no reason to think that the extension of the term in my mouth depends on the existence or availability of any special class of experts in this sense. The term just means what it does. It may be difficult or hard to determine whether something is in the extension; this is a special problem of what we are going to know. Sometimes we may not know what terms are in the extension, what objects are in the extension or not, for a very long time. But the experts provide no help as far as actually determining the extension of the term. They only help us find out after a while which things actually fall into the extension of the term. (1986, 244)

He ends his essay with this reiteration: "There is no special linguistic role to be given to any special substratum of the community. The community can in fact have a completely prevailing erroneous misconception either about a natural kind term or about a proper name provided the appropriate historical connections exist. Any suggestion that some special subclasses of theory are going to save the situation is, I think, wrong" (1986, 247).

4. Putnam reiterates this view of explanation later in his 1989 essay "Model Theory and the 'Factuality' of Semantics" (reprinted in *Words and Life* [1994], 354–358), as well as, though with perhaps a somewhat different emphasis, in his more recent work (e.g., *The Threefold Cord* [1999], esp. 144–145).

5. In *The Many Faces of Realism* (1987, 39), he mentions explicitly Devitt, Glymour, Boyd, and Barwise and Perry. Putnam continues to this day (see, e.g., Putnam 1995a, 65, 1992, 35, 1994, 358) to reject purported attempts to define or reduce reference in terms of causation.

6. In Putnam 2001, he states that he no longer accepts the theory of truth that he espoused in *Reason, Truth, and History*.

7. For example, besides his book *Pragmatism: An Open Question*, he has published essays with titles like "Pragmatism," "Pragmatism and Realism," "James's Theory of Truth," and "The Real William James."

8. In *Between the Absolute and the Arbitrary* (1997), Elgin uses the term "constructivism" rather than "constructionalism." Throughout most of her writings, however, the latter term is used.

9. Searle is not even mentioned in *Reconceptions in Philosophy* (Goodman and Elgin 1988) or in *Considered Judgment* (Elgin 1996), nor in any of Elgin's post-1990 essays.

10. This is not to say that she denies that the concept of rigid designation is coherent. Rather, she takes the concept, and the rigid–nonrigid distinction, to be pragmatic, not metaphysical. See Elgin 1997, 169n15.

11. In spite of his take here that Kripke is less mistaken and more misguided, Rorty clearly disagrees with specific aspects of Kripke's view, for example, that it makes sense to talk of "this X" independent of some category or description. For Rorty, "Thinghood, identity, is itself description-relative" (1991b, 4). This opposition to Kripkean commitments extends to general ontology. In his recent book, *Philosophy and Social Hope*, Rorty claims that natural kinds are not given:

> Bank accounts are made, giraffes are found. Now the truth in this view is simply that if there had been no human beings there would still have been giraffes, whereas there would have been no bank accounts. But this causal independence of giraffes from humans does not mean that giraffes are what they are apart from human needs and interests. On the contrary, we describe giraffes in the way we do, *as* giraffes, because of our needs and interests. We speak a language which includes the word "giraffe" because it suits our purposes to do so. (1999, xxvi)

12. However, in his 1984 review of Searle's *Intentionality*, Rorty sounds slightly harsher in his assessment of the underlying commitments of both Searle and Kripke: "Do we *have* to carve things up into the subject and the object (or into language and the world, intentional states and their objects, what is in the head and what is not) in the first place? Are Kripke-style causal theories of reference and Searle-style theories of intentional causation alternative theories about how nature works, or are they alternative patchwork repairs of a badly-functioning and obsolescent contrivance?" (1984a, 4).

6   Across the Pond: Eco, Apel, and Habermas

1. Carrying the semiological mode even further, Eco (1984) considers whether a mirror image is, or at least functions like, a proper name or rigid designator:

> In an extreme attempt to find one more relation between mirror images and words, we might compare mirror images to proper names. . . . [But] there is a difference between a mirror image and a proper name, in that a mirror image is an *absolute proper name* as it is an absolute icon. In other words, the semiotic dream of proper names being immediately linked to their referent . . . arises from a sort of *catoptric nostalgia*. . . . Such catoptric apparatus would be a rigid-designa-

tion apparatus. There is no linguistic contrivance which would provide the same guarantee, not even a proper name, because in this event two conditions of absolutely rigid designation would be missing: (1) the original object might well not exist at the moment and also might never have existed; (2) there would be no guarantee that the name corresponds to that object alone and to no other having similar characteristics.

We therefore come to discover that the semantics of rigid designation is in the end a (pseudo-) semantics of the mirror image and that no linguistic term can be a rigid designator (just as there is no absolute icon). If it cannot be absolute, any rigid designator other than a mirror image, any rigid designator whose rigidity may be undermined in different ways and under different conditions, becomes a *soft or slack designator*. As absolutely rigid designators, mirror images alone cannot be questioned by counterfactuals. In fact, I could never ask myself (without violating the pragmatic principles regulating any relation with mirrors): "If the object whose image I am perceiving had properties other than those of the image I perceive, would it still be the same object?" But this guarantee is provided precisely by the threshold-phenomenon a mirror is. The theory of rigid designation falls a victim of the magic of mirrors. (1984, 211–213)

Given the distortions of "fun house" mirrors, I would add that one could indeed ask oneself whether the object whose image one is perceiving would be the same object if it had properties other than those presently perceived!

2. In his earlier works, especially *The Role of the Reader*, Eco's account of haecceity and individuation is intimately tied up with a Peircean semiotic view. Here he claims that "this object is only such insofar as it is thought under a certain profile" (1979, 181). Being a sign, anything, including any "thisness," must involve an interpretation (or representamen) and that carries with it the unlimited semiosis noted above. This necessarily includes an element of habit, or law, required for the general applicability of the notion of "thisness" (e.g., "this" entails "not that").

3. Eco cites this example from Peirce on a number of occasions, e.g., Eco 1976, 131; Eco and Sebeok 1983, 203; 1990, 157.

4. Though Eco does not delve into the nature of cause, obviously, from a semiological point of view, whatever counts as a cause is some form of sign that presupposes an underlying abductive relation.

5. The connection to Wittgenstein, via Steinman here, is neither accidental nor incidental for Eco. In *Kant and the Platypus*, he makes an explicit connection to Wittgenstein by citing the latter's remarks that one must not confuse the meaning of a name with the bearer of a name (see Wittgenstein 1953, para. 40). Eco claims that "acts of reference are possible only insofar as we know the meaning of the terms used for referring" (2000, 288), a view, he suggests, that runs counter to Kripke's notion of rigid designation.

6. Cf. Apel 1980, 112: "Both [understanding and explanation] are included, in fact, in the sign-mediated knowledge of something *as* something: mediation between subject and object in the form of an interpretation of the world *and* mediation between human subjects in the form of the interpretation of language."

7. Having noted the importance of intentionality in relation to reference, Apel nonetheless rejects a descriptivist view of reference. In the context of discussing Wittgenstein and hermeneutic understanding, he remarks that Wittgenstein "draws attention to the fact that the meaning function of words is fixed by their standard usage in such a manner that the intentional act of meaning something is not only superfluous but also hardly has a chance of asserting its intention against such a usage . . . it is not the fact that in speaking we 'parade the meanings before our minds' which is decisive for the meaning of verbal utterances but rather that the utterances occur in a language-game in which meaning, on the one hand, and understanding on the other, are fixed by means of a public rule, an institutional 'habit'" (Apel 1980, 26).

8. "Linguistics *qua* science of man's linguistic competence—linguistics competence in general and linguistic competence with reference to specific languages—is not concerned with the *ad hoc* 'understanding' of individual utterances" (Apel 1980, 193).

9. See Mendieta 2002, 91–96. He discusses several other aspects of Apel's overall views, especially in terms of discourse ethics, that are not included here.

10. A second major influence, though one outside the present scope, was Mead.

11. While not explicitly claiming that Habermas holds a descriptivist view, Cristina Lafont (1999) notes his reliance and resonance with Searle's speech-act views and lobbies hard for supplementing Habermas's views with a direct reference view.

12. Habermas has never mentioned Fultner or Thompson in print. About Lafont, he has only quipped that she "follows her own agenda of defending realism all the way down" (Aboulafia, Bookman, and Kemp 2002, 223).

13. Habermas acknowledges that Peirce's semiotic analysis encompasses much more than linguistic forms of expression. He calls the expansion of the world of symbolic forms beyond the limits of linguistic forms of expression "the great achievement of Peircean semiotic" (1992, 107).

7   Individuation and Similarity

1. See Margolis 2002 for a detailed discussion of Putnam vs. Rorty.

2. Elgin (1980) makes this same point with regard to the notion of scientific progress.

3. The reason we "are well aware which of the two incompatible predictions is genuinely confirmed," for Goodman, finally boils down to pragmatic considerations. English (at least in this case) works better than the gruesome language.

4. Goodman repeats this theme throughout his writings: There are many different equally true descriptions of the world, and their truth is the only standard of their faithfulness. And when we say of them that they all involve conventionalizations, we are saying that no one of these different descriptions is *exclusively* true, since the others are also true. None of them tells us the way the world is, but each of them tells us *a* way the world is (1972, 31).

Frames of reference, though, seem to belong less to what is described than to systems of description. . . . If I ask about the world, you can offer to tell me how it is under one or more frames of reference; but if I insist that you tell me how it is apart from all frames, what can you say? We are confined to ways of describing whatever is described. Our universe, so to speak, consists of these ways rather than of a world or of worlds. (1978, 2–3)

5. Even Nagel (1961) accepts the presence of "characterizing value judgments" (as opposed to "appraising value judgments") as part of science. These characterizing value judgments are a version of what I am calling cognitive values.

6. Another argument for the interest-dependence of theories is that theories are, in large part, metaphorical (cf. Kuhn 1962, 1977, 1983; Hesse 1974, 1980, 1983; Rothbart 1984). Quite simply, metaphors reflect and display our interests and languages; these metaphors are an integral part of our theories.

7. Such a treatment of individuals might seem strange because our commonsense notion of individuals is that they are clearly demarcated objects, each with a distinct spatiotemporal continuity. However, Quine (1976) and Goodman (1972) have both argued that there is no good reason to forbid the conception of individuals that consist of widely scattered and very unlike parts. (Quine, for example, see nothing wrong with speaking of mass terms, such as sugar, as individuals.) Leonard and Goodman (1940) pursued this conception of individuals to the point of attempting to construct a calculus to accommodate it.

8. There has been some debate whether events can be treated as individuals. Davidson (1970), I think, has argued conclusively that they can.

9. See also Thomson 1965 for further argumentation for a nonrealist treatment of experimental replicability.

10. In fact, Kripke's presentation of his Gödel–Schmidt counterexample to what he calls thesis (3) of the cluster account of reference begs the issue. Kripke says: "For example, it is argued, if we say, 'Gödel proved the incompleteness of arithmetic,' we are, of course, referring to Gödel, not to Schmidt" (1980, 85n36). This begs the issue because by saying, "we are, of course, referring to Gödel" Kripke seems to think that this instance of "Gödel" clearly refers to an independently located object. But it doesn't. Who is he referring to here? It won't help to say, "Well, to Gödel, of course," because that is just what is at issue. Kripke seems to take it that we could, if need be, rely on ostension to pick out Gödel.

11. Indeed, much of the discussion above about partitioning could be interpreted as being more explicitly related to similarity than to individuation. For example, the green–grue question is a question of whether emeralds are similar with respect to color. Of course, one of the points of this chapter is that there is no clear distinction between issues of individuation and issues of similarity.

12. For an interesting and detailed discussion of similarity and its significance for philosophy of science, see Barnes 1982.

13. The issue of natural kinds has been one that has generated a lot of attention within the philosophy of biology. A large body of literature has flowered concerning the notion of species versus individuals (or species as sets versus species as individuals). See, e.g., Hull 1978, Kitts and Kitts 1979, Dupre 1981, Holsinger 1984, and Kitcher 1984. Similar conceptual difficulties as those noted in the text above exist for asexual and nonbiological entities.

14. It is interesting to note that with regard to this point, a footnote of Kripke's sounds quite reminiscent of his thesis (5) of the cluster account (viz., the statement, "If X exists, then X has most of the ϕ's" is *known* a priori by the speaker). Kripke says in the text (with regard to the baptismal reference fixing): "Several features of this baptism are worthy of note. First, the identity in the definition does not express a (completely) necessary truth: though each of these items is, indeed, essentially (necessarily) gold, gold might have existed even if the items did not" (1980, 135). His note 69 reads:

Assuming, of course, that they are all gold; as I say below, some may be fool's gold. We know in advance, *a priori*, that it is not the case that the items are *typically* fool's gold; and all those items which are actually gold are, of course, essentially gold. (1980, 135n69)

Now, it is not obvious to me that there is any difference between "If Aristotle exists, then Aristotle has most of the ϕs" and "If gold exists , then gold has most of the ϕ's." Although Kripke explicitly states that we must distinguish between the reference-fixing properties of an object and the (I take it) essential properties of an object, this reminder does not prove to be so helpful. For example, suppose one of the reference-fixing properties is an essential property, and we know it (supposing that there are essential properties and that we can in fact recognize them). It would seem, then, that Kripke is committed to the a prioricity thesis. A possible response to this claim is that even if one of the reference-fixing properties is an essential property, that establishes a necessary truth, not a priori knowledge. One might say, it might be the case that an essential reference-fixing property is (necessarily) true of an object, but it doesn't follow that we know this a priori. However, it seems to me that if we fix the reference of a term a priori and if, when doing that, we know that one of the reference fixing properties is essential, then we know a priori that if that thing (stuff) exists, then it has—if not most of—one of the ϕ's. For example, suppose in 1947 (before Israel became a sovereign state, but knowing that it soon would be), someone said, "Anyone born in Israel is an Israeli citizen." It seems to me that the speaker knows a priori that if someone is born in Israel after time t (where time t is when Israel attains statehood), then that person is an Israeli citizen (i.e., if X exists, then X has one of the φ's). It might be argued that being a citizen, or being an Israeli citizen, is not a natural kind, but, of course, that is part of what is at issue (viz., what a [natural] kind is). Besides, the point here is that Kripke sounds quite a bit like the cluster account of reference that he criticizes.

8   Haecceities and Essentialism

1. I use "object" here to refer to both individuals and kinds. For example, as I will note below, species can be thought of as individuals. As will be seen, the distinction between individuals and kinds has been important. It is a distinction that I reject (at least as it is usually presented).

2. I am not making an "existence" restriction here. That is, I am not saying that for an object to have essential properties, it must have them in order for that object to exist, but simply in order for it to be what it is. I take the issue of essences and essentialism as issues of identity, not of existence.

3. I will return to this issue, and strengthen my claims here, shortly. First, I need to explicitly address the distinction between individuals and kinds.

4. Extensionally, there are cases where kinds are indistinguishable from individuals that make up the kind (e.g., "even prime numbers" and "2").

5. Actually, there is a sense in which I do not think that Searle is committed to essentialism here. I will make this explicit at the end of this chapter when I discuss what I see as a legitimate way of talking about essentialism.

6. This commitment is borne out in such claims as the following: "In order that a name should ever come to be used to refer to an object in the first place there must be some independent representation of the object. This may be by way of perception, memory, definite description, etc., but there must be enough Intentional content to identify which object the name is attached to" (Searle 1983, 259).

7. I should add at this point that, just as I see much of what Searle claims as correct to an extent, so, too, I see much of what Kripke claims as correct to an extent. At the end of this chapter I will argue for what is basically right about both of their views on essences. First, however, just as I criticized Searle, I want to now criticize Kripke.

8. This sounds like Searle's claim that being a person is analytically true of this person (e.g., de Gaulle).

9. Of course, for Kripke, "a clearly identifiable object" is meant metaphysically. Nixon is Nixon whether we know it or not, and "Nixon" is a rigid designator because it refers to that object in all possible worlds.

10. An important objection that might be raised here is that I have misrepresented Kripke's position when I accuse him of being committed to essentialism through the notion of rigid designation. I claim that there must be some property (or properties) common to, say, Nixon in all possible worlds such that "Nixon" refers to that object in all of those worlds. That property (or properties), I suggest, is what is essential to Nixon. What else, I asked, could guarantee that Nixon is referred to by "Nixon" in all possible worlds? One answer to this question—other than the requirement of essential properties—is that Kripke simply stipulates that "Nixon" refers to the same object in all possible worlds. Indeed, this seems to be Kripke's explicit position. He says:

Don't ask: how can I identify this table in another possible world, except by its properties? I have the table in my hands, I can point to it, and when I ask whether it might have been in another room, I am talking, by definition, about *it*. I don't have to identify it after seeing it through a telescope. If I am talking about it, I am talking about it, in the same way as when I say that our hands might have been painted green, I have stipulated that I am talking about greenness. Some properties of an object may be essential to it, in that it could not have failed to have them. But these properties are not used to identify the object in another possible world, for such an identification is not needed. Nor need the essential properties of an object be the properties used to identify it in the actual world, if indeed it is identified in the actual world by means of properties (I have up to now left the question open). . . . So, we do not begin with worlds (which are supposed somehow to be real, and whose qualities, but not whose objects, are perceptible to us), and then ask about criteria of transworld identification; on the contrary, we begin with objects, which we *have*, and can identify, in the actual world. We can then ask whether certain things might have been true of the objects. (1980, 52–53)

I want to say (repeat) several things about this view. As I have said above, the issue that I see as the important one is not that of transworld identity or transworld identification or transworld individuation, but of identity–identification–individuation in this world. Kripke's quote seems to me to indicate that we start with an identified object ("I am talking, by definition, about *it*") and we can then simply stipulate that we are talking about that object. Much of what I am arguing for in this chapter and the previous one is that Kripke is mistaken in suggesting that he can do just that. (This will come out clearer in this chapter and the next.) When Kripke says that he is, by definition, talking about *it*, I want to ask: about what? Kripke seems to presume that we can clearly separate out issues of individuation from issues of identification. I am suggesting that we can't. We cannot, contra Kripke, simply stipulate that we are talking about, say, Nixon and presume that we are referring to Nixon in all possible worlds merely by using the name "Nixon." Indeed, I am somewhat perplexed that Kripke would want to make such a move, since it seems (to me, anyway) that this divorces the name from any public, historical, linguistic context—the very point for which he criticizes Searle's theory of names. Although it may be true that a move to postulating the stipulation of (the identity of) an object across possible worlds relieves Kripke from a commitment to essentialism, the cost, I would argue, is too great. The issue is whether or not one can stipulate in this world the identity (or individuation) of an object. To the extent that this can be done, it is possible only given a public language and only to the extent that the language community accepts such a stipulation. As Kripke himself says, I cannot refer to Schmidt by (the use of) "Gödel." Nor, I want to add, can I do so by stipulating that I am referring to Schmidt by (the use of) "Gödel" (unless the language community agrees, and, as a result, "Gödel" becomes another name for Schmidt). Additionally, I cannot separate out the issues of the individuation of an object (say, Nixon) from the issues of the identification of that object. That is, I think Kripke is simply wrong to claim that he is talking about it (say, Nixon) and that this makes no commitment to talking about the means of identifying *it*. When Kripke says he's talking about *it*, and I ask, about what, Kripke cannot respond by saying that my question misses the point because it is asking for the identification of the object that has already been individuated (by stipulation). Kripke's position seems to be committed to the following: in a given possible world Nixon is not only not a president, but Nixon is not even a human; rather, Nixon is a particular dime. When I ask: how do you know that this dime is Nixon and not that dime, Kripke's answer, it seems to me, can only be: because I said so! If indeed this is Kripke's move to avoid a commitment to essentialism, then I suggest that he has avoided the commitment, but only at the cost of incoherence.

11. Of course, what I have said about rigid designation and essentialism with respect to names applies mutatis mutandis with respect to natural kinds.

9 Neptune and Nemesis

1. A literary example of the social nature of names comes from Jhumpa Lahiri's novel, *The Namesake*. In the following passage, a young boy, Gogol Ganguli, is being registered on the first day at school:

"Welcome to elementary school, Nikhil. I am your principal, Mrs. Lapidus."

Gogol looked down at his sneakers. The way the principal pronounces his new name is different from the way his parents say it, the second part of it longer, sounding like "heel."

She bends down so that his face is level with his, and extends a hand to his shoulder. "Can you tell me how old you are, Nikhil?"

When the question is repeated and there is still no response, Mrs. Lapidus asks, "Mr. Ganguli, does Nikhil follow English?"

"Of course, he follows," Ashoke says. "My son is perfectly bilingual."

In order to prove that Gogol knows English, Ashoke does something he has never done before, and addresses his son in careful, accented English. "Go on Gogol," he says, patting him on the head. "Tell Mrs. Lapidus how old you are."

"What was that?" Mrs. Lapidus says.

"I beg your pardon, madam?"

"That name you called him. Something with a *G*."

"Oh that, that is what we call him at home only. But his good name should be—is"—he nods his head firmly—"Nikhil."

Mrs. Lapidus frowns. "I'm afraid I don't understand. Good name?"

"Yes."

Mrs. Lapidus studies the registration form. She has not had to go through this confusion with the other two Indian children. She opens up the folder and examines the immunization record, the birth certificate. "There seems to be some confusion, Mr. Ganguli," she says. "According to these documents, your son's legal name is Gogol."

"That is correct. But please allow me to explain—"

"That you want us to call him Nikhil."

"That is correct."

Mrs. Lapidus nods. "The reason being?"

"That is our wish."

"I'm not sure I follow you, Mr. Ganguli. Do you mean that Nikhil is a middle name? Or a nickname? Many of the children go by nicknames here. On this form there is a space—"

"No, no, it's not a middle name," Ashoke says. He is beginning to lose patience. "He has no middle name. No nickname. The boy's good name, his school name, is Nikhil."

Mrs. Lapidus presses her lips together and smiles. "But clearly he doesn't respond."

"Please, Mrs. Lapidus," Ashoke says. "It is very common for a child to be confused at first. Please give it some time. I assure you he will grow accustomed."

He bends down and this time in Bengali, calmly and quietly, asks Gogol to please answer when Mrs. Lapidus asks a question. "Don't be scared, Gogol," he says, raising his son's chin with his finger. "You're a big boy now. No tears."

Though Mrs. Lapidus does not understand a word, she listens carefully, hears that name again, Gogol. Lightly, in pencil, she writes it down on the registration form.

Ashoke hands over the lunch box, a windbreaker in case it gets cold. He thanks Mrs. Lapidus. "Be good, Nikhil," he says in English. And then, after a moment's hesitation, he is gone.

When they are alone, Mrs. Lapidus asks, "Are you happy to be entering elementary school, Gogol?"

"My parents want me to have another name in school."

"And what about you, Gogol? Do you want to be called by another name?"

After a pause, he shakes his head.

"Is that a no?"

He nods. "Yes."

"Then it's settled. Can you write your name on this piece of paper?"

Gogol picks up a pencil, grips it tightly, and forms the letters of the only word he has learned thus far to write from memory, getting the "L" backward due to nerves. "What beautiful penmanship you have," Mrs. Lapidus says. She tears up the old registration form and asks Mrs. McNab to type up a new one. Then she takes Gogol by the hand, down a carpeted hallway with painted cement walls. (*The Namesake*, 57–59)

2. I need to make an important distinction here. In response to the following discussion of Searle's and Kripke's commitment to intentionality and private reference, one might object that a commitment to intentionality does not commit Searle or Kripke to private language. The reason for this is that speakers intend to refer to public, not private, entities (i.e., entities that are "out there" independent of any speaker's intentions). Being committed to intentionality, then, does not entail being committed to private reference because the objects being referred to are public. I want to claim that this objection fails because it rests on a particular conception of individuation of objects, a topic discussed in the previous two chapters.

3. This critique of the role of intention applies not simply to the notion of private reference, but to reference in general.

4. Rhees (1954, 81–82) makes the same point: "I know a headache when I feel it, and I know I felt giddy yesterday afternoon, because I know what giddiness is. . . . But the identity—the sameness—comes from the language . . . without language I could not have told whether this feels the same, either; if only because I could not have asked."

5. Anscombe makes much the same point:

Let us suppose that the thought in [a man's] mind is "you silly little twit!" Now here too, it is not enough that these words should occur to him. He has to mean them. This shews once more, that you cannot take any performance (even an interior performance) as itself an act of intention; for if you describe a performance, the fact that it has taken place is not proof of intention; words for example may occur in somebody's mind without his meaning them. So intention is never a performance in the mind, though in some matters a performance in the mind which is seriously *meant* may make a difference to the correct account of the man's action—e.g., in embracing someone. But the matters in question are necessarily ones in which outward acts are "significant" in some other way. (1957, 49)

It seems to me that not only is Anscombe arguing against a private notion of intentionality, but also she is alluding to the same point that Elgin (1983) makes, of the interrelation between intention and interpretation.

References

Abel, Reuben. 1982. "What is an explanandum?" *Pacific Philosophical Quarterly* 63: 86–92.

Aboulafia, Mitchell, Myra Bookman, and Catherine Kemp (eds.). 2002. *Habermas and Pragmatism.* New York: Routledge.

Alvarez, Luis, Walter Alvarez, Frank Asaro, and Helen V. Michel. 1980. "Extraterrestrial cause for the Cretaceous-Tertiary extinction." *Science* 208: 1095–1108.

Anscombe, G. E. M. 1957. *Intention.* Oxford: Oxford University Press.

Apel, Karl-Otto. 1980. *Towards a Transformation of Philosophy.* London: Routledge and Kegan Paul.

Apel, Karl-Otto. 1981. *Charles S. Peirce: From Pragmatism to Pragmaticism.* Amherst: University of Massachusetts Press.

Apel, Karl-Otto. 1984. *Understanding and Explanation.* Cambridge, Mass.: MIT Press.

Apel, Karl-Otto. 1991. "Is intentionality more basic than linguistic meaning?" In Lapore and Van Gulick 1991, 31–55.

Apel, Karl-Otto. 1994. *Karl-Otto Apel: Selected Essays,* volume 1: *Towards a Transcendental Semiotics.* Atlantic Highlands: Humanities Press.

Apel, Karl-Otto. 1996. *Karl-Otto Apel: Selected Essays,* volume 2: *Ethics and the Theory of Rationality.* Atlantic Highlands: Humanities Press.

Apel, Karl-Otto. 1998. *From a Transcendental-semiotic Point of View.* Manchester: Manchester University Press.

Apel, Karl-Otto. 2001. "Pragmatism as sense-critical realism based on a regulative idea of truth: In defense of a Peircean theory of reality and truth." *Transactions of the Charles S. Peirce Society* 37: 443–474.

Asquith, Peter D., and Ronald Giere (eds.). 1981. *PSA 1980,* volume 2. East Lansing: Philosophy of Science Association.

Asquith, Peter D., and Thomas Nickles (eds.). 1983. *PSA 1982*, volume 2. East Lansing: Philosophy of Science Association.

Barnes, Barry. 1982. *T. S. Kuhn and Social Science*. New York: Columbia University Press.

Bernstein, Richard (ed.) 1985. *Habermas and Modernity*. Cambridge, Mass.: MIT Press.

Boer, Steven E. 1972. "On Searle's analysis of reference." *Analysis* 32: 154–159.

Boersema, David. 1988–1989. "Is the descriptivist/cluster theory of reference 'wrong from the fundamentals?'" *Philosophy Research Archives* 14: 517–538.

Boersema, David. 2002a. "Peirce on names and reference." *Transactions of the Charles S. Peirce Society* 37: 351–362.

Boersema, David. 2002b. "Wittgenstein on names." *Essays in Philosophy* 3, no. 2 (June). Available at www.humboldt.edu/~essays.

Boersema, David. 2005. "Eco on names and reference." *Contemporary Pragmatism* 2: 167-184.

Boersema, David. 2007. "Geach on proper names." In *Proceedings of the Twenty-First World Congress of Philosophy*, volume 6: *Epistemology*, edited by Dermot Moran and Stephen Voss, 37–42. Ankara: Philosophical Society of Turkey.

Brandom, Robert (ed.). 2000. *Rorty and His Critics*. Oxford: Blackwell.

Brody, Baruch A. 1980. *Identity and Essence*. Princeton: Princeton University Press.

Burch, Robert. 1979. "James and the 'new theory of reference.'" *Transactions of the Charles S. Peirce Society* 15: 283–297.

Burke, Tom. 1994. *Dewey's New Logic*. Chicago: University of Chicago Press.

Canfield, John V. 1977. "Donnellan's theory of names." *Dialogue* 16: 104–127.

Cartwright, Richard. 1968. "Some Remarks on Essentialism." *Journal of Philosophy* 65: 615–627.

Chomsky, Noam. 2000. *New Horizons in the Study of Language and Mind*. Cambridge: Cambridge University Press.

Cohen, Robert S., Paul K. Feyerabend, and Marx W. Wartofsky (eds.). 1976. *Essays in Memory of Imre Lakatos*. Dordrecht: D. Reidel.

Cohen, Robert S., and Marx W. Wartofsky (eds.). 1965. *Boston Studies in the Philosophy of Science*, volume 2: *In Honor of Philipp Frank*. New York: Humanities Press.

Cooke, Maeve. 1994. *Language and Reason*. Cambridge, Mass.: MIT Press.

Davidson, Donald. 1970. "The individuation of events." In Rescher 1970, 216–234.

Davidson, Donald, and Gilbert Harman (eds.). 1972. *Semantics of Natural Language*. Dordrecht: D. Reidel.

Davis, M., P. Hut, and R. A. Muller. 1984. "Extinction of species by periodic comet showers." *Nature* 308: 715–717.

Devitt, Michael. 1981. *Designation*. New York: Columbia University Press.

Devitt, Michael. 1984. *Realism and Truth*. Princeton: Princeton University Press.

Devitt, Michael. 1987. *Language and Reality*. Cambridge, Mass.: MIT Press.

Devitt, Michael. 1989. "Against direct reference." *Midwest Studies in Philosophy* 14: 206–240.

Devitt, Michael. 1998. "Reference." *Routledge Encyclopedia of Philosophy*, volume 8: 153–164. New York: Routledge

Dewey, John. 1976–1990. *John Dewey: Collected Works, 1882–1953* (37 volumes). Edited by J. A. Boydston. Carbondale: Southern Illinois University Press.

Dews, Peter. 1986. *Autonomy and Solidarity: Interviews with Jürgen Habermas*. London: Verso.

Donnellan, Keith. 1966. "Reference and definite descriptions." *Philosophical Review* 75: 281–304.

Donnellan, Keith. 1972. "Proper names and identifying descriptions." In Davidson and Harman 1972, 356–379.

Donnellan, Keith. 1974. "Speaking of nothing." *Philosophical Review* 83: 3–31.

Dupre, J. 1981. "Natural kinds and biological taxa." *Philosophical Review* 90: 66–90.

Eco, Umberto. 1976. *A Theory of Semiotics*. Bloomington: Indiana University Press.

Eco, Umberto. 1979. *The Role of the Reader*. Bloomington: Indiana University Press.

Eco, Umberto. 1984. *Semiotics and the Philosophy of Language*. Bloomington: Indiana University Press.

Eco, Umberto. 1987. "Meaning and denotation." *Synthese* 73: 549–568.

Eco, Umberto. 1989. *The Open Work*. Cambridge, Mass.: Harvard University Press.

Eco, Umberto. 1990. *The Limits of Interpretation*. Bloomington: Indiana University Press.

Eco, Umberto. 1992. *Interpretation and Overinterpretation*. Cambridge: Cambridge University Press.

Eco, Umberto. 1994. *Six Walk in the Fictional Woods*. Cambridge, Mass.: Harvard University Press.

Eco, Umberto. 1995. *The Search for a Perfect Language*. Cambridge: Blackwell.

Eco, Umberto. 1998. *Serendipities*. New York: Columbia University Press.

Eco, Umberto. 2000. *Kant and the Platypus*. New York: Harcourt Brace.

Eco, Umberto, Marco Santambrogio, and Patrizia Violi (eds.). 1988. *Meaning and Mental Representation*. Bloomington: Indiana University Press.

Eco, Umberto, and Thomas A. Sebeok (eds.). 1983. *The Sign of Three*. Bloomington: Indiana University Press.

Elgin, Catherine Z. 1976. "Analysis and the picture theory in the *Tractatus*." *Philosophy Research Archives* 2: 1116.

Elgin, Catherine Z. 1979. "Quine's double standard: Indeterminacy and quantifying in." *Synthese* 42: 353–377.

Elgin, Catherine Z. 1980. "Lawlikeness and the End of Science." *Philosophy of Science* 47: 56–68.

Elgin, Catherine Z. 1983. *With Reference to Reference*. Indianapolis: Hackett.

Elgin, Catherine Z. 1984. "Review of Richard Rorty's *Consequences of Pragmatism*." *Erkenntnis* 21: 423–431.

Elgin, Catherine Z. 1987. "The cost of correspondence." *Philosophy and Phenomenological Research* 47: 475–480.

Elgin, Catherine Z. 1991a. "What Goodman leaves out." *Journal of Aesthetic Education* 25: 89–96.

Elgin, Catherine Z. 1991b. "Understanding: Art and science." In French, Uehling, and Wettstein 1991, 196–208.

Elgin, Catherine Z. 1993. "Scheffler's symbols." *Synthese* 94: 3–12.

Elgin, Catherine Z. 1996. *Considered Judgment*. Princeton: Princeton University Press.

Elgin, Catherine Z. 1997. *Between the Arbitrary and the Absolute*. Ithaca: Cornell University Press.

Elgin, Catherine Z. 1997. "The power of parsimony." *Philosophia Scientiae* 2: 89–104.

Elgin, Catherine Z. 2000a. "Interpretation and understanding." *Erkenntnis* 52: 175–183.

Elgin, Catherine Z. 2000b."Reorienting Aesthetics, Reconceiving Cognition." *Journal of Aesthetics and Art Criticism* 58: 219–225.

Evans, Gareth. 1973. "The causal theory of names." *Aristotelian Society Supplementary Volume* 47: 187–208.

Evans, Gareth. 1985. *Collected Papers*. Oxford: Clarendon Press.

Fischer, A. G., and M. A. Arthur. 1977. "Secular variations in the pelagic realm." In *Deep-water Carbonate Environments, Society of Economic Paleontologists and Mineralogists Special Publication* 25 (ed. H. E. Cook and P. Enos): 19–50.

Flew, Antony (ed.). 1975. *Logic and Language*. Garden City, N.Y.: Doubleday Anchor Books.

Flew, Antony (ed.). 1979. *A Dictionary of Philosophy*. New York: St. Martin's Press.

Fodor, Jerry. 1990. *A Theory of Content*. Cambridge, Mass.: The MIT Press.

Fodor, Jerry. 2006. "What is universally quantified and necessary and a posteriori and it flies south in the winter?" *Proceedings and Addresses of the American Philosophical Association* 80: 11–24.

Forbes, Graeme. 1998. "Proper names." In *Routledge Encyclopedia of Philosophy*, volume 7: 752–757. New York: Routledge.

Frege, Gottlob. 1994. "On sense and reference." In Harnish 1994, 142–160.

French, Peter, Theodore Uehling, Jr., and Howard Wettstein (eds.). 1991. *Philosophy and the Arts: Midwest Studies in Philosophy*, volume 16. Notre Dame: University of Notre Dame Press.

Gardiner, Mark Quentin. 2000. *Semantic Challenges to Realism: Dummett and Putnam*. Toronto: University of Toronto Press.

Geach, Peter. 1957. *Mental Acts*. London: Routledge and Kegan Paul.

Geach, Peter. 1962. *Reference and Generality*. Ithaca, N.Y.: Cornell University Press.

Geach, Peter. 1969. "The Perils of Pauline." *Review of Metaphysics* 23: 287–300.

Ghiselin, M. 1974. "A radical solution to the species problem." *Systematic Zoology* 23: 536–544.

Goodman, Nelson. 1965. *Fact, Fiction, and Forecast,* 2nd edition. Indianapolis: Bobbs-Merrill.

Goodman, Nelson. 1972. *Problems and Projects*. Indianapolis: Bobbs-Merrill.

Goodman, Nelson. 1978. *Ways of Worldmaking*. Indianapolis: Hackett.

Goodman, Nelson, and Catherine Z. Elgin. 1988. *Reconceptions in Philosophy*. Indianapolis: Hackett.

Gorner, Paul. 2000. *Twentieth Century German Philosophy*. Oxford: Oxford University Press.

Gould, Stephen Jay. 1981. *The Mismeasure of Man*. New York: W. W. Norton.

Gould, Stephen Jay. 1983. *Hen's Teeth and Horse's Toes*. New York: W. W. Norton.

Habermas, Jürgen. 1971. *Knowledge and Human Interests*. Trans. Jeremy J. Shapiro. Boston: Beacon Press.

Habermas, Jürgen. 1973. "A Postscript to *Knowledge and Human Interests*." *Philosophy of the Social Sciences* 3 (1973): 157–189.

Habermas, Jürgen. 1979. *Communication and the Evolution of Society*. Trans. Thomas McCarthy. Boston: Beacon Press.

Habermas, Jürgen. 1984. *The Theory of Communicative Action*, volume 1. Trans. Thomas McCarthy. Boston: Beacon Press.

Habermas, Jürgen. 1987. *The Theory of Communicative Action*, volume 2. Trans. Thomas McCarthy. Boston: Beacon Press.

Habermas, Jürgen. 1991. "Comments on John Searle: 'Meaning, Communication, and Representation.'" In Lapore and Van Gulick 1991, 17–29.

Habermas, Jürgen. 1992. *Postmetaphysical Thinking*. Trans. William Mark Hohengarten. Cambridge, Mass.: MIT Press.

Habermas, Jürgen. 1998. *On the Pragmatics of Communication*. Ed. Maeve Cooke. Cambridge, Mass.: MIT Press.

Habermas, Jürgen. 2001a. *On the Pragmatics of Social Interaction*. Trans. Barbara Fultner. Cambridge, Mass.: MIT Press.

Habermas, Jürgen. 2001b. *The Liberating Power of Symbols*. Trans. Peter Dews. Cambridge, Mass.: MIT Press.

Hanna, Joseph F. 1969. "Explanation, prediction, description, and information theory." *Synthese* 20: 308–344.

Hanna, Joseph F. 1978. "On transmitted information as a measure of explanatory power." *Philosophy of Science* 45: 531–562.

Harding, Sandra. 1981. "The norms of social inquiry and masculine experience." In Asquith and Giere 1981, 305–324.

Harnish, Robert M. (ed.). 1994. *Basic Topics in the Philosophy of Language*. Englewood Cliffs, N.J.: Prentice-Hall.

Hesse, Mary. 1974. *The Structure of Scientific Inference*. London: Macmillan.

Hesse, Mary. 1980. *Revolutions and Reconstructions in the Philosophy of Science*. Brighton: Harvester Press.

Hesse, Mary. 1983. "Comments on Kuhn's 'Commensurability, Comparability, Communicability.'" In Asquith and Nickles 1983, 704–711.

References   265

Hilpinen, Risto. 1994. "Peirce on language and reference." In Letner 1994, 272–303.

Hirsch, Eli. 1971. "Essence and identity." In Munitz 1971, 31–49.

Holsinger, Kent E. 1984. "The nature of biological species." *Philosophy of Science* 51: 293–307.

Hookway, Christopher. 2000. *Truth, Rationality, and Pragmatism.* Oxford: Oxford University Press.

Hull, David. 1965. "The effect of essentialism on taxonomy." *British Journal for the Philosophy of Science* 15: 314–326.

Hull, David. 1978. "A matter of individuality." *Philosophy of Science* 45: 335–360.

Humphreys, Paul W., and James H. Fetzer (eds.). 1999. *The New Theory of Reference.* Dordrecht: Kluwer Academic.

Ingber, Warren. 1979. "The descriptional view of referring: Its problems and prospects." *Journal of Philosophy* 76: 725–738.

Ishiguro, Hide. 1969. "Use and reference of names." In Winch 1969, 20–50.

James, William. 1970. *The Meaning of Truth.* Ann Arbor: The University of Michigan Press.

James, William. 1995. *Pragmatism.* New York: Dover.

Kettner, Matthias. 1996. "Karl-Otto Apel's contribution to critical theory." In Rasmussen 1996, 258–286.

Kitcher, Philip. 1984. "Species." *Philosophy of Science* 51: 308–333.

Kitts, D. B., and D. J. Kitts. 1979. "Biological species as natural kinds." *Philosophy of Science* 46: 613–622.

Kripke, Saul. 1977. "Speaker's reference and semantic reference." *Midwest Studies in Philosophy* 2: 255–276.

Kripke, Saul. 1980. *Naming and Necessity.* Cambridge, Mass.: Harvard University Press.

Kripke, Saul. 1986. "A problem in the theory of reference: The linguistic division of labor and the social character of naming." In *Philosophy and Culture: Proceedings of the XVIIth World Congress of Philosophy,* 241–247. Montreal: Editions du Beffroi.

Kuhn, Thomas S. 1962. *The Structure of Scientific Revolutions.* Chicago: University of Chicago Press.

Kuhn, Thomas S. 1977. "Second thoughts on paradigms." In Suppe 1977, 459–482.

Kuhn, Thomas S. 1983. "Commensurability, comparability, communicability." In Asquith and Nickles 1983, 669–688.

Lafont, Cristina. 1999. *The Linguistic Turn in Hermeneutic Philosophy*. Cambridge, Mass.: MIT Press.

Lapore, Ernest, and Robert Van Gulick (eds.). 1991. *John Searle and His Critics*. Oxford: Blackwell.

Leonard, Henry, and Nelson Goodman. 1940. "The calculus of individuals." *Journal of Symbolic Logic* 5: 44–55.

Letner, Kenneth Laine (ed.). 1994. *Peirce and Contemporary Thought*. New York: Fordham University Press.

Linsky, Leonard. 1977. *Names and Descriptions*. Chicago: University of Chicago Press.

Liszka, James J. 1996. *A General Introduction to the Semeiotic of Charles Sanders Peirce*. Bloomington: Indiana University Press.

Luntley, Michael. 1999. *Contemporary Philosophy of Thought*. Oxford: Blackwell.

Madarasz, Norman. 2002. "Intentionalism *contra* intersubjectivism: The Apel–Habermas, and Searle debate." *International Studies in Philosophy* 34: 113–126.

Mandelbrot, Benoit. 1982. *The Fractal Geometry of Nature*. San Francisco: W. H. Freeman.

Margolis, Joseph. 1986. *Pragmatism without Foundations*. Oxford: Blackwell.

Margolis, Joseph. 2002. *Reinventing Pragmatism*. Ithaca: Cornell University Press,.

Mayr, Ernst. 1942. *Systematics and the Origin of Species*. New York: Columbia University Press.

McCarthy, Thomas. 1978. *The Critical Theory of Jürgen Habermas*. Cambridge, Mass.: MIT Press.

McKinsey, Michael. 1978. "Kripke's objections to description theories of names." *Canadian Journal of Philosophy* 8: 485–497.

McMullin, Ernan. 1983. "Values in science." In Asquith and Nickles 1983, 3–28.

Mendieta, Eduardo. 2002. *The Adventures of Transcendental Philosophy*. Lanham: Rowman and Littlefield.

Moore, Patrick. 1988. *The Planet Neptune*. New York: John Wiley.

Munitz, Milton (ed.). 1971. *Identity and Individuation*. New York: New York University Press.

Murphy, John. 1990. *Pragmatism: From Peirce to Davidson*. Boulder: Westview Press.

Nagel, Ernest. 1961. *The Structure of Science*. New York: Harcourt, Brace.

Pape, Helmut. 1982. "Peirce and Russell on proper names." *Transactions of the Charles S. Peirce Society* 18: 339–348.

Peirce, Charles S. 1931–1935. *Collected Papers of Charles Sanders Peirce,* volumes 1–6. Ed. Charles Hartshorne and Philip Weiss. Cambridge: Belknap Press.

Peirce, Charles S. 1958. *Collected Papers of Charles Sanders Peirce,* volumes 7–8. Ed. A. Burks. Cambridge: Belknap Press.

Peirce, Charles S. 1998. *The Essential Peirce,* volume 2. Ed. the Peirce Edition Project. Bloomington: Indiana University Press.

Plantinga, Alvin. 1974. *The Nature of Necessity.* Oxford: Oxford University Press.

Putnam, Hilary. 1973. "Meaning and reference." *Journal of Philosophy* 70: 699–711.

Putnam, Hilary. 1975a. *Mathematics, Matter, and Method.* Cambridge: Cambridge University Press.

Putnam, Hilary. 1975b. *Mind, Language, and Reality.* Cambridge: Cambridge University Press.

Putnam, Hilary. 1978. *Meaning and the Moral Sciences.* London: Routledge and Kegan Paul.

Putnam, Hilary. 1981. *Reason, Truth, and History.* Cambridge: Cambridge University Press.

Putnam, Hilary. 1983. *Realism and Reason.* Cambridge: Cambridge University Press.

Putnam, Hilary. 1987. *The Many Faces of Realism.* LaSalle: Open Court.

Putnam, Hilary. 1988. *Representation and Reality.* Cambridge, Mass.: MIT Press.

Putnam, Hilary. 1990. *Realism with a Human Face.* Cambridge, Mass.: Harvard University Press.

Putnam, Hilary. 1992. *Renewing Philosophy.* Cambridge, Mass.: Harvard University Press.

Putnam, Hilary. 1994. *Words and Life.* Cambridge, Mass.: Harvard University Press.

Putnam, Hilary. 1995a. *Pragmatism: An Open Question.* Oxford: Blackwell.

Putnam, Hilary. 1995b. "Pragmatism." *Proceedings of the Aristotelian Society* 95: 291–306.

Putnam, Hilary. 1996. "Pragmatism and realism." *Cardozo Law Review* 18: 153–170.

Putnam, Hilary. 1997. "James's theory of truth." In Putnam, R. A., 1997, 166–185.

Putnam, Hilary. 1998. "The Real William James: Response to Robert Meyers." *Transactions of the Charles S. Peirce Society* 34: 366–381.

Putnam, Hilary. 1999. *The Threefold Cord*. New York: Columbia University Press.

Putnam, Hilary. 2000. "Richard Rorty on reality and justification." In Brandom 2000, 81–87.

Putnam, Hilary. 2001. "When 'evidence transcendence' is not malign: A reply to Crispin Wright." *Journal of Philosophy* 98: 594–600.

Putnam, Hilary. 2002. *The Collapse of the Fact/Value Dichotomy and Other Essays*. Cambridge, Mass.: Harvard University Press.

Putnam, Hilary. 2004. *Ethics without Ontology*. Cambridge, Mass.: Harvard University Press.

Putnam, R. A. (ed.). 1997. *The Cambridge Companion to William James*. Cambridge: Cambridge University Press.

Quine, W. V. O. 1953. *From a Logical Point of View*. Cambridge, Mass.: Harvard University Press.

Quine, W. V. O. 1960. *Word and Object*. Cambridge, Mass.: MIT Press.

Quine, W. V. O. 1969. *Ontological Relativity and Other Essays*. New York: Columbia University Press.

Quine, W. V. O. 1972. *Methods of Logic,* 3rd edition. New York: Holt, Rinehart and Winston.

Quine, W. V. O. 1976. "Whither physical objects?" In Cohen et al. 1976, 497–504.

Rasmussen, David M (ed.). 1996. *A Handbook of Critical Theory*. Cambridge: Blackwell.

Ratner, Sidney, and Jules Altman (eds.). 1964. *John Dewey and Arthur F. Bentley: A Philosophical Correspondence, 1932–1951*. New Brunswick: Rutgers University Press.

Raup, D. M., and J. J. Sepkoski. 1984. "Periodicity of extinctions in the geologic past." *Proceedings of the National Academy of the Sciences* 81: 801–805.

Recanati, Francois. 1993. *Direct Reference*. Oxford: Blackwell.

Rescher, Nicholas (ed.). 1970. *Essays in Honor of Carl G. Hempel*. Dordrecht: D. Reidel.

Rhees, Rush. 1954. "Can there be a private language?" *Proceedings of the Aristotelian Society Supplement* 28: 77–94.

Rorty, Richard. 1959. "Review of *Experience and the Analytic*, Alan Pasch." *Ethics* 70: 75–77.

Rorty, Richard. 1961a. "Pragmatism, categories, and language." *Philosophical Review* 70: 197–223.

Rorty, Richard. 1961b. "Realism, categories, and the 'linguistic turn.'" *International Philosophical Quarterly* 2: 307–322.

Rorty, Richard (ed.). 1967. *The Linguistic Turn*. Chicago: University of Chicago Press (2nd edition, 1992).

Rorty, Richard. 1976. "Realism and reference." *Monist* 59: 321–340.

Rorty, Richard. 1979. *Philosophy and the Mirror of Nature*. Princeton: Princeton University Press.

Rorty, Richard. 1980. "Kripke vs. Kant." *London Review of Books* (4 Sep): 4–5.

Rorty, Richard. 1982. *Consequences of Pragmatism*. Minneapolis: University of Minnesota Press.

Rorty, Richard. 1984a. "What's it all about?" *London Review of Books* (17 May): 3–4.

Rorty, Richard. 1984b. "Life at the end of inquiry." *London Review of Books* (2 Aug): 6–7.

Rorty, Richard. 1989. *Contingency, Irony, and Solidarity*. Cambridge: Cambridge University Press.

Rorty, Richard. 1990. "Pragmatism as anti-representationalism." Introduction to Murphy 1990, 1–6.

Rorty, Richard. 1991a. *Objectivism, Relativism, and Truth*. Cambridge: Cambridge University Press.

Rorty, Richard. 1991b. *Essays on Heidegger and Others*. Cambridge: Cambridge University Press.

Rorty, Richard. 1992. "A pragmatist view of rationality and cultural difference." *Philosophy East and West* 42: 581–596.

Rorty, Richard. 1995. "Philosophy and the future." In Saatkamp 1995, 197–205.

Rorty, Richard. 1998a. *Truth and Progress*. Cambridge: Cambridge University Press.

Rorty, Richard. 1998b. *Achieving Our Country*. Cambridge, Mass.: Harvard University Press.

Rorty, Richard. 1999. *Philosophy and Social Hope*. New York: Penguin.

Rorty, Richard. 2000. "Response to Hilary Putnam." In Brandom 2000, 87–90.

Rothbart, Daniel. 1984. "The semantics of metaphor and the structure of science." *Philosophy of Science* 51: 595–615.

Royce, Josiah. 1913. *The Problem of Christianity*, volume 2. New York: Macmillan.

Russell, Bertrand. 1905. "On denoting." *Mind* 14: 479–493.

Salmon, Nathan. 1981. *Reference and Essence*. Princeton: Princeton University Press.

Saatkamp, Jr., Herman J. (ed.). 1995. *Rorty and Pragmatism*. Nashville: Vanderbilt University Press.

Salmon, Nathan. 1981. *Reference and Essence*. Princeton: Princeton University Press.

Schwartz, Stephan P. (ed.). 1977. *Naming, Necessity, and Natural Kinds*. Ithaca, N.Y.: Cornell University Press.

Searle, John. 1958. "Proper names." *Mind* 67: 166–173.

Searle, John. 1969. *Speech Acts*. Cambridge: Cambridge University Press.

Searle, John. 1979. *Expression and Meaning*. Cambridge: Cambridge University Press.

Searle, John. 1983. *Intentionality*. Cambridge: Cambridge University Press.

Searle, John. 1984. *Minds, Brains, and Science*. Cambridge, Mass.: Harvard University Press.

Sleeper, R. W. 1986. *The Necessity of Pragmatism*. New Haven: Yale University Press.

Slote, Michael A. 1975. *Metaphysics and Essence*. New York: New York University Press.

Smith, Quentin. 1999. "Direct, rigid designation and a posteriori necessity: A history and critique." In Humphreys and Fetzer 1999, 137–178.

Soames, Scott. 2002. *Beyond Rigidity*. Oxford: Oxford University Press.

Soames, Scott. 2005. *Reference and Description: The Case against Two-Dimensionalism*. Princeton: Princeton University Press.

Standage, Tom. 2000. *The Neptune File*. New York: Walker.

Steinman, Robert. 1982. "Naming and evidence." *Philosophical Studies* 41: 179–192.

Strawson, Peter. 1950. "On referring." *Mind* 59: 320–344.

Strawson, Peter. 1959. *Individuals*. London: Methuen.

Suppe, Frederick (ed.). 1977. *The Structure of Scientific Theories*. Urbana: University of Illinois Press.

Thibaud, Pierre. 1987. "Peirce on proper names and individuation." *Transactions of the Charles S. Peirce Society* 23: 521–538.

Thomson, Sir George. 1965. "Some thoughts on the scientific method." In Cohen and Wartofsky 1965, 81–92.

Thompson, John B. 1981. *Critical Hermeneutics: A Study in the Thought of Paul Ricoeur and Jürgen Habermas*. Cambridge: Cambridge University Press.

Tiles, J. E. 1988. *Dewey*. London: Routledge.

Waismann, Friedrich. 1965. "Verifiability." In Flew 1965, 122–151.

White, Stephen K. 1988. *The Recent Work of Jürgen Habermas*. Cambridge: Cambridge University Press.

Whitmire, D. P., and A. A. Jackson. 1984. "Are periodic mass extinctions driven by a distant solar companion?" *Nature* 308: 713–15.

Whorf, Benjamin Lee. 1956. *Language, Thought, and Reality*. Cambridge, Mass.: MIT Press.

Williamson, Timothy. 1996. "Reference." In *The Encyclopedia of Philosophy. Supplement*, 499–502. New York: Macmillan.

Winch, Peter (ed.). 1969. *Studies in the Philosophy of Wittgenstein*. London: Routledge and Kegan Paul.

Wittgenstein, Ludwig. 1953. *Philosophical Investigations*. New York: Macmillan.

Wittgenstein, Ludwig. 1958. *The Blue and Brown Books*. Oxford: Blackwell.

Wittgenstein, Ludwig. 1967. *Zettel*. Oxford: Blackwell.

Wittgenstein, Ludwig. 1968. "Notes for Lectures on 'Private Experiences' and 'Sense Data.'" *Philosophical Review* 77: 275–320.

Wittgenstein, Ludwig. 1969. *On Certainty*. Oxford: Blackwell.

Wittgenstein, Ludwig. 1979. *Wittgenstein's Lectures, Cambridge, 1932–1935*. Ed. Alice Ambrose. Totawa: Rowman and Littlefield.

Index

Abduction, 139–140
Abilities to designate, 24–26. *See also* Designating chains
Abstract entities
  accounted for by causal theory, 36–37
  as problem for causal theory, 28, 34, 40, 66, 71, 76, 135, 166–167, 242n4
Anscombe, G. E. M., 223
Apel, Karl-Otto, xi, 103, 142–153, 159, 166, 215, 228, 236
A priori (a prioricity), 7,8, 17–19, 30–32, 150, 186, 187, 189, 190, 240n9, 252n14
Attributive use, 9, 14, 26, 27
Axioms of reference, 4

Baptism
  accounted for by causal theory, 23, 29, 37, 38, 40, 60, 216, 241n1, 252n14
  as problem for causal theory, 58, 63, 145, 146, 232, 234, 241n1, 252n14
Baptismal, 23, 37, 44, 52, 60, 74–75, 112, 135, 221, 224, 241n1, 252n14
Brody, Baruch, 197
Bühler, Karl, 158
Burch, Robert, 71–75, 77

Categories, 109, 112–113, 116, 118, 120, 155, 166, 172, 178, 181, 236, 242n2
Causal theory of reference

statement and defense of, 23, 24, 34, 39, 45, 60, 96, 99, 100
critiques of, 26, 29, 57, 67, 83, 100, 113, 123, 136, 227, 228
Cerberus, 6, 27, 30
Churchill, Winston, 69, 114, 226, 228
Cleveland Browns, 193, 195–196
Cluster theory. *See also* Descriptivist theory of reference
statement and defense of, 2–6, 9–22, 39–48, 50–51
critiques of, 2, 7–8, 39–48, 50–51, 62–65, 84, 121, 123, 157, 168, 170, 178, 191–193
Coherence, 108, 109, 134, 170, 171, 223, 232, 236
Communication, 3, 24, 26, 29, 37, 80–81, 88, 132, 145–153, 157–163, 225, 236, 255n13
Communication situations, 24, 26. *See also* Designating chains
Communicative action, 153, 155, 157, 158–162, 163
Community, 23, 29, 38, 40, 70–71, 91, 94, 101–102, 111, 118, 127–130, 141, 147–149, 151, 154, 157, 162, 184, 210–212, 220–224, 231–234, 247n3, 255n10
Conferring, 80, 166, 228, 235
Constructionalism, 105, 107–109, 116, 248n8